The Challenge of Rethinking History Education

Every few years in the United States, history teachers go through what some believe is an embarrassing national ritual. A representative group of students sit down to take a standardized U.S. history test, and the results show varied success. Sizable percentages of students score at or below a "basic" understanding of the country's history. Pundits seize on these results to argue that not only are students woefully ignorant about history, but history teachers are simply not doing an adequate job teaching historical facts. The overly common practice of teaching history as a series of dates, memorizing the textbook, and taking notes on teachers' lectures ensues.

In stark contrast, social studies educators such as Bruce A. VanSledright argue instead for a more inquiry-oriented approach to history teaching and learning that fosters a sense of citizenship through the critical skills of historical investigation. Detailed case studies of exemplar teachers are included in this timely book to make visible, in an easily comprehensible way, the thought processes of skilled teachers. Each case is then unpacked further to clearly address the question of what history teachers need to know to teach in an investigative way. *The Challenge of Rethinking History Education* is a must read for anyone looking for a guide to both the theory and practice of what it means to teach historical thinking, to engage in investigative practice with students, and to increase students' capacity to critically read and assess the nature of the complex culture in which they live.

Bruce A. VanSledright is Professor in the Department of Curriculum and Instruction at the University of Maryland, College Park.

The Challenge of Rethinking History Education

On Practices, Theories, and Policy

Bruce A. VanSledright

Routledge
Taylor & Francis Group

NEW YORK AND LONDON

First published 2011
by Routledge
270 Madison Avenue, New York, NY 10016

Simultaneously published in the UK
by Routledge
2 Park Square, Milton Park, Abingdon, Oxon OX14 4RN

Routledge is an imprint of the Taylor & Francis Group, an informa business

Typeset in Bembo and Helvetica Neue
by Florence Production Ltd, Stoodleigh, Devon
Printed and bound in the United States of America
on acid-free paper by Edwards Brothers, Inc.

Library of Congress Cataloging in Publication Data
    VanSledright, Bruce.
    The challenge of rethinking history education: on practices,
    theories, and policy/Bruce A. VanSledright.
        p. cm.
    1. United States—History—Study and teaching (Secondary)
    2. History—Study and teaching (Secondary)—United States.
    I. Title. E175.8.V35 2010
    973.071—dc22   2010017581

ISBN13: (hbk) 978–0–415–87378–9
ISBN13: (pbk) 978–0–415–87379–6
ISBN13: (ebk) 978–0–203–84484–7

Contents

Introduction

About a decade ago, I taught a diverse group of fifth graders over some 16 weeks to learn to think historically in an effort to deepen their historical understandings of the American past. We pursued history as an investigative endeavor in which we began with historical questions that have long animated the work of other investigators. My purpose was to test an idea borne out by my own and others' research that investigating the past through rich questions and teaching students how to think their way toward answering them would enhance their historical understandings in ways that common, textbook-centered practices typically do not. A closely tethered goal was to use this process of investigating others' lives to help students come to better understand who they were and are becoming with the hope that this would begin to create in them the capacity to critically read and assess the nature of the complex culture in which they lived.

Following that experience, interested groups—history teachers, teacher educators, state department of education officials, social studies curriculum supervisors, and the like—would invite me to talk to them about that work. Almost invariably, someone, often an interest-piqued history teacher, would get around to asking, *so what do you need to know to teach the way you did and where and under what circumstances are teachers to learn how to do it?* At first, I found the question disarming because, quite frankly, I had not given it adequate thought. In the years since, I began to appreciate the question's brilliance, for it goes on my view to the heart of the matter: The knowledge history teachers need to possess in order to significantly deepen their students' historical understandings, as complex, multi-valenced, and socioculturally diverse as those might be. This book is my attempt to address the two-part question largely by way of analogies, descriptions, and illustrations.

In doing so, I am seeking to enter into a conversation with a number of different groups who occupy a variety of roles in addressing that knowledge question and approach it from contrasting standpoints. The primary groups I am thinking of include teacher educators, historians, history teachers, history education researchers, and various stripes of policymakers from local school system coordinators, to state education department officials, and on to those who shape educational policy at the federal level. This is a disparate list, characterized by divergent—but also, I hope, at least a few convergent—interests in the question. All have some influence over the process of constructing the opportunities children have to learn in history classrooms and what they take from those experiences.

Yet, as we know, these groups speak in different vocabularies and operate from and within different communities of practices. This makes my effort here especially challenging. And I will be the first to admit that readers may find my efforts questionable. As a result, I wish to offer some suggestions to readers up front about how the book is structured, ones that may offer some sense about which portions of it might appeal to some more than others. Of course, like all authors, my desire would be that all groups and individual readers find the entire text accessible and compelling. But that may border on unwarranted wishful thinking.

In the first two chapters, I labor to make the case that the general cluster of common approaches to history education for over a hundred years in the United States is largely broken. There is simply no solid evidence to say that what we typically do and have repeatedly done matters significantly in producing young Americans who hold deep understandings of history. In these opening chapters, I sketch out an argument using counterpoised illustrations that I hope show where we have gone wrong and contrast that analysis with one that portends a more potent approach to history education. There are, of course, historical antecedents for what I am advocating—one in particular, the 1960s and 1970s Amherst history project—and I draw from those antecedents to make my case on the assumption that a book on rethinking history education should pay some *homage* to the history of its ideas.

In my view, the large middle section of the book, Chapters 3 through 6, go directly to the first part of the question: what do teachers need to know to teach history as an investigative process? This investigative approach is an uncommon one. However, research indicates that it shapes and cultivates deeper historical understandings of the sort epitomized by the experts than do our more common and traditional ways of teaching history in school. To take up the question, with an appreciative nod to Joseph Schwab's idea of commonplaces, I devote chapter-length treatments to (a) subject matter knowledge, (b) knowledge of learners and theories of learning that support this investigative approach, and (c) knowledge of corresponding teaching practices. In the latter especially, I illustrate in considerable detail with the pedagogical machinations of my invented, history-teacher protagonist, Thomas Becker. I trace his work as he teaches a typical curriculum-prescribed unit on Cherokee Indian removal and dislocation in the 1830s. I then devote the sixth chapter to outline, again in some detail, the types of assessment practices Becker engages in with his charges, ones that are aligned with and therefore support his investigative approach.

In Chapter 7, I undertake some summative theorizing. That is, I try to fit the different types of knowledge Becker holds into a theoretical composite, a small-t theory of history education as investigation into the past, if you will. I attempt to show how those forms of knowledge overlap, cohere, correspond, and align. I note how unaligned aspects of this knowledge terrain can produce confusing results for students because of the mixed messages they entail. I stress the critical importance of alignment to achieving the enhanced learning results such an approach can produce. Readers will find in this chapter as well as elsewhere that I occasionally repeat ideas and constructs at the risk of belaboring them. This is a consequence of the degree of integration I am trying to stress and the theorizing that underpins it.

The final chapter addresses the second part of the question, where and under what circumstances are history teachers to learn to teach as I have been describing. Policies and contributory practices are important here. I frame the rethinking of history education as a systemic reform problem. As such, I attempt to speak to most of the audiences I noted in the foregoing. I argue that they all have important, though different roles to play in rethinking and thus re-imagining history education along the lines I lay out. I describe how I envision their different and sometimes overlapping roles and suggest collaborative steps each might take if they were disposed to rethinking history education in ways that promote student understanding.

★ ★ ★ ★ ★

Much of this book, and the research I undertook to write it, was made possible by a grant from the Spencer Foundation. I especially wish to thank Lauren Jones Young at the Foundation for her encouragement on this project. It is important to note that, despite the Foundation's support, the work here does not necessarily represent its views or an endorsement of the arguments it contains.

I want to acknowledge a debt to two historian colleagues, and I hope still friends of mine, Daniel Ritschel and David Sicilia, who often listened generously as I ranted on about my ideas and tried to persuade them of their wisdom. I also wish to thank my colleague, Chauncey Monte-Sano, and current and former students who also supported and listened to my mutterings about it and/or occasionally read and commented on the work in draft stages. The principal of the students is Kimberly Reddy, but also Liliana Maggioni, Kevin Meuwissen, Jennifer Hauver James, and those in my University of Maryland Graduate Seminar on History/Social Studies Education, Christopher Budano, Jeffrey Shaw, Brie Walsh, and Eric Watts. The groups of history majors that were thinking of becoming secondary history teachers, whom I taught through several iterations of an introductory course on history teaching, were most kind and attentive while I tested out a number of the ideas in the book on them initially. In the end, though, all errors of omission and commission are entirely of my own making. My editor at Routledge, Catherine Bernard, has been long-suffering in support of this book and I thank her for her efforts. Finally, I acknowledge the memory of my friend and mentor, Jere Brophy, who through good humor and his characteristic wry wit always found time to offer me words of encouragement. I only wish that he was still here to read and critique this book.

January 2010

CHAPTER 1

Seeking a More Potent Approach to Teaching History

Fifty-three years old on his next birthday and from solid Anglo New England stock, Bob Brinton has been teaching U.S. history for almost three decades. By some lights, he is a master. Much admired and respected, he heads up the social studies department at Oak Hollow High School in a large suburban school district in the mid-Atlantic region. The district adjoins an urban core. Once a predominantly wealthy suburb with a panoply of country clubs and spacious homes surrounded by smartly manicured lawns, the portion of the district served by Oak Hollow has slowly evolved as the urban environment next door expanded, seeping over its invisible geographic borders into its suburban neighbors' back-yards. As a result, Oak Hollow's student population grew increasingly less European-American and more African, Asian, and Latino/a American. Despite these rather profound demographic changes, Bob Brinton's teaching has remained largely unaffected. He approaches his U.S. history classes much as he has done throughout his long tenure.

Brinton's favorite historical period is the American Civil War, largely because he so admires Abraham Lincoln. Brinton is somewhat the Lincoln aficionado. He has read most of the best-sellers on Lincoln and finds him a true, red-white-and-blue American hero, who historian John Bodnar might refer to as a quintessential patriot of the officialized history of the nation.[1] Brinton spends 12 class sessions on Lincoln. In fact, his entire treatment of the Civil War turns on Lincoln's axis. Little is said about the war itself, the lengthy military campaigns, the profound death, destruction, and dislocation, the soldiers who gave up their lives on both sides of the line, or of the raft of causes historians have explored for why the war was fought. Rather, Brinton entreats his charges to Civil War history as Lincoln biography, beginning with his early years in Illinois and ending with his assassination.

What drives Brinton's curricular and pedagogical choices is his conviction that America has lost its connection to the patriot–statesman–hero, one, on his view, perfectly epitomized by the life and presidency of a man commemorated in the massive edifice anchoring the west end of the Mall in Washington, DC. Brinton sees his role as refurbishing and then burnishing that patriot–hero archetype in the minds of his high school students. He labors intently to show his pupils how great leaders, such as Lincoln in particular, have shaped what he considers to be the most incredible national experiment known to human kind, the creation and development of the United States of America.

Brinton is unapologetic about his flag waving and the trafficking he does in American exceptionalism. He wants to burn the image of Lincoln—the savior of the Union, the slave emancipator—onto the neural networks of those 16-year-olds sitting in front of him. He wants them to cherish Lincoln as much as he does, to understand the sacrifice such great patriot heroes are willing to undertake in service of the nation. He has no difficulty noting that we Americans have not seen a national leader of Lincoln's caliber since, perhaps (and only perhaps), Franklin Delano Roosevelt. He laments the loss of such great American leaders and appears to be in the business of challenging his students with the memories of the Lincoln he narrates to embrace the archetype fully as a means of kindling the embers of national leadership so long lost.

Brinton, unsurprisingly, loves to talk about Lincoln to his students. It might be better said that he talks at them, for most of the 12 class sessions are spent with Brinton telling stories about the humble Lincoln of lore who rose from the lowly log cabin to reside in the White House and preside over what Brinton believes was the most dangerous threat to American national development the nation ever faced. Brinton has a well-worn notebook containing almost 75 pages of lecture notes that frame his talks to his students, although he seldom cracks the notebook's cover anymore. He can recount the stories the pages contain at will. Students spent a good share of the time taking notes on Brinton's talks, following a time-honored tradition in history courses.[2]

Brinton is a powerful storyteller; always has been. His students generally report enjoying his talks, feeling stimulated listening to his verbal nuances and dramatic flourishes. Students regularly vote him as their favorite teacher and clamor to get into his sections. Rarely is there a seat left open in his classroom of 32 chairs. However, students can be heard occasionally to complain about how his tests are difficult because he is so picky about details, especially true with regard to the 40-item multiple-choice exam at the end of the Lincoln unit. Brinton also is known to complain that his students do not do as well as he would like them to on that test. He wonders why their memories are so thin, especially since his stories are so rich and vivid.

A good measure of students' difficulties in doing well on Brinton's test on knowledge of the Civil War can be traced to his insistence that they carefully read the textbook, *The History of the United States*, Daniel Boorstin and Brooks Mather Kelley's treatment of the subject. This treatment spans almost 30 pages and deals with much more about the Civil War than Lincoln's role in it alone. Because Brinton devotes so much of his classroom time presenting Lincoln, he relies on the textbook chapter and his students' consumption of it to fill in missing details that round out the story. It is a pedagogical choice rationalized on the basis, he says, of the importance of Lincoln and his role in preserving the nation and ending slavery. For their part, some students confess that they find the textbook sleep-inducing and therefore do not attend to it well enough to score successfully on the roughly one-third of the 40-item exam that deals directly with textbook substance not discussed in class. They say that they wish Brinton would either take time in class to review the textbook chapter, or dispense with assigning it altogether and simply test them on his Lincoln narratives.

★ ★ ★ ★ ★

Directly across the hall from Bob Brinton, Nancy Todd teaches five sections of the same U.S. history curriculum every day to students who were not lucky enough to get into one of his sections. Todd has been teaching for six years and has been mentored by Brinton since her arrival at Oak Hollow. Brinton likes her very much and enjoys mentoring her. He remains puzzled, however, by her teaching practice, largely because she approaches it much differently than he does. She spends less time on Lincoln per se and focuses more on the historical scholarship surrounding the causes of the Civil War and what its conclusion portended for those who experienced its destructive consequences.

Todd sees Lincoln as a complex man, very much a person of his time, conflicted about race, slavery, and its impact on the union of states, but also someone who adhered to a view of African-Americans that was imbued with a sense of their intellectual and personal inferiority. He pitied them and lamented their condition, but was far from understanding them as the equal of whites. In her three-period pedagogical rendition, Lincoln is neither glorified nor commemorated, but treated as a man thrust into an untenable situation, who chose to do what he thought he had to in order to solve what appeared to be intractable national problems. Yet, and much unlike Brinton, she seldom shares her view of Lincoln directly with her students. Instead, she insists that students read Lincoln "in the flesh" as it were and begin building their own interpretations of the man and the sixteenth President.

She begins her three-session treatment of Lincoln, much as she did many historical topics in the school district's U.S. history curriculum, with questions: Who was this man, Abraham Lincoln? Are the labels, "Savior of the Union" and "The Great Emancipator," fair and accurate ones? Like Brinton, Todd keeps notebooks. However, in her notebooks, Todd had collected and collated selected source documents, speeches Lincoln had made, archival records, newspaper accounts and editorials, descriptions of Lincoln's policies and their effects, written by historians both more recent and at some remove from the present. Students are given copies of these source materials and invited to read them carefully.

Todd teaches her students that history involves an exercise in which investigators, armed with perplexing, but intellectually fertile questions of the sort just noted, pour over documents and the *residua* from the past as they work to answer their questions. The documentary record is to be understood as a form of evidence for making claims about, say, who Lincoln was and whether or not the labels and descriptors often associated with him—modest and unassuming, brilliant and perspicacious, national savior, emancipator, patriot—are valid. It is the students' task to study some of this source material with an eye to building an interpretation or understanding of Lincoln and his role in the Civil War. Claims about and interpretations and understandings of Lincoln that develop from the sources she supplied need to be supported by evidence drawn directly from those sources.[3]

Convinced that they are all capable of such efforts, Todd teaches her students how to build arguments relying on such evidence-based claims.[4] In short, she models for them how historical accounts are written, a practice that characterizes activity in the discipline of history. Students then get a turn to write their own. The invitations to write concern Lincoln vis-à-vis the questions she presents to them that guide their perusal of the source material. She assesses the students primarily on their capacity to build an evidenced-based account and demonstrate budding prowess in citing sources. She is preparing them for the appearance of just such a question on the unit exam.

It seems that there was always a student or two, perhaps in an effort to condense and simply their task, who ask about drawing from the Boorstin and Kelley textbook. Todd reminds these students that the textbook holds no privileged epistemological status in her classroom and needs to be understood as only one additional source. She also cautions about relying too heavily on the textbook, for, on her view, it contains no traces of the source material its authors had used to build their account, despite its authoritative, omniscient tone.[5] There would be no way to check the accuracy of its claims short of going to other source materials, many of which she just gives them anyway, she often gently needles.

After one class period and a portion of the next, during which she roams the room observing how students are using the sources and providing guidance where she thinks necessary, she brings the class back to frontal attention. She begins with the label "Savior of the Union." She calls on a student, asking her to address whether the label is accurate. After this student provides a response, several others are summoned to do the same. After 15 minutes, Todd has covered the chalkboard with student interpretations of Lincoln. With what remains of this class period, an intense debate frequently ensues. Students differ in their assessments of Lincoln. Some believe that Lincoln indeed deserves the label while others find it exaggerated, preferring to draw in other historical agents as also important to the effort at preserving the union. As students offer their assessments of the label's accuracy, Todd sometimes pauses to remind them to indicate the sources upon which they are drawing.

In the class period that follows, time is spent judging the claim that Lincoln was the "Great Emancipator." Students' evaluations almost always vary. Some insist that Lincoln's own words betray his racist sympathies, that he saw the slaves as intellectually and morally inferior. Others note that Lincoln appeared increasingly uncomfortable with the ways slaves were treated. While not necessarily disagreeing with their classmates' claims, another cluster of students argues that the Great Emancipator label was more, rather than less accurate because, after all, Lincoln did spearhead an effort that would later result in the end of slavery. A student will typically remark that Lincoln was only responding to a long line of abolitionist rhetoric, and, being the pragmatic politician that he was, believed that to salvage a union of states, he had to play the abolitionists' game.

During such discussions, Todd guides and occasionally cajoles students. She typically says little other than to ask questions about evidence for claims and query students about where they think the preponderance of the evidence lays. Near the conclusion of this sort of class, Todd brings the discussion to an end by observing two matters about which she has often reminded them: that it was often in the nature of historical investigations to end in some dispute with multiple accounts competing for attention, and that it is exceptionally important to make every effort to judge historical agents such as Lincoln in the context of their past, rather than from the viewpoint of our present. She then will spend five minutes describing the unit test that would occur the following day.

* * * * *

Here again, Todd's pedagogical choices differ from Brinton's in crucial ways and, as her mentor, a bit to his ongoing chagrin. Although U.S. history courses are not tested under the state's accountability regime, the school district in which Oak Hollow sits has pursued a long-standing policy of centralized unit exams. Curriculum specialists in each subject domain develop test banks. Teachers are required to base 80 percent of their unit tests on test-bank items. But teachers are free to develop items of their own for the remaining 20 percent. All items in the history test bank are multiple choice, focusing students principally on recalling (or recognizing) correct details from a list of distracters. Because the history curriculum must be standardized in order to standardize items in the test bank, the history textbook serves as the central repository of details, ideas, and historical figures around which items are written. Brinton draws all of his items from the test bank, exercising his 20 percent professional latitude by using all the Lincoln questions available. He also has been known to submit Lincoln questions to the curriculum office, successfully getting on average one or two questions accepted every year.

Todd uses her degree of professional freedom to invite her students to write. Typically, her unit exams include one or two items in which she supplies students several excerpted source documents, often containing conflicting perspectives or otherwise discrepant accountings. She then poses an investigative question. Drawing from the accounts and citing them as evidence, students are to craft an argument that stakes out a position vis-à-vis that question. The Civil War unit exam she often uses contains one such prompt on Lincoln:

> Some claim that Lincoln can be understood as the Great Emancipator. Others claim that this label exaggerates his legacy. Using the documents I have supplied you and drawing from them to support a position, address the following question: Is the label Great Emancipator an accurate one in describing Lincoln and his policies?

As she was wont to do, she tells students that the question is designed to be provocative, but can create the sense of a false dichotomy, and therefore students are free to stake out middling positions as long as they adequately defend their stance with documentary evidence. Students sometimes wonder if they can cite sources beyond those provided on the exam. Todd will note that this is acceptable and encouraged, but such sources must be identified.

Todd reminds students that she will be relying on the scoring rubric she often uses in grading these interpretive essays, one she always lays out for them early in the semester. Because the prompt effectively requests the assumption of a position for which there was no definitive correct answer, Todd's rubric contains criteria focused more on procedural components. It hinges on four categories:

(a) Stakes out a position and argues it effectively;
(b) Defends position by clearly citing evidence from documentary sources;
(c) Shows evidence of having assessed the reliability of sources; and
(d) Demonstrates understanding (of events, persons, and ideas) by displaying the capacity to reason within the historical context.

Each category is scored on the three-point system with 2 being the highest score and 0 being the lowest. By this point in the semester in which they deal with the Civil War, and following persistent pedagogical effort on Todd's part to that point, students are typically averaging scores between 6 and 7 relative to the maximum 8 possible points they could attain on such essays.

Although Todd chooses to focus her students' attention concerning the Civil War around investigative issues and complex, thick historical questions (e.g., What was the impact of the abolitionist movement on the outbreak of the war? Should the South have been permitted to secede from the Unites States and form a separate country? Why did Southerners believe their cause was just, despite the apparent ravages of slavery?), her students consistently do somewhat better on the standardized multiple-choice test items than do Brinton's students. The only exception to this rule is with regard to the Lincoln items, over which Brinton's students most often hold a slim edge. This only adds to his mild vexation for he is convinced his students should perform much better than Todd's, especially on the Lincoln questions. Despite getting somewhat better grades on average and finding her investigative approach engaging, Todd's students often grumble about how hard her course is, how much work and writing they have to do to succeed. In private moments, though, a number of them concede that they learn much, find the investigative approach engaging, and believe that they develop a much deeper understanding of history through Todd's efforts. Nonetheless, some of them say that they would prefer to take the course with Brinton, if only because they think his version is easier to master.

FROM COMMON TO UNCOMMON TEACHING PRACTICES

Those familiar with the research on history teaching will recognize Brinton's approach as fairly common pedagogical practice.[6] His efforts might be even construed as better than average. Students clamor to get into his sections. They claim to find his Lincoln lectures interesting and believe that with average effort they can do well in his course. He is a compelling storyteller, whose delivery and cadence keeps students awake and reasonably engaged. His take on Lincoln is in line with the most high school textbook treatments and with common public memories and understandings of his greatness as a leader during a deeply troubling period in American history.

As such, Brinton traffics largely in an inspiring, commemorative, heritage-infused approach to teaching U.S. history. After Maurice Halbwachs,[7] we might call it part of a collective-memory project, one in which school-based versions of United States history play an important role in socializing and Americanizing the young, habituating them to celebrating and revering national heroes who sacrificed much to fuel the development of the most powerful (some might also say exceptional) nation on Earth. Along with the typical United States history textbook, teachers such as Brinton can serve as crucial conduits through which the schools' version of collective-memory is delivered.

This collective-memory project, to use this term as shorthand, can be characterized in its school form by a nationalist-oriented commitment to rendering the history of nation building in the United States as one of relentless progress in overcoming the difficulties that beset a democratic experiment, one bent on wresting *unum* from *pluribus*. Respect for the difference that beliefs in *pluribus* allow underwrites southern states exercise of secession from the union, for example. In valuing *unum* over *pluribus,* Lincoln's greatness lies in the ways in which he draws the line, refusing to acknowledge Southern secession, and going to war to preserve the nation as constituted by its amalgamated states. This is Brinton's view at least. Lincoln becomes the patriot hero because he prevents the nation-building experiment from crumbling. The *United* States triumph over forces designed to render them *Divided* States. On Brinton's view, there may be a no more important national leader than Lincoln in this regard, the likes of whom are desperately needed to arrest the country's twenty-first-century slide toward political and cultural polarization.[8] Brinton's narrative register puts the importance of a strong, unified nation at the center, with patriot heroes such as Lincoln (along with Jefferson, Theodore Roosevelt, and FDR) orbiting in tight, commemorative arcs around that center.

It is probably fair to say that thousands of U.S. history teachers across the country put this narrative register on display in some form every day. That register is reinforced by the textbook, by local and national history assessments, in the media, and by national leaders with about equal frequency. The narrative is official United States history and that official history is the narrative. It is crucial to the maintenance of the collective-memory project and its role in birthing distinctive American identities. Without it—that is, the capacity to recount at least the rough contours of the nation-building narrative arc and the heroes responsible for its progress and success—one cannot claim that identity fully, or so the sentiment goes.[9] History teachers such as Brinton are deeply and unapologetically complicit in the project's instructional design and delivery.

Not so Todd, which is what most profoundly perplexes Brinton. Todd is a rare iconoclast in her treatment of United States history, someone who seldom appears in accounts of research on history teaching.[10] Although there is an implicit narrative arc to her treatment of U.S. history because she follows the textbook's general periodization scheme, it is more nod to chronology than narrative. Rather than simply retrace the officialized narrative, Todd wants her students to openly investigate the American past on which that narrative is based. She asks questions and requires her students to ask and then address those questions with her. How was it that African slaves ended up in Jamestown in 1919? What was their experience like? What can be argued were the causes of the American Revolution? What happened at the so-called Boston Massacre, and what effect did it have? Why are Lewis and Clark so celebrated in American history? Was Andrew Jackson really the "people's President"? What was life like for average workers and ex-slaves in the south after the Civil War? We American's talk a lot about our freedom birthright, but why were indigenous Americans repeatedly denied this birthright? Is the idea of Manifest Destiny a positive or negative force in American history, or both? If such questions disrupt the narrative arc in some ways, Todd accepts it because she finds that the narrative borders on possessing powerful ideological components and to present it without question participates in subtle indoctrination. In spite of firm convictions in this regard, she has not dared to share these views with Brinton.

Like many teachers who teach against the grain of common practice, Todd closes her classroom door, asks her meaty historical questions, provides her students with source material they can use to investigate and address those questions, and they have at it, so to speak. She also quietly but deliberately teaches her students how to go about this process, what sort of epistemological stances they will need to adopt to understand sources as evidence (rather than as what really happened), to identify and attribute them, assess their perspective, and judge their reliability and value in making historical claims. Her classroom functions frequently like a history seminar in which participants debate ideas, cite evidentiary support for their positions, dispute others' claims, and, in the end, agree to disagree. In contrast to the collective-memory tableau that primarily infuses Brinton's practice, Todd could be said to be engaged in a disciplinary approach, one history specific that looks on the former approach with some skepticism. Two very different teaching approaches, distinguished by visions of the American past that are partly at odds and marked by disparate under-standings of what students need and are capable of, residing a mere 30 feet from one another on the second floor of Oak Hollow High School.

VEXING DIFFERENCES?

What can we say about the differences in these two approaches, the ones epitomized by Brinton and Todd? Such differences trouble policymakers and educational reformers. How can two teachers, both professionally certified and licensed in the state of their practice, conceptualize the very same subject matter so differently and go about it as though they had never encountered one another? Of course this is not the first time such questions have animated discussions about ways of teaching history. Over 40 years ago, following the Soviet Union's launch of Sputnik, the threat that the United States had fallen behind its Cold War arch enemy rattled the nation. What students were learning in schools and how they went about it became the focus of educational reformers, largely on the assumption that changes in practices and approaches were direly needed if the United States was to catch up to its rival. Much of the reformist energy was targeted at the study of mathematics and science. However, education in the social sciences and history did not escape attention. With respect to history education, and specifically American history, the most notable attempt to reformulate how the subject was taught and learned took place under the aegis of the Amherst Project, with Richard Brown as its director.

RETHINKING HISTORY EDUCATION: THE AMHERST PROJECT AS ANTECEDENT

In an address to the annual convention of the National School Boards Association in 1965, Richard Brown observed, "I do not need to tell you people who are so closely connected with education that there is raging on every side nothing less than a revolution in American education." He then observed, "The revolution is, in fact, long overdue, nowhere more so than in the teaching of history. As a nation we have little sense of our history. We have less sense of what history is. What passes for it far too often is a frightful blend of antiquarianism and patriotism." Amplifying his critique, Brown added, "The critical qualities, the reasoned temper and judgment and perspective that a study of history ought to provide, are precisely those intellectual qualities which, as a society, we lack the most."[11] These worries, Brown told his audience, were the source of work on the Amherst Project. Cautiously optimistic, Brown anticipated that the Project would indeed bear fruit, and it did for over a decade.

Thirty-one years later, and two years following the initial release of the National History Standards, Brown was asked to write a retrospective on that project for the journal, *The Social Studies*. Scholars have debated the impact of the broad-based New Social Studies reform movement, a federally funded effort designed to change teaching by focusing students' attention away from common lecture and memorization approaches, typical of teachers such as Bob Brinton, and toward the disciplinary referents and inquiry-based practices of the subjects they studied in school, United States history in the case of the Amherst Project. The Amherst Project had in mind teachers such as Nancy Todd. The larger reform movement originated out of the Woods Hole Conference in the late 1950s and was prompted by the Cold War arms race and fears that American education had lost its capacity to retain an intellectual and technological edge over the Soviets.[12] Many have claimed that the revolution the movement hoped to achieve ended largely in limited success because it resulted in few lasting changes in the way subject matter in general and history in particular were taught in school.[13] While acknowledging the critics' claims, Brown's retrospective is less sanguine about reports of the movement's many failures.

Brown asks, "What happened? How did the tiger get away? Was the 'revolution' overstated? Misconceived? Was it, after all, simply one more swing of the pendulum that throughout the twentieth century, has oscillated between basic education and progressivism? What, if anything, was its [the Amherst Project's] legacy?" Answering his own question, Brown observes, "however one characterizes it, the message has never gone entirely out of fashion. Evidence abounds that, in the nineties, it is beginning to receive new attention. Remarkably, a quarter of a century later, two units of the Amherst Project . . . are still in print." Laying out one example of the project's impact after another, he continues, "Even the cosmetics that dress up modern textbooks and find their way into the controversial National History Standards for United States History bear witness to some impact . . . of what has gone before." Shifting to prognostication, Brown argues, "The signs of renewed interest are bound to increase. An age venturing onto the Information Superhighway can expect changes aplenty in what is demanded of education, even in what it considers 'education' to be. The premium clearly will be on students learning how to learn, in order to be able to use information literally at their fingertips."[14] History teachers such as Nancy Todd reflect the premium placed on teaching students how to learn and thereby reflect Brown's prophetic sentiments.

"The polestar of the Amherst Project," Brown noted, "was the idea that students learn best when they are acting as inquirers, pursuing into evidence questions that grow out of their own lives. [. . .] We [project directors and participants] saw both "knowledge" of the historical past and the development of inquiry skills as important goals that would be best achieved together. Neither was an end in itself."

The first phase of the Amherst Project began in the late 1950s when Van R. Halsey, then Assistant Dean of Admissions at Amherst College, assembled a group of area high school history teachers and college historians to discuss what pre-collegiate students should know about history at the point of their graduation from high school. Halsey began with the historians. Unanimous in their conclusion, the historians said they assumed entering students would know virtually nothing, even though the historians were aware that students had taken American history courses, for example, in at least three iterations before college. Halsey then asked the historians to explain what they would like students to know.

Despite the absence of a unanimous response to this question, the historians generally agreed that they cared less about students possessing a fixed body of knowledge and more about them having the capacity to work with cognitive tools that formed a critical approach to the history they might study. The historians, Brown explains, "wanted students to understand that 'history' was at best an interpretation of what had happened in the past, and they wanted students to be able to doubt."[15] The high school teachers retorted by wondering how they were to accomplish this feat if the only curriculum materials they had to work with were history textbooks that conveyed the idea that the America past was a known story, recorded in an unassailable narrative, and designed principally to be memorized and recalled by students. The teachers wanted different materials to supplement the textbooks, materials that would "enable students to question evidence, to doubt, to interpret—to see, in short, what the historian did and therefore what 'history' was."[16]

Armed with these responses, in the summer of 1959 groups of history teachers and historians sat down to design new curriculum units to be tried out informally by the teachers. From there on, the Project expanded its reach across the country with the help of publishing companies who produced the units en masse. Federal funding followed and the staff of the project expanded. Between 1965 and 1970, workshops on how to teach history as an inquiry into the past aided by the published curriculum units proliferated.

Difficulties ensued, however. Amherst Project participants soon learned that knowing how to teach these new curriculum materials, and the investigative practices that underpinned them, required that attention be paid to history teachers' knowledge about the discipline and its structure and to the preparation of teachers. But educating better teachers was not sufficient. The obsession in schools with relaying a stabilized narrative of U.S. national development, presented to students as a *fait accompli*, was so deeply rooted that the Project turned its attention to changing the culture of schools themselves. Educational development teams were designed and put in place across the country. The workshop approach toward changing practices and approaches became the signature pedagogy of the Project. And then, just as the workshop approach began to make headway, the Federal funding ran lean and Americans became increasingly distracted by the troubles of the war in Vietnam.[17] By about 1975, the Project had lost its momentum. The *Nation At Risk* report with a symbolic signaling of the importance of returning to age-old, basic forms of education and schooling emerged off the presses in 1983.

AN ENDURING LEGACY?

Despite the demise of the Amherst Project, Brown's cautious optimism and hopeful prognostications, offered up in his retrospective accounting, show some signs of coming to fruition. Although the accountability movement—ushered in by the passage of the *No Child Left Behind* act in the early twenty-first century with an operationalized emphasis on testing relatively low-level cognitive capacities—could be understood as tempering Brown's prophetic enthusiasm, one could argue that the landscape of history education in the United States continues to change, and perhaps fairly dramatically. Through engagements with history teachers under the auspices of the Teaching American History grant program, historians, who for much of the latter half of the twentieth century sat on the sidelines, have found renewed interest in what happens in history courses at the pre-collegiate level. Historians have also begun talking more about their own teaching practices, as well as the role they play in the preparation of history teachers.[18]

A conference at the University of Virginia and Monticello in the summer of 2006, attended by over 45 historians, history teachers, and history education researchers resulted in a white paper, "The Next Generation of History Teachers: A Challenge to Departments of History at American Colleges and Universities." It was sent to all post-secondary history departments in the United States. On the paper's cover page, the challenge was framed this way: "We believe that historians in higher education might educate, in more purposeful ways, the future teachers among their own students. In fact, it seems to us, historians might benefit from interesting themselves in these issues even if they have not done so before. *We urge every department to devote at least one department meeting . . . to discussing this message and its recommendations.*"[19]

In a nod to Brown's prophesy, digitized, Internet-based archival source materials have proliferated in recent years, making access to them easier for history teachers and therefore their use in classrooms more common.[20] The Library of Congress' American Memory website, host for thousands of digitized documentary and photographical Americana, posted millions of hits by the year 2000 alone. Teachers report employing more of these source materials as part of their pedagogical armamentarium on a regular basis and students indicate reading and studying them more frequently.[21] Sensitized to these recalibrations of focus toward original source materials, United States history textbooks have changed somewhat to include more of them, either in the texts themselves (often as sidebars) or in supplemental materials.

Since about 1980, a veritable cottage industry of research has arisen that focuses on how teachers teach history, what students learn as a result of that teaching, and how the relationship between the two could be improved. Much of that work blossomed after 1990, especially in North America. In 1998, 25 historians, history educators, and researchers assembled at Carnegie Mellon University to present papers and debate the explosion of work in the field, make reform recommendations, and seek some consensus about future directions. In 2005, the National Research Council (of the National Academies) released a volume titled, *How Students Learn: History in the Classroom*, with chapters authored by distinguished research scholars who had made careers from studying how school-age students learn the subject and what implication that work had for history teaching.[22] The blurb on the back cover of the book states, "The nation turns to the National Academies . . . for independent, objective advice on issues that affect people's lives worldwide." The research undertaken from 1980 onward made giving advice about new ways of teaching history possible, a feat nearly unthinkable in the first three-quarters of the twentieth century. That advice bears at least some lineage to the work of the Amherst Project.

So what is the legacy of the Amherst Project? Did it—like the New Social Studies Movement of which it was a part—end without much success as some resolute critics have claimed? Larry Cuban, who spent a good share of his career documenting what he has called "persistent instruction" (i.e., teaching as telling) suggests that despite the promise of efforts such as the Amherst Project, little has changed about the ways in which teachers teach history and therefore the project's legacy was less fecund than perhaps Brown's retrospective implies.[23] However, the types of changes I described in the foregoing portend at least several good reasons to be optimistic, that perhaps the legacy of the Amherst Project, and the antecedents that led to it, remains with us in the present. Surely, the volume *How Students Learn: History in the Classroom* and the chapter authors' positions reflect a good many of the principles embedded in the Amherst Project's efforts some 40 years later. Yet, persistent instruction in history education continues to be a fact of schooling, and has been documented many times by researchers interested in the study of history education.[24]

Given these realities, we witness a tension, for example, between (a) the classroom proliferation of archival source materials (in addition to the textbook) and history teachers' endorsements of their use as a means of enhancing their students' historical investigative capabilities and (b) what might be termed an obsession with covering, say, a commemorative United States nation-building narrative drawn directly from those 1,000-plus-paged textbooks. To cover the narrative typically translates into history teachers reiterating it to silent clusters of students, some of whom scribble notes in notebooks and memorize the details for the tests that ask for selective recall. Investigations of the past using non-textbook sources involves asking questions about what that past means, reading the documents carefully to address the questions, and offering interpretations. The former mirrors persistent instruction; the latter represents a closer alignment with the "polestar" tenet of the Amherst Project. The differences between Brinton and Todd exemplify this tension.

Yet, the fact that we can observe such a tension, that in spite of the press for persistent instruction in history classrooms and the draw to teach history as the nation state's collective memory, teachers such as Nancy Todd (and those who appear in National Academies volume) do exist. The legacy of the Amherst Project may not be entirely lost. As Brown alludes, we may be standing at the edge of a propitious moment, one that continues to foment changes in and reconceptualizations of history education, those epitomized by the practices and approach of the Nancy Todds of the classroom world. Nonetheless, close observers of such change note how slow and fitful it remains. Therefore, it is fair to ask, if the work of teachers such as Nancy Todd represents the legacy of the Amherst Project, if it signals a more potent and desirable approach to teaching America history, why are examples of it not more commonplace? Why do few teachers emulate her? Why do we not see a quicker evolution toward the kinds of teaching and learning relationships depicted in detail in the National Academies' volume? There are a number of complex ways to respond to these questions. I take them up in Chapter 2 on the way toward building a case for the importance of understanding impediments for realizing change.

I begin the next chapter by noting that in many ways what Bob Brinton does in his history courses is eminently familiar, seen as necessary, and understood as intellectually tidier than the approach Nancy Todd pursues, in part accounting for its persistence. However, from that point on, I explain that perceived necessity, familiarity, and an easy tidiness come at potentially heavy cost, requiring much closer attention to the potency of Nancy Todd's alternate approach. In the chapters that follow the next one, I engage that attention by unpacking what teachers such as Todd know and what that knowledge enables them to do by way of pedagogical decision making, choices that enable their students to learn how to learn in ways that Brinton's classroom moves do not.

CHAPTER 2

On the Limits of Collective Memorialization and Persistent Instruction

So why is what Nancy Todd does in her classroom quite rare while Bob Brinton's practice remains common? One of the principal reasons is that the pull of teaching the nation-building narrative arc—the nation's collective memory—in U.S. history courses is indelible. It is staunchly rooted in the need to socialize the young and cultural outsiders into what Arthur Schlesinger, Jr. (after Gunnar Myrdal) called the "American Creed."[1] Deeply implicated in patriotic identity-formation politics, the story arc and its representation in U.S. history textbooks serve to carry the symbolic meaning of what it is to be an American, epitomized in Brinton's class by Abraham Lincoln. To claim that identity, one needs to be able to repeat that storyline, to call it one's own, to say "we" and "our" when referring to America and to its history.

A history teacher's job then is to compel his charges to acquire that narrative and repeat it and its details on command. Exercising this effort intimates pressing on the storyline, imploring students to read and consume the textbook, reinforcing those details in class each day, and assessing possession of them at the end of the unit.[2] The learning-as-acquisition metaphor is pronounced. There are many plot twists, much detail, many events to address—and more accumulate each day. The ticking classroom clock becomes the enemy and the race to get through it all becomes both *de rigueur* and *raison d'etre*. In history education, such practices become embedded into the teaching culture and are passed from one generation to the other largely through years of apprenticeships in observation. Hence, persistent instruction.

Not only is there pull from within the history teaching culture, but there is pressure emanating from outside it. In a nation that has built itself off the backs of waves of immigrants, the push to use history education to Americanize the hordes of "outsiders" lobbies incessantly. To sow allegiance to the nation state requires constant maintenance. Cultural leaders, who are sympathetic to Schlesinger's fear of a disuniting America, worry that the onslaught of immigrant *pluribus* will undermine the possibility of *unum*. In 2006, for example, the Florida House of Representatives went so far as to legislate how United States history was to be taught, mandating that it be a progressive story of nation building, fact based, and testable.[3] In 1995, the United States Senate passed a resolution denouncing the 1994 United States History Standards on the grounds that the Standards' authors violated the American Creed by sullying the arc of the nation-state narrative with too many examples drawn from the seamier underbelly of the American past.[4] To challenge the narrative register of progress in achieving the nation's ideals is to defy the nation's civil religion. Few history teachers or school people find that kind of defiance attractive.

Teaching history as an investigative act, as a program of digging into the nation's past in order to understand it more deeply (blemishes and all)—as the Amherst Project pursued and as Nancy Todd attempts— threatens to collide directly with the socializing Americanization mission persistent instruction in American history is designed in good measure to accomplish.[5] Even though they may be more than willing, it is rare to find history teachers who are not daunted by running the risk portended by such a collision, or at least not without some support and guidance that makes traversing it more manageable. As a result, there are few opportunities to witness the teaching of American history in ways that represent the investigative, inquiry-based approaches practiced by Nancy Todd.

Even though Bob Brinton's collective-memory approach to teaching U.S. history and the persistent instruction it fosters is widespread among history teachers and may be seen as a necessity, its practice entails a variety of consequences that present a mixed record of accomplishments and limitations. By my lights, the latter more than outweigh the former, requiring a serious rethinking of how it is that history is taught in school. To support this claim, I trace out six consequences of pursuing a collective-memory approach drawn from three decades of history education research and linked to the legacy of the Amherst Project and its critique of common practice. The first two consequences, some would argue, are salutary. However, they are offset by four additional consequences that appear far less so.

CONSEQUENCES OF PURSUING A COLLECTIVE-MEMORY APPROACH

1 Acquiring the Freedom-Quest Narrative

There is evidence to suggest that students who are engaged by the sort of collective-memory approach Brinton pursues in his history classes (and for those who have it reinforced for them away from school) retain and can recount the general contours of a nation-building narrative. In one study, a group of 24 American college undergraduates were asked to write an essay response to the question, what is the origin of the United States? Twenty-three of them crafted essays that bore uncanny similarities.

Persecuted Anglos fled Europe and the source of their oppressive overlords and traveled to the New World in search of freedom. The birth of the United States, the 23 reasoned, was the result of a quixotic struggle to overthrow European-style tyranny and establish a new nation founded on individual liberty and the unregulated pursuit of happiness. Following this birth, a period of two centuries ensued in which the people further distanced themselves from the Old World, engaging in limitless progress as they settled and populated the geographic expanse that was western North America. With copious amounts of hard work and the goal of individual liberty beckoning them from every horizon, patriots and pioneers threw off their Old World trappings and were born anew. The nation they built stood for liberty, democracy, and the right to live and produce all their minds and hearts could desire, unobstructed by regulators who would tamper with their yearnings. The result was a nation state, populated by freedom seekers who created the best and most powerful experiment in nation building the world had yet to see.[6]

Impressed by the similarities in these freedom-quest narratives, psychologist James Wertsch observed that such renditions are powerful because they can be compressed into succinct storylines, contain thematic elements that are seductive and thus memorable, and can be easily repeated because they become tied to self-identifications with core features of the storyline and what it represents symbolically. Wertsch refers to them as schematic narrative templates. They function as powerful cultural tools that allow their carriers to claim an allegiance to the nation state and its institutions in a world where such allegiances are seen as important to success in identity development.[7] Students need few historical details in order to acquire and utilize the template. And learning the narrative template in school can begin early.

Elements of it appeared among 9- to 11-year-old students in study in Kentucky. As with the college students, the younger ones saw national progress as generally linear and rational, moving steadily forward as Americans became progressively smarter and developed crucial new inventions as a consequence of their freedoms. The children also tended to imagine history through a lens of much reduced scope in ways reminiscent of the reductionist and telescopic narratives the college students produced.[8] Already by upper elementary school, these students had developed several of the precursory ingredients of the freedom-quest narrative template echoed by older students and found in most U.S. history textbooks.

Some key patriots and pioneers that populate the template are also retained in memory. The list is, however, quite short and hardly diverse. In a study of approximately 1,000 entering college students over a period of a decade in Buffalo, New York, a historian invited them on the first day of his survey American history course to list without reflection ten names they could remember after they saw the prompt, "American history from its beginning through the Civil War."[9] The results revealed rather remarkable consistency in their recollections. Presidents especially, similar national leaders, and generals topped the lists. Fourteen of the same names appeared consistently across samples of students during the ten-year span of the study. President responses (e.g. Washington, Jefferson, Lincoln, Jackson) were so common that students were asked to produce a similar list without naming any presidents. These second lists turned up consistent notations of the same set of celebrated and mythologized American patriots and pioneers noted by historian, John Bodnar.[10] Betsy Ross, Paul Revere, Harriet Tubman, and Lewis and Clark were top recollections. Presidents, generals, patriots, and pioneers are all part of the supporting cast of characters that give a degree of substance to the freedom-quest narrative template. This substance, albeit thin, is the stuff of common U.S. history classroom stories and the lore of textbooks.

The results of the study prompted its author to remark that "they are evidence that cultural imagery seems to be reproduced in our young people with startling consistency and regularity."[11] By way of a conclusion, he observed, "the consistency and extraordinary uniformity in the images offered up by these students indicates that [political leaders] and their followers have little cause for concern: the structure of myth and heroes, martyrs and mothers, is firmly in place."[12]

At its best, the school-based collective-memory approach that Brinton endorses manages fairly well at binding a freedom-quest narrative arc to the historical memories of students who encounter it. At the very least, the approach successfully reinforces the narrative template that is sold in many forms of mass culture from historical theme parks to the U.S. Park Service's commemorative sites to television's The History Channel. If the goal of the collective-memory approach is to inculcate in students a fore-shortened, thematically linear, simple, and upbeat storyline of national development (with an abbreviated list of American heroes, martyrs, and mothers thrown in), then some research evidence indicates that the results remain salutary.

2 Consumers of the Past

Because teachers such as Brinton rely so heavily on talking *at* their students while narrating the storyline, students become astute about their roles as consumers of what is being pedagogically reproduced. This consumer role fits reasonably well within a culture that prizes consumption, particularly economic consumption. In this sense, the history classroom in which it is the student's task to participate in the collective-memory project as a consumer of its wares, provides some preparation for participation in the buying of what mass culture has to sell on the Internet, at the shopping mall, in the food court, and at the Nike and I-Tunes stores. Unfortunately for history teachers, the market competition is fierce. Such teachers need to be gifted storytellers and exciting performers to keep students from being distracted. Nonetheless, sitting in on the live performance of a Brinton narration about Lincoln is something consumption-piqued students recognize as familiar. It both reminds and reinforces.

3 Low Cognitive Challenge

However, there is some price to be paid for the passive, consumptive nature of their narrative acquisitions. Students in history classes taught by the likes of Brinton do not learn to reason historically in any but the most superficial ways. There is little about what is offered there that is intellectually challenging. Reading and making sense of the *residua* of the past, attempting to cull together ideas and defending them by working with a concept of evidence, evaluating claims made by others, and working from a carefully honed, criterial framework that allows one to sort less from more powerful claims are generally lost on Brinton's students. On confronting discrepant historical accounts (e.g., Lincoln the apparent abolitionist who neverthe-less wrote of the racial inferiority of the slaves about whose plight he sympathized), Brinton's pupils are left rather helpless, absent a defensible system for arbitrating those claims.[13] Complex literacy practices required for making deeper sense of an unstable past are reduced to the ostensibly simple task of being sure to get the author's (i.e. Brinton's or Boorstin and Kelley's) main idea. It is possible to imagine that Todd's students score slightly better on the unit exams, in part, because they know how to think about and wrestle with ideas, know how to read the items on the test and think their way through them because Todd spends a good share of her time teaching them how to think and read in precisely that way.

4 The Narrative Register and Resistance by Students of Color

Some students respond to the narrative register with suspicion, cynicism, and occasional resistance. One such study that revealed these kinds of outcomes took place in Detroit in the 1990s. Researchers compared differences among European-American and African-American adolescents on a task in which they had to sort into a top-ten list both names and events drawn from the U.S. past by order of their perceived importance. The European-American students, not unlike the collegians in the Buffalo study, ranked as most important key names and events marking traditional elements of the freedom-quest, nation-building narrative and the presidents, patriots, and pioneers often associated with it. For the European-American students, George Washington and John Kennedy were most often at the top of their lists and the Civil War (because it saved the union of states) and the Declaration of Independence and Constitution periods were most pivotal. The Civil Rights Movement, the Civil War (because it signaled an end to slavery), and Emancipation From Slavery ranked at the top of the African-American students' lists, as well as did Martin Luther King and Malcolm X. A close third to the latter two was Harriet Tubman. Neither Tubman nor Malcolm X was ranked by any of the European-American students.

In an effort to understand more about the differences, the researchers asked students to explain what influenced their decisions. For the European-American students, the textbook and teachers' lectures served as most important in forming their selections, suggesting the power of those sources in mediating ideas about what was historically significant. The African-American students, by contrast, talked about the influence of parents and relatives especially, and lumped teachers, television, and film together as of secondary importance. In interviews with a subsample of students, several African-Americans registered suspicion about the whitewashing agenda textbook and school curricula were perceived to promote. They claimed that the books and lectures tended to ignore or marginalize contributions of African-Americans and otherwise sanitize or omit a long history of racial oppression, struggle, and violence necessary to overcome it. Several students argued that the narrative transmitted in the classroom supported an ongoing conspiracy to keep African-Americans in a type of perpetual bondage. Turning toward localized, specific narratives conveyed by family and community members became an exercise in cultural survival.[14]

As these data suggest, knowing the narrative and some of its roman-ticized heroes and their patriotic national sacrifices and accomplishments does not necessarily result in the appropriation of or self-identification with that narrative. Instead, in this case, the collective-memory approach appears to promote and reinforce among some Americans counter narratives that, with enough repeating, serve to nurture a suspicious view of it and the larger school system that serves as its sanctioning agent. If proponents of collective memory, such as Bob Brinton, cannot find means for countering competing local narratives, or by broadening the approach's appeal through genuine inclusion, it risks saliency among some groups, and ironically may actually increase resistance.[15] Rather than enhance *unum*, one consequence is that the persistent instruction of a collective-memory approach can exacerbate the contentiousness of *pluribus* the more it insists on a program that can be understood as suffused with prejudicial aims by those who feel excluded from its primary narrative arc. As historian David Lowenthal has noted, it is the celebratory excesses of the collective-memory approach to the American past, its often irrational exuberance and desire to secure allegiance to *particular* remembrances of nation (e.g., Brinton's worshipful treatment of Lincoln), that can imperil its success.[16]

5 National Assessments

Every four or five years since the late 1980s, the National Assessment of Educational Progress (NAEP) history exam is given to a sample of fourth, eighth, and twelfth graders from across the United States. What typically follows is considerable hand wringing and teeth gnashing. Scores repeatedly suggest that students do not know very much of the nation's history.[17] It might be more accurate to say that they cannot remember many details of that history that test developers and policymakers think are important to know. Students at all levels blow relatively easy multiple-choice items that some believe are so crucial to the nation's collective memory that they are simply baffled at how so many students could be so ignorant. Finger pointing frequently follows and U.S. history teachers are caught in the middle of policymakers' angry recriminatory strafing. By implication, history teachers are put on notice that they must shape up and do what they do with increased intensity and greater compulsion, or they'll be shipped out, presumably to some teacher prison in an uninhabitable area of the central Nevada desert. This approach is a bit like saying to history teachers that the verbal berating will continue until morale improves. All the disappointment and vitriolic rhetoric aside, the point is that the tests reveal that American students who sit for this NAEP United States history exam exhibit a marked tendency to have faulty memories when it comes to remembering historical details.[18] Brinton regularly sees this same pattern among his students following administrations of his multiple-choice unit exams.

If Brinton's pedagogical strategy of narrating the U.S. nation-building story and forefronting the legacy of its patriot and pioneer heroes combined with a stress on the history textbook's similar commemorative treatment is common to history classrooms across the country, then the results on such national tests portend at least a mild indictment of this practice.

Students simply do not exit the experience with much lasting understanding of the American past, or at least cannot recall much of the substance that frames out that past. Students do appear to emerge with some sense of a nation-building narrative arc, one that should provide Brinton, other teachers, and the disappointed policymakers with a measure of cold comfort. Yet, as these periodic national assessment results indicate, asking for a more intricate history complete with plot complexities, supporting particulars, and an occasional wart or two appears to request too much, provoking new rounds of criticism every half decade or so.

History as patriot–hero autobiography and/or shiny freedom-quest plotline may be necessary, but it is hardly sufficient for developing in students a deeper understanding of the American past. Brinton has not read the aforementioned research. It stands to reason, though, that should he encounter it, he would be profoundly disappointed in his students and resolved to do more of what he was already doing and do it more intently until his charges got it.

6 Waning Interest

Another casualty of a steady, passive routine of listening to and reading about the celebratory story of national development common to most U.S. history courses is interest in and engagement with the subject. Not all history teachers are as gifted a storyteller as is Brinton. In fact there is some indication that Brinton is relatively rare in this regard.[19] Many history teachers find lecturing and storytelling for four or five periods every day simply exhausting. The ubiquitous videotape/DVD and worksheet strategies they rely on provide much-needed respite from a draining workload, even though history teachers know students despise the latter. As a consequence, studies periodically unearth evidence of how unimpressive most students find their history courses. History frequently ranks at the bottom of favorite subjects on a list of typical high school courses.[20] Biology, mathematics, physics, foreign language, physical education, and English all rank higher, despite many of these subjects being perceived by students as far more difficult. History shorn of its mystery, portrayed as a *fait accompli*, and whose blemishes are airbrushed to appear as minor irritations loses much of its otherwise riveting appeal.[21]

IMAGINING AN ALTERNATIVE

Todd succeeds in avoiding many of the problems common to the persistent teaching practice of the collective-memory approach. Her students report finding her questioning, investigative approach invigorating and engaging, even in as much as they remain uncertain about it because it does not altogether seem like regular school to them.[22] They look forward to attending her class, even though they know it will require more effort than Brinton's students might need to expend. They claim that reading Lincoln in the original sources, for example, is compelling because they say it gives deeper insight into understanding him than a textbook version alone would. They find the original Lincoln fascinating, warts and all, and perhaps mostly because of the warts. Despite the intellectually challenging thought her approach demands, her students also report appropriating the tools and criteria she has taught them for reading and assessing competing historical accounts. They have come to appreciate the importance of the concept of evidence and its role in making historical claims. It gives them arbitration purchase on the many claims that they encounter in their daily experience and provides guidance in making thoughtful decisions. Ultimately, they find that participating actively, even as novices, in a culturally valued community of practices—the type of researching, thinking, and writing that historians do—connects them to a wider adult world in ways that doing the routine of high school seldom provides.

However, Todd's students do not come to mythologize and valorize Lincoln as Brinton's students do. Nor are they willing to engage in much hero worship with respect to the traditional American patriot and pioneer archetypes. Like Brinton's students, they learn and understand some constituent elements and the general contour of the freedom-quest narrative and can repeat it easily. But what distinguishes them from Brinton's students is that they also possess a critique of that narrative register. They are quick to point out, as a consequence of the kinds of questions Todd lays out before them and the investigations they undertake as a result, that the freedom-quest narrative applied to only certain portions of the American population for many years, that African slaves, women, immigrants, and indigenous inhabitants were systematically denied from participating in and acquiring the benefits of that quest. Many of them are capable of reasoning about and holding in their minds America, the land of the free, home of the brave, and most envied and powerful nation on the planet, together with America, the unfinished democratic experiment whose population constantly wrestles in the present with its pockmarked, divisive, volatile, and contradictory past.

These two competing images, in spite of the way that they grate against each other, seem more real to Todd's students and are more consistent with their experience of the world than the progressive, heroic nation-building narrative register of the textbook. Although the promise of a neat, simple, stabilized storyline remains deeply seductive (and what may account in part for students' desire to be in Brinton's class), Todd's students have learned to deal with its implausibility as a consequence of Todd's pedagogical approach.

★ ★ ★ ★ ★

It is probably fair here to wonder if I am using Brinton's and Todd's cases to create a manufactured dichotomy that allows me to use the former's teaching practices as a handy foil against which I can champion the latter's. This is a reasonable concern; I have several responses I wish to offer in defense of my comparisons.

As I have stressed, Brinton's collective-memory approach to teaching history can be thought of as common across the country, an exercise in persisting instruction. There are a number of history teachers who excel at being powerful storytellers, who participate daily in the revered collective-memory approach, who draw heavily (or exclusively) from standard U.S. history textbooks, and succeed at building the freedom-quest narrative arc into the historical consciousness of American youth. These history teachers do well at engaging their students most of the time with their animated lectures and compelling storylines. As such, Brinton's efforts represent a good example of what we would appreciate finding if we walked through the secondary school, U.S. history classroom door. His orientation to historical knowledge and history itself, his epistemological mindset, his pedagogical choices and practices all go some distance in defining the basis of the sorts of opportunities students typically receive in learning about the nation's past.

However, as much as we might want to praise Brinton's practices, *it is becoming increasingly difficult to ignore the mounting research on the limits of his persistent-instruction/collective-memorialization approach to teaching history*:

(a) less than salutary results on national assessments of student knowledge;
(b) reports of alienated students disliking history courses and finding them moribund because the storyline is presented as a *fait accompli*;
(c) cognitive helplessness when they encounter conflicting historical accounts because they lack tools and criteria for judging among them; and
(d) students of color (the ever-growing proportion of public school inhabitants) reporting suspiciousness about the nature of a storyline that seldom includes them as key agents in stories of national triumph.

All of these limitations should occasion serious pause. As I have observed elsewhere, continuing to encourage more of the practices Brinton exemplifies on the expectation that it will erase the limits just noted is akin to over-filling the gas tank of an automobile on the belief that it will make the car's seized engine operate more effectively.[23]

My argument is this: Even though Brinton's efforts may appear to be what we might expect in history teaching, *it is largely a broken approach.* Because it primarily traffics in a nationalist collective-memory project and is more about heritage commemoration than teaching history itself, as David Lowenthal might say, it works on principals of indoctrination instead of open investigation, advocates celebration over education, and privileges acquisition of prepackaged ideas rather than participation in a community of practice that generates those ideas.[24] Historian Michael Frisch observes that

> alienated students cannot be bullied into attention or retention; that authoritarian cultural intimidation [in the history classroom] is likely to be met by a further and more rapid retreat; and that there may well be, in that alienation itself, statements about the claims of the present on the past worth our respect, attention, and response.[25]

He then adds, "I have concluded in my own [U.S. history] teaching that the evidently massive, uniform subsurface reefs of cultural memory [students possess] are, in this sense, part of the problem, not resources for a solution."[26] If Frisch is correct, and the research in history education repeatedly bears out his claims, then more of the same will simply not do.

Most of us recognize Brinton's approach as history teaching, and a good example at that. Perhaps we all encountered and can wistfully recall a teacher like him. In the presence of his approach's familiarity, it is difficult to imagine that there could be alternatives that we might still think of as teaching history. However fixated we might be on insisting that what Brinton does defines history teaching, there is nothing about his collective-memory approach that is necessary or inevitable, nothing about requiring that the nation and its progress be located at the center of the narrative, little that makes a narrative at all inexorable. To this end, my characterization of Nancy Todd serves as an apt counterpoint. A look into history classrooms such as Todd's gives us a viable alternative to consider and around which we can explore learning consequences that turn out to be more intellectually potent and engaging for students.

Albeit in a manner that may miss the mark with some students (but is any public high school history teacher fully successful with all her 30-plus students all the time?), Todd engages her charges' intuitive investigative proclivities, their desire to know why things turned out as they did, their need to raise questions about what the past means for them, to wonder whether there might be other stories we might tell about that past. Although her students may occasionally complain about how difficult this enterprise often is, a visit to her classroom more often than not presents the observer with adolescents who are wide-eyed interrogators of the past that has gone before them. They poke and prod, question and judge. They read, and not simply for that one main idea an author ostensibly had in mind when he or she told a story about his or her experience. Todd's students read critically, assessing sources, considering their perspectives, evaluating their worth in addressing questions posed by Todd. She continues to push them to the point where she imagines that they eventually will begin asking their own smart historical questions.

Todd has succeeded in providing her students with criteria for making decisions about what to believe about the past based on the evidence they can cull from an examination of past's multiple accounting practices. Unlike Brinton's high schoolers, Todd's are not intellectually helpless when they encounter conflicting messages. They know how to read carefully, assess proficiently, build a model (or models) of what might have happened, and construct defensible arguments for the historical claims they wish to make.

Todd's students are learning that the past and history are two different animals. The former is much larger, widely temporal in scope, and riddled with contradictions and complexities. The accounts an investigator of that complexity can generate are multiple and subject to almost infinite revisions. The story in the standard U.S. history textbook, they have come to find, is only one such accounting effort. It retains no more inherently elevated an epistemological status than another account save for the way it uses evidence to support its claims. Because the textbook contains few if any traces of the evidentiary trail on which it rests its claims to historical knowledge, it cannot be fully trusted to get it right. Trusting the textbook because some invisible authorities said so, or the book's authorial tone implied that it got the story correct, smacks for Todd's students of the parental claim that the parent must be obeyed simply because she or he is in charge. For most adolescents, and especially Todd's, those sorts of rationales for obedience generate considerable skepticism and the demand for more powerfully defended warrants.

Perhaps most importantly, Todd's history course is as much about teaching potent life capabilities as it is about teaching history. And Todd will aver to preparing her students with those capabilities as her most important purpose for teaching history the way she does. She recognizes that few if any of those adolescents who grace her classroom will become professional historians. Building a teaching purpose around that type of preparation, she acknowledges, would be almost silly. She understands the landscape to be about using her history courses as a means of cultivating in her charges the ability to read their world and make sound, astute decisions about what to take from it, what to believe. She wants them to be good Jeffersonian democrats; ones who engage, question, and assess requests for sociopolitical, cultural, marketplace allegiance; ones who pause to think in the face of claims that sound too good to be true; ones who exercise an eminently healthy modicum of skepticism before rendering a commitment. In a world where communication is instant, horizons are vastly foreshortened, and information and ideas bombard from every direction (especially outside of school), Todd wants her students to be ready. However, she also wants them to know some history and to learn about the freedom-quest narrative. And know it they do because they typically score as well as or better than Brinton's on the school district standardized assessments (assuming those test results are accurate and valid measures of that narrative's ideas).[27]

Todd makes different pedagogical choices than Brinton. Her choices are framed by a different set of understandings and conceptualizations about what history is, how it references the past, and to what end. She worries that the collective-memory approach to teaching U.S. history is more indoctrination than education, more nation-state celebration than serious historical study, and emphasizes acquisition of at the expense of participation in. She wonders what sort of preparation for life in a hectic, complex twenty-first-century world it provides. Such doubts and questions have spurred her to explore and pursue pedagogical options that tend to defy common practice, but yet yield more educationally defensible outcomes for students, or so she reasons. And there is some evidence in the research literature on history education that lends credibility to the educational potency of her choices and the subsequent rationalizations she pursues.[28]

By my lights, Todd's pedagogical choices and moves provide a window through which to imagine what history education could be for adolescents and youth in American public schools. The consequences of her choices on the academic development of her students appear rich and intriguing. They represent additional value in that students have opportunities to learn about the same nation-building narrative Brinton and others like him teach their students, while also receiving experiences in historical study that teach crucial ideas useful beyond that narrative and beyond school itself. This is not to criticize the Brintons of the U.S. history teaching corps, but rather to call attention to a different way of conceptualizing and rethinking how that subject can be taught and to what ends.

* * * * *

At this point I want to return to the question concerning why, if Todd's efforts show so much promise, more history teachers do not emulate her. Why is it that what she does appears so rare? There are some obvious reasons to which I have already alluded. To the extent that the state is responsible for socializing its young into understanding the cultural tools that are perceived by adults to be crucial to the development of their identities as Americans, it makes good sense to instill in them a triumphal narrative arc that commemorates and celebrates national heroes and their emblematic historical accomplishments. From Founding Fathers to military geniuses, and from Manifest Destiny to Promontory Point, Utah, there is much to tell and repeating the story often can serve to anchor it in historical consciousness. Those who learn to repeat it, while using pronouns such as "we" and "our" throughout, bespeak their nation-state allegiances. They can rightly call themselves Americans.

Teachers such as Brinton understand themselves to be conduits and carriers of this important socializing collective-memory project. Most Americans would recognize that project as a central mission of schools, insisting on its necessity. Veering off its path means to be doing something other than teaching U.S. history, just as teaching the German language in a Spanish class would be perceived as a grievous error in direction and conceptualization. Nancy Todd makes this "error" at her peril. She knows it, but continues on anyway. Other history teachers are much more reluctant to stray off the time-honored path. Experience has taught people to know what a U.S. history class looks like, and many—parents and administrators in particular—would likely be at least somewhat dismayed by Todd's choices and practices, thinking them, perhaps, curious, but otherwise suspect in the context of a history course. Many teachers learn quickly to avoid the potential for that kind of controversy.

Another fairly obvious reason for the rarity of history teachers such as Todd is a function of the rarity itself. It is problematic to understand and then emulate a set of practices you have never seen. Put another way, history teachers who have become discouraged because their persistent-instruction effort does little to interest students, find themselves to be less than compelling storytellers, and/or cannot sustain the energy it takes to be a consistently good narrator, may deeply desire a conceptually different alternative to what they are dong. However, if those teachers have no one like Todd from whom to learn, they tend to find the learning curve steep and genuinely distinct ideas and approaches difficult to envision. Even historians, in the courses they teach at the collegiate level to grade-school history-teachers-in-waiting, rarely spend much time revealing the inner workings of historical practice, how knowledge is produced, how ideas get debated, and the ways in which evidence for claims is mustered and defended, preferring instead to reserve those sorts of intellectual experiences for their graduate students.[29] Where are teachers to learn how to deal with the complexities of a Nancy Todd approach?

Less obvious reasons for the rarity of history teachers such as Todd involve understanding how complex and challenging the practice is, especially if history teachers in their apprenticeships of practice have experienced only a steady stream of storytellers, narrators, and lecturers from early grade school on. Doing what Todd does in her classroom requires deep knowledge of the subject matter, an understanding of the structure of the discipline of history, as Jerome Bruner might say,[30] and a fundamentally different epistemological orientation to how knowledge is produced than the one that typically animates work in the collective-memory effort. History teachers in Todd's vein also must believe that their students can learn to investigate the past, reason intelligently about what they find, build evidence-based interpretations, and construct oral and written arguments that can stand up to scrutiny. Additionally, they must possess the fortitude to be persistent in the face of initial resistance from students who have never learned history except as relatively passive recipients of the heritage-inspired, celebratory accounts they encountered since elementary school and in the wider culture since birth.

Despite the important gains in historical thinking and understanding history teachers will witness should they persist, they run the risk of losing some control over their students. This, most teachers will tell you, is an ardent, palatable, daily fear. Asking students to actively construct historical ideas from the *residua* of the past can mean that they may well go off in all sorts of unpredictable directions. Managing those directions by insisting that the use of evidence arbitrate an outcome still can mean that a variety of interpretations and ideas are in play simultaneously. Such results are endemic to the discipline of history; some might say it is the discipline's lifeblood. Nonetheless, engaging novice learners in this manner creates dilemmas for history teachers that take considerable energy to manage. It can be psychologically draining in the same way Brinton's daily routine of animated storytelling is physically fatiguing.

History teachers, such as Todd, trade one sort of exhaustion for another. That is why purpose becomes so important to sustaining teachers who approach their history classrooms in a more disciplinary, investigative vein. They come to see advantages in the broader educative and intellectual power such an approach produces in students, advantages generally absent from the common collective-memory regimen. The few who traverse Todd's path appear willing to trade off some classroom control to gain richer, longer-lasting learning outcomes, ones that have the potential to arrest the less than salutary consequences we currently witness. That

Todd's students score as well as if not better than Brinton's on school assessments, as one example, suggest that the trade-offs are worth pursuing in spite of the challenges inherent in the approach.

＊ ＊ ＊ ＊ ＊

I am maintaining that it would benefit us to accept the general premise that the approach teachers such as Todd take to teaching history—rare as it is—portend important cognitive and academic advantages and may be more intellectually and culturally potent than collective-memory approaches typically are. For the reasons I have labored to show, it is time to rethink again the approach we take in history education, to revisit the legacy of the Amherst Project and take Richard Brown's prophesy seriously. Doing so leaves us to consider at least two key questions. The first is this: What does a teacher like Todd need to know in order to teach as she does? And the second is: Where would he or she learn it and under what circumstances? My goal is to address these two questions in the chapters that follow. I attempt to bring teachers such as Todd and the sorts of knowledge they work from into sharp relief. By necessity, I work from a set of assumptions that it may help to explain.

First, I assume that many history teachers are caught up in practices that resemble Brinton's. Yet, for a variety of reasons, some salient ones related to the restlessness and boredom of their students, such teachers are at least interested in thinking about modifying their practices in ways that engage those students in more exciting learning experiences in their history classrooms. Some have taken advantage of the burgeoning number of historical source materials on the Internet, using them with their students to augment the narrative they present and the one offered up by the text-book. As a result, students, many for the first time, can get opportunities to read history from the perspectives of those who lived it, an experience that entices.[31] This assumption's currency is borne out by my many anec-dotal conversations with history teachers who find the daily plight of storytelling in the presence of disengaged students pedagogically wearisome. Their curiosity, they say, is piqued by almost anything that might adjust practices in ways that motivate their charges. An investigatory approach to teaching history is one such matter that brings them to conferences and colloquia to learn. Not all history teachers are so inclined; but many are.

Second, I assume that there is significant merit for students in learning history in ways that reflect how the past comes to be understood within the discipline. If students benefit, then I assume history teachers are benefiting as well, since most teachers I talk to are deeply interested—we might say invested—in their students learning what they have to teach.

I have already noted a number of these benefits in my descriptions of what Nancy Todd does and to the ends she pursues.

Third, teachers who seek a path toward history teaching that represents a type of knowledge and a cluster of practices tied up in an investigative angle rarely, if ever, have had what constitutes that knowledge and those practices systematically unpacked for them.[32] As I noted, this makes the learning curve steep and daunting. Engaging that curve therefore can feel like a lonely enterprise, and because it is, perhaps it seems unattractive. Reading something that resembles a road map across the complex bumpy landscape of teaching this way may help. Here is a hint of the road map I pursue.

Most of the middle of the book treats the question concerning what teachers might need to know in order to teach in ways that resemble an investigative, discipline-based approach. Specifically, I focus the third chapter on history as a subject matter and attempt to address what about it history teachers need to know in order to teach in an investigative vein. I consider it from several different angles—for example, epistemological, substantive, and procedural—all rooted in a conception of history that is linked directly to my sense of what happens in the discipline, to the practices that originate there. Then in the fourth chapter, I consider what history education research has taught us about what it means for learners to understand history as a subject matter as defined in Chapter 3. I take up who these learners might be, the range of their capacities, and some ideas about the sociocultural contexts from which they come that may affect the nature of their understanding of history.

Next, I draw Chapter 5 together under the auspices of planning and teaching. What kinds of pedagogical moves do teachers need to make, how do they think about and plan for these moves, and what alternatives might be entertained when different sorts of classroom situations arise. Following this, I devote a chapter to ideas about knowledge such history teachers would need to possess concerning how to design assessment practices that generate data to tell what degree of success is being achieved. Knowing about these assessments, what they measure, and what they reveal about learning can go some distance in rationalizing a practice that, as we have seen, is rare in public education. The ability to provide data on what students are learning, for example, is a powerful means of understanding whether the effort is succeeding, and if it is, how to communicate to parents in what ways. I also add to this discussion ideas about the relationship of the types of assessments I believe teachers who pursue an investigative approach might need to know and employ, while also considering issues facing them that relate to more common assessment practices driving standard, history-curriculum-coverage efforts and the limits of those efforts.

To provide some sense of actual practice from which to unpack the ideas I convey, I provide examples of history teachers (composite illustrations of one in particular, Thomas Becker, throughout the middle part of the book, that are drawn from my research program in history education and from that of others[33]) going about planning, teaching, and assessing in ways that are reminiscent of Nancy Todd. This will allow me to tease apart those ideas, separate them for closer analysis and dissection, and then reassemble them again near the end in Chapter 7. This chapter summarizes how the pieces fit together into a *small-t* pedagogical theory of history education as investigative practice.

Finally, I devote the last chapter to dealing broadly with the second question: Where are history teachers to learn the ideas I have heretofore described? Although I broach this topic, I go beyond typical discussions of teacher education programs conceptualized as those delivered by faculty in colleges of education. I take up the role history departments can and do perform, the long apprenticeships of observation budding history teachers experience, the role collegial mentorship could play in bringing about the further education of history teachers in the spirit of the approach I am advocating and illustrating, and the job curriculum specialists in school systems can perform to enhance the likelihood that their history teachers might follow the path of Nancy Todd (and Thomas Becker in the forthcoming chapters) and reap the rewards she (he) does. I also consider the influence of various policymaking bodies with an eye to what they currently do that could be reshaped to support teachers like the Nancy Todds and Thomas Beckers.

CHAPTER 3

The Case of Thomas Becker

Using Knowledge of History as a Domain to Structure Pedagogical Choices

Thomas Becker sat at his desk, staring at the blank notepad and assorted history books and articles in front of him. Tomorrow, he was to begin a series of lessons on Andrew Jackson's Indian-removal policies that would culminate in a look at the 1838 Trail of Tears, an experience in which approximately 15,000 southeastern Native Americans were forcibly marched to "Indian territory" (later known as Oklahoma) as a means of clearing land east of the Mississippi River for Anglo settlers.

Becker had just read the school's textbook version of Jackson's approach toward the natives and was left unimpressed. The textbook's account of Jackson's Indian policies was scarcely a page and a half and barely glossed events that stretched over a decade from 1830 to 1840. Becker did marvel in passing at how astute textbook authors were at condensing rich complex events into such compressed accounts. Becker stared at the wall and then the ceiling, imagining how he might teach his 15- and 16-year-olds about this historical period and about U.S. policy toward Indians in the first half of the nineteenth century.

Despite the textbook's telescopic treatment, Becker was convinced that Jackson's approach toward the southeastern Indians represented a congealing of attitudes and policies pursued by his leadership predecessors. That hardening of approach resulted in swift and powerful actions. Promises were frequently broken and treaties were fundamentally nullified at Jackson's discretion. The cavalry was called in and the Indians were set to the march. By Becker's lights, Jackson's administration laid down important precedents for interacting with Indians that would be followed again and again by future national leaders.[1] Becker wanted his tenth graders to understand how this worked, how the history of using the U.S. army in forceful dislocations of Indian tribes could be traced at least to Jackson in the 1830s. Historical context and precedence for the bloody post-Civil War military campaigns against the Indians on the far western frontier would be laid down here in the east in the 1830s, or so Becker reasoned. But how to take up this topic?

Becker had been teaching American history at Sentinel High School for four years. Until this year, however, he had not taught early nineteenth-century American history, having been assigned to courses focusing on periodizations following the Civil War and Reconstruction. Becker had graduated from college with a degree in American history. Not sure whether he wanted to teach or pursue an advanced degree in history, financial considerations pushed him to consider combining a master's degree with a teacher-certification program. It took him just over two years to finish the combination degree and obtain teaching licensure. He enjoyed the study of graduate-level history while also learning to teach. For his master's thesis in history, he focused on the changing nature and application of democratic principles during the early nineteenth century. He found Jackson to be a compelling and conflicting case.

Jackson is sometimes referred to as the "People's President" for his efforts at expanding how the new nation conceptualized its citizens' franchise. Yet, Jackson was no friend to Native Americans, who arguably could be thought of as the first citizens of the nation. One could think of Jackson as a democrat in some senses and a tyrannical despot in others. Becker had read widely about Jackson. Some of his favorite then-recent treatises include work by Robert Remini, Ronald Takaki, and Anthony Wallace.[2] A year or so ago he had picked up and read Gloria Jahoda's, *The Trail of Tears*, and found it intriguing and saddening simultaneously.[3] Jahoda's account tells the story more from the Cherokee, Seminole, and Choctaw perspective. He found in it parallels with Takaki's, *A Different Mirror*. Becker was also well read in the archival source material on Jackson, having combed speeches, treaty language, policy statements, and congressional debates about Jackson's policies. Jackson was very much a man of his times, patriot, nationalist, military hero, frontiersman and paternalist, occasional autocrat, and racist all rolled into the same persona. Becker wanted his students to understand Jackson as just such a man, providing them with a historically contextualized window through which to view that early nation as it attempted to move forward with its ideals, on the one hand, and struggle to overcome (often unsuccessfully) past contradictions of those ideals on the other.[4]

To his twenty-first century sensibilities, Jackson seemed profoundly enigmatic to Becker. He imagined that his students might see him the same way. How could someone, who professed to believe in democracy the way Jackson did, be so apparently cruel toward the natives, and especially the Cherokee who had adapted fluidly to the white man's colonizing world? This would be a good generative question for the lessons on Indian policy, Becker thought. It would track nicely onto his preceding treatment of Jackson the democrat, who widened the franchise and championed changes in voting practices. In many ways, mused Becker, Jackson epitomized nineteenth-century, new-nation tensions, while at the same time symbolizing the conflicted nature of America's efforts at closing the distance between its professed ideals and its gritty undemocratic realities.

It was getting late and Becker needed to make some curricular and pedagogical decisions. One generative question was not enough. He wanted students to further their investigation of Jackson, to deepen their understanding, to get a more balanced view than a textbook-only treatment would provide. As with most accounts drawn from the past, the story of Indian policies during the 1830s and their consequences could be told from a variety of perspectives. Knowing how a history gets produced, a perspective shaped, and outcomes developed was as much a teaching goal for Becker as was inviting his students to understand Jackson, the man, the aspiring democrat, and the seventh President of a nation emerging full force into the nineteenth century.

Becker was searching for a set of questions—five fertile ones would be ideal—that could become the grist for the mill of his students' efforts to dig into the past of Jackson, the natives, Indian policies, their consequences, and a sense of continuity amidst historical change. Different perspectives were central to this undertaking. Becker wrote his broader generative question on the notepad. Below it and indented, he began to scrawl out those five questions. The questions would frame out the students' investigative focus. They would also help him select the kinds of materials the students would read as they dug about in the past seeking to answer the questions Becker had laid out before them. Students would work in five groups of five to six students each. He would either supply them with the readings or point them to websites that contained archival material on Jackson, the natives, and policies, and included some firsthand accounts from a variety of perspectives. What the latter would be at this juncture he wasn't sure. But experience taught him where to look and how to make selections. He first needed the investigative questions.

Those questions slowly began to emerge: (a) What were Jackson's Indian-removal policies and what insight do they provide us into the mind of the man? (b) In considering his treatment of the Native Americans, can we fairly call Jackson the "people's President?" If so, which people are we speaking about, and what does this tell us about how leaders such as Jackson conceptualized what it meant to be an American in the early nineteenth century? (c) How did the Cherokee, Choctaw, and Seminole tribes, for example, respond to efforts at removing them from their homelands? What were their positions? How did they communicate them? (d) What exactly was the Trail of Tears and what were its consequences for white settlers in the southeast and for the natives moved to the west? And (e) In what ways were Jackson's policies and tactics with regard to the natives a historically precedent setting and how can we tell? How did the idea of Manifest Destiny relate to such possible precedents?

Tacitly, by this point, Becker was also working from another set of questions, more epistemic in nature. They derived from his abiding concern that students understand how we come to know about the past, a concern that figured in all his curricular units. What allows us to make claims that we know what occurred during that period from 1830 to 1840? On what basis can we say that there are warrants for the histories that are produced? What evidence can we draw from? How do we work with that evidence to assemble interpretations? What evidence is considered reliable and historically significant and what of it remains marginal to our investigations?

Rather than simply provide students with a range of perspectives on Jackson and Indian affairs in the decade under consideration and be content with whatever understandings students produced, Becker sought to develop in them a healthy intellectual skepticism toward knowledge claims in history, to help them see that there are a variety of legitimate stories that can be told. He would also insist that, despite history's tentativeness and partiality, it was not that any old account would do. Accounts or interpretations that result from questions asked about the past would need to stand up to the test of evidentiary support, something Becker had been gradually teaching his charges. These lessons on Jackson and Indian removal would be no exception. Becker would weave these more tacit, epistemic matters into the fabric of the lessons, as he had been doing since the semester began, and since he began teaching.

The substantive questions that would drive Becker's pedagogical moves throughout the series of lessons were about as complete as he could render them at this late night point. It was time to begin framing out the procedures by which students would tackle those questions. He began to sketch out an introduction to the lessons in which he would pose the larger generative question to the class and then include the five sub-questions. In doing so, he imagined that this practice was an effort to model for students how to ask rich historical questions that could animate investigations. He hoped that eventually students could engage also in the process of posing questions themselves. For now, he was convinced that they were not yet ready because they had had little experience of coming up with rich, meaty questions in school history courses.

After introducing the five questions, Becker would follow with a clearly articulated plan in which students would be grouped five or six to a question. He pondered for a moment whether to take the time to let students decide which questions seemed most intriguing to them and shape the groups that way, or to simply assign students. He deferred for the moment on the decision, instead scribbling on his notepad the need to remind students of the rules for pursuing their questions. He then listed out those six rules:

- All source materials and texts he would provide would be read by all group members.
- All would make a concerted effort to make a contribution to the production of an interpretive response to the question they were assigned.
- Group discussions should be dominated by fairness, openness to ideas, the right to speak and be heard, and the right to file a minority report if the group was not unanimous in their interpretive response to the question.
- Responses needed to be supported by evidence from the materials and cited in the footnote style he had previously taught them to use.
- Both oral and written responses would need to be generated.
- Students would assume different group roles (e.g., recorder, oral presenter, written-account assembler) as they went about producing their responses.

Becker knew from previous exercises drawing on this approach that his students were beginning to make sense of how to so engage, largely because he had begun giving them a grade on group effort, of which the students had partial input.

It was time to begin assembling materials. He had been building a set of files of readings related to Indian-government relations during the 1830s. Many of the documents were original sources from the period, especially writings by natives, particularly the Cherokee. He had photocopied sections of the books from his personal library. He also had extracted some documents from Internet digitized archives, favoring the Library of Congress' "American Memory" site and the National Archives site. He pulled these from his briefcase and began to sort them into piles based on the five questions. Once the piles were complete, he put each into its own file folder and wrote the respective investigative question across the top. Then he went back through each folder to be sure that a variety of perspectives were represented. For example, he included a copy of the Treaty of Dancing Rabbit Creek; writings by Choctaw Chief David Folsom, Cherokee Chief John Ross and his wife Quatie Ross; correspondence between Jackson and his military commanders sent to remove the Indians; excerpts from the Treaty at New Echota signed by U.S. Commissioner Schermerhorn; and the like.[5]

Becker knew that the need to sort through the differences among these perspectives would make the students' interpretive work tricky and some would complain that such exercises were too difficult. But he would assure these students that this was doing history, that the need to be as true and faithful to the past as possible, while also understanding such a possibility is largely denied because no one could go back to see what really happened, what people really thought and said in any definitive way.[6] History was a thoroughly interpretive discipline, its problems and questions ill-structured, bearing heavy reliance on incomplete residue from the past to teach us about our forbearers, necessitating no shortage of historical imagination to generate more complete ideas and mental models. He reassured himself that this issue—the one of interpretive difficulty and its prompting of complaint—was registered typically by the same handful of students who were so good at doing school (reading, getting the right answer and reproducing it for a grade) that his approach to teaching history ruffled their academic security blankets.[7] He also reminded himself that most of the rest of his students took to these exercises with considerable excitement and interest.

It was late. Becker had made about as much progress as was to make. He would finish the remaining adjustments to the plan tomorrow; time for sleep.[8]

KNOWLEDGE OF THE DISCIPLINE'S STRUCTURE

How does Becker understand the subject matter of history, in this case concerning Andrew Jackson and Indian policies and relationships during the 1830s? How does that understanding help him shape his curricular and pedagogical choices? In what ensues, I unpack the sorts of knowledge of history I believe Becker works from in formulating his plans.

At the outset, it is important to note two matters. First, it should be clear that Becker is following a periodization scheme common to school U.S. history curricula across the country. The scheme is typically organized chronologically, begins with a cluster of chapters on colonization along the Atlantic coast, moves on to a consideration of what many textbooks refer to as the "Forming of the New Nation," followed by the growth of that nation (and sometimes its inherent growing pains) during the early nineteenth century, then onto "A Nation Divided," and so forth. United States history curricula in public schools generally follow the chronological progression and colligatory conceptual divisions used by textbook publishers as they ply their chapter-by-chapter tour of the nation-building process. Focus frequently turns on cultural leaders such as presidents and assorted national level politicians, generals, and capitalists, who are mostly of Anglo stock and male. Becker's consideration of Jackson is part of this same package, appears in Sentinel High School district's U.S history curriculum guidelines, and resurfaces in state standards documents. Becker's treatment of Jackson's Indian-removal policies, while not explicitly mentioned in any formal school district or state documents, does go to one of the district's curriculum objectives that hinges on students developing an understanding of issues related to national growth and development during the first four decades of the nineteenth century, or at least this is how Becker interpreted the lessons' application.

Second, Becker is somewhat the expert on Jackson and early nineteenth-century American history. This provides him with crucial advantages as he weighs the range of options at his disposal. Possessing more rather than less knowledge about specific topics one will teach opens up the terrain on which decisions can be made. This probably seems self-evident. But it is not a trivial point here. Teachers such as Nancy Todd and Thomas Becker use the investigative approach they do because they are confident in their knowledge of the topics they teach and understand their disciplinary referents and historiographic patterns.[9] To teach this series of lessons, as Becker will, requires that he read history and keep reading it. As a physician works to stay abreast of the latest developments in diagnostic practices and surgical and pharmacological treatments, so too history teachers such as Becker work to stay reasonably current with scholarship around the topics they teach. However, there is more to it than simply reading additional histories produced by historians and other scholars of the past. Becker works from an understanding of what Jerome Bruner or Joseph Schwab might call the structure of the discipline.[10]

In history, what might that structure look like? This is a difficult question to address in any definitive way for there is no agreed-upon structure of the discipline of history. Philosophers and theoreticians of history have offered a variety of differing conceptualizations.[11] Here, I provide a bit of a hybridized version that I believe squares with Becker's understandings (ones that enable him to work through the lessons he proposes the way he does) and borrows from a number of treatments of such a structure by theoreticians. Bear in mind that I am being cautious here. Not all will agree with this conceptualization, the one that Becker holds. However, we need something to work with in order to unpack the types of subject matter knowledge history teachers might need in order for them to teach as I am proposing. The one here provides some useful analytic and theoretic power.

Epistemological Underpinnings

Let me begin by sorting through the types of epistemological under-standings Becker appears to possess that enable him to plan the way he does here. This is intellectual heavy lifting. However, in many ways it is pivotal to making sense of Becker's grip on the subject matter he will teach. Without these epistemological, warrants-for-historical-knowledge commitments, it would be difficult for Becker to imagine the kinds of investigations he invites his students to pursue. And it would be even more difficult to envision how he would manage the enterprise in the classroom. Teaching history for him is underpinned and defined by the epistemic stance to historical knowledge he holds.[12]

For decades after the historical guild professionalized its practices in the late nineteenth century, it pursued what historian Peter Novick refers to as the Rankean objectivity ideal.[13] In brief, the effort involved understanding and reporting the past as it really was. Influenced by positivism and modernism's burgeoning reliance on the scientific method, historians of Rankean persuasion strove to adopt the method and underlying philosophy as they sought to render the past on its own terms, letting the voices and minds of human ancestors speak in their own words. This effort or goal has served as an ideal that has animated much of the work in the discipline for over a century. However, as ideals often go, it has never been fully attainable. Historians such as Fred Morrow Fling, Carl Becker, and Charles and Mary Beard in the first half of the twentieth century and a raft of historians such as Frank Ankersmit, Joan Wallach Scott, and Hayden White in the latter half of the same century pointed out how the past cannot be made to speak in its own language. Such scholars noted that historians mediate the past in their retellings of it, that their own sociocultural positionalities cannot be shorn in order to free that past to reveal itself independently of those who seek to retell it.

Historians and historical investigators are all products of their own times and locations. Their present positions inexorably shape their understandings and retellings of the past. The possibility of Rankean objectivity thus remains an ideal. Investigators of the past may do all in their power to tell the truth about the past, to let it speak in its own language, but this effort is denied. It is denied because the historian cannot fully stand outside her/his own mind in order to understand the minds of those he/she investigates.[14] Moreover, investigators to date have not developed the capability to do time travel and, as such, cannot go back to the era of their investigations to observe history enacted and record its outcome. And they cannot conduct experiments in genuine reenactments of the past and observe and record the results much as a physicist might. In effect, the past has been lost to us in the present. All that remains is its residue in the form of documents, notes, diaries, postings, pictures, pottery shards, and the many stories investigators have told about them. These must all be interpreted, within the historical context of the period in which they originated, but also by investigators who occupy a contemporaneous time zone replete with its own, often contrasting norms, values, and emotional valences.[15] As David Lowenthal notes, the past can indeed be a foreign country.[16]

Thomas Becker is fully aware of the ways in which the objectivity ideal is elided by the limitations and encumbrances of actual historical practice. This is why he finds the textbook accounts of the American nation-building process so unimpressive. They tend to mask the sources from which they draw their knowledge claims, speak in authoritative, omniscient voices as though the past was communicating directly through the author(s), render invisible the many different ways the nation-building story might be told, and hide the interpretive, investigative machinery that made the story possible in the first place and remains the lifeblood of the community of practices called the discipline of history.[17] Historiography, that study of how historians have written about the past and to what end, exists as it does because of the deep interests investigators possess in understanding the shifting, changing, revisionist nature of historical knowledge. Becker learned to appreciate these points in his historiography course in graduate school. It took him some time to reach that understanding, though.

Becker, like many prospective history teachers, had his epistemological understandings of knowledge in the field shaped by textbook authors and teachers who presented the subject's storyline as if it had been carved timelessly in granite, as though everyone in some era came to a consensus about just what the narrative of nation building was to say. Those ideas were reinforced by everyday encounters with the past in the media and at his visits to historical theme parks. A few details here and there might appear askew or in conflict, but there was little that upset the fundamentals of the narrative register he learned in school.

Little about his undergraduate history degree challenged his epistemic stance, one that left him convinced that the story appearing in the books and sounding off the lecterns was anything other than the truth about the nation, that the objective ideal had been attained. His senior research paper on early nineteenth-century democratic developments began to raise questions for him, however. His pouring through archival material and reading different historian's accounts of Jackson, for example, demonstrated to him that a unitary account was hardly possible. The past was too complex, too conflicting in the images it presented. Jackson, the "people's President" and "Indian slayer," became more and more difficult for Becker to bend into one coherent storyline the longer Becker spent in researching him. Jackson, like his nineteenth-century counterparts, was a man of his time, with a particular conception of democracy in his head that Becker did not initially comprehend from his twenty-first-century perch, framed out by beliefs in a relatively unmalleable narrative arc of the American nation, land of unbridled liberty, unvanquishable progress, and justice before the law. Uneasy, he went to graduate school for some resolution. More historical research and a powerful historiography seminar later, he emerged having reworked his epistemological position. Sure, one could speak in terms of historical facts, but it was the meaning to which investigators subjected those facts that gave history its substance, and it seemed, those meanings were constantly in a state of being reshaped.

Becker's initial reaction to this apparent realization gave him a moment of cynical pause. History, he began to think, was whatever we wanted it to be, whatever story we might come up with, something bordering on mere opinion. However, his next educational transformation came as he learned about the concept of evidence in historical writing and research. This involved coming to understand that, what may distinguish a bona fide history recognized within the field from someone's mere opinion about past events, hinges on its having passed guild-sanctioned tests, those that require a historical account to defend its claims by substantive use of evidence. He learned for the first time that all those book reviews that appear in the leading research journals in American history were part of the vetting process. Footnoting practices were also central. Peer review before publication was yet another part.

In time, Becker began to make distinctions between the past, History, and histories. The past was that temporally vast landscape strewn with its relics and *residua*, the partial, complex, and conflicted archive of material from which investigators would draw in order to make sense of what came before them. By Becker's lights, History—with a capital H—became the officialized, sanctioned story that, say, a nation state wanted to tell about itself.[18] The typical high school history textbook served as a good example. Becker came to define histories—plural and in the lower case—as those multiple stories one might tell about a nation state, a civil-rights struggle, a president, a midwife, a labor strike, or a suffrage movement.[19]

Structures of Historical Knowledge

These epistemological gyrations eventually led Becker to a process in which he constructed a sense of the structural terrain of history, the subject matter he was to teach. He was helped down the path by a course in his teacher education program that related history education research on teaching and learning the subject, especially in the context of American history, to the exercise of learning to teach it. It involved two interrelated but, from his perspective, analytically distinct forms of domain knowledge.[20]

The first type of knowledge was construed as substantive. It was divided into two parts, foreground and background subtypes. The foreground subtype derived its moniker from the role it typically played in how people think about the subject. When people talk of history, they often mean— in everyday parlance—History, the official story, for example, that narrates the tale of nation building, something with a title such as *The Story of the American Nation* or *The United States and Its People*. At one level of sophistication or another, it is a product of investigators' efforts to make sense of the past. It is the finished product, the end result of research into the past. Its key concepts turn on revolution, democracy, capitalism, government operations, laws and policies, decision making, checks and balances—all organized by colligatory, chronological themes. However, such a history could be of shorter temporal scope, encompassing the American Revolution period or the Civil War or the Great Depression. It might also show a temporal range, if more circumscribed yet, by tracing out experiences and telling the story of someone's life or a particular labor union's efforts or the vicissitudes of the civil rights movement in a southern city during the first half of the 1950s. The vehicle for the most part pivoted on narrative or storytelling in an effort to explain to readers the past of its focus.

Knowledge of the background type (still substantive in nature) derived its metaphorical reference from the fact that it tended to reside as an organizational force in the mind of the investigator. Creating a history (or History) requires a sense of the relationships between progress and decline, periods of continuity and those of change. It also necessitates thinking about causation or, put more specifically, multiple causative factors that can account for, say, an era of rapid change following a time of relative historical stability and permanence—such as the rapid movement toward industrialization and urbanization after decades of reliance on agrarian living arrangements. These background ideas and concepts assist investigators in organizing and framing out the ways in which they shape their stories or narratives.[21] Investigators explain the past of the industrial revolution (the events and developments foregrounded) to their readers using (background

A CHARACTERIZATION OF HISTORY DOMAIN KNOWLEDGE*

Substantive Knowledge Types

(1) Foreground/First-Order Conceptual and Narrative Ideas and Knowledge

- Interpretations of the past that come from who, what, where, when, and how questions. Often rendered chronologically in narrative, explanatory, or expository style.
- Examples: Stories of nation building, capitalism, socialism, economic production, military exploits, democracy, political parties, names, dates, etc.

(2) Background/Second-Order Conceptual Ideas and Knowledge

- Concepts and organizing ideas that investigators impose on the past in the practice of researching, interpreting, and making sense of it.
- Examples: Causation, significance, change over time (e.g., progress, decline), evidence (i.e., author perspective, source reliability, nature of sources), historical context, human agency, colligations (e.g., the American Revolution Period, the Progressive Era).

Procedural Knowledge Type

Strategic Practices

- Knowledge of how to research and interpret the past. This knowledge is rule bound and criteria laden. It is subject to decisions about its proper practice from within the community of historical inquirers, but also remains open to ongoing debate.
- Examples of procedures:
  - Assessing status of sources:
    Identifying and attributing sources, assessing perspective, judging reliability.
  - Building mental maps or models.
  - Using historical imagination while interpreting within historical context.
  - Constructing evidence-based arguments.
  - Writing an account.

* Adapted from Bruce Van Sledright and Margarita Limon, "Learning and Teaching Social Studies," in Patricia Alexander and Philip Winne (Eds.), *The Handbook of Educational Psychology, 2nd Edition* (Mahweh, NJ: Lawrence Erlbaum Associates, 2006, pp. 545–570).

organizing) concepts about what constitutes such change, what caused it, and whether it denotes progress or something else.

The narrative arc—and the causative claims inevitably embedded in it—function as an overcoat, carrying the perspectives, predilections, and conceptual organizational predispositions of the investigator woven deeply and implicitly into its fabric. Such perspectives and predilections involve a degree of historical imagination, empathy, and contextualization, and implicate degrees of moral judgment and theories of human agency. These mental operations also rely on a sense of what counts as historically significant, an understanding of what that concept means, and how its definition has been shaped and reshaped historiographically. Above all the narrative must be underpinned by evidentiary support drawn from the past itself.

Imagination, empathy, and historical contextualization are required because often the residual evidence necessary for substantiating historical claims is both conflicted and sparse. To make a narrative case, that is, to make the story work, requires imagination to fill in blanks or to resolve testimonial conflicts. Empathic regard—the capacity to understand the past on its own terms, as in to judge historical actors and their actions within the contexts of the lives they lived—tempers how this imaginative process is wielded and how moral judgments are rendered, to the extent that they are. Investigators must understand these concepts, how to use them, and how they operate in the background-shaping space where they work to form the narrative, the history. We see the mayfly spread its wings and light off the river's surface, fluttering around our face fully formed and elegant in its fragility. But the background work that forms this hatched, aquatic beauty is in its underwater emerging or nymphal state. So too with histories; their foregrounded structure is what readers see and read. Their background formative period is nymph like, taking shape beneath sight lines of direct view, submerged in the working mind of the investigator.[22] Yet, careful readers sense these subsurface characteristics implicitly through the perspectival contours and veneers of the surface narrative.[23]

A second type of historical knowledge might be referred to as syntactic, procedural, or strategic. Here, the term strategic knowledge and practices will suffice. Becker came to classify the processes and specific cognitive operations the historical investigator undertook in her or his investigative work as just such knowledge. These included the capacities to (a) ask rich historical questions, (b) comprehend where to find evidentiary source materials that would address the question posed, (c) assess the status and nature of those sources (judge their reliability as evidence, make assessments of where evidentiary preponderance lay, make sense of the perspective of an author, identify type of source and origin and attribute it to a socioculturally positioned particular author), and (d) construct an evidence-supported account first mentally and then in writing. It was not difficult for Becker to see that, as an investigator plied the trade of engaging in this activity, the use of background concepts, ideas, and types of knowledge would also be brought to bear.

For example, to ask rich questions (strategic process), one must know something about what is constituted as historically significant (substantive

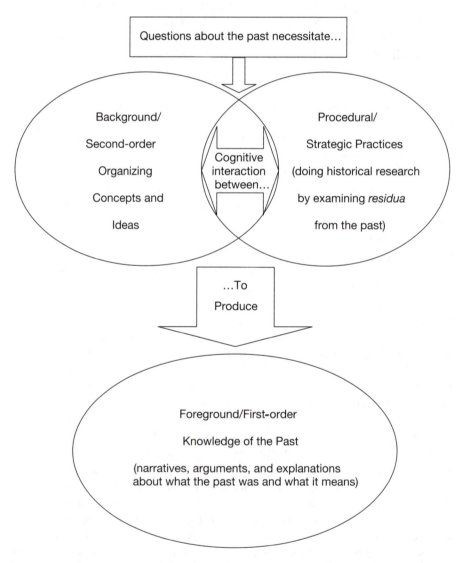

Figure 3.1 A characterization of the relationship between types of domain knowledge

background concept) and be able to distinguish it from the historically trivial. Second, to assess the nature of a source (strategic process) requires a sense of the historical context in question, how an author may have thought about his or her world during that period (background concepts). And a third example turns on knowing something about ideas such as causation, continuity and change, and human agency (background concepts) in order to build a cognitive, evidence-supported account that addresses the historical question asked (strategic process). An account or a history (foreground knowledge) *emerges from* the complex, cognitive interplay of applying strategic processes while deploying background, organizing concepts. Figure 3.1 characterizes the arrangement between and among these ideas and practices.

Becker was committed to helping his students learn the nature of this interplay so that they would come to a deeper sense of how History (or *histories*) is (are) formed. Rather than found or received, History (or a *history*) arises from a set of human cognitive operations that are guided by rules and guild-sanctioned norms and criteria (see Box "A Characterization of History Domain Knowledge" and Figure 3.1). Absent the interplay of substantive types of knowledge and strategic processes, History or histories are not possible. Nonetheless, even History remains necessarily unstable and ill-structured as a knowledge domain because humans (historical investigators) are prone to shifting the nature of the questions they ask of the past. As questions change, so do the ways in which those questions get answered. New *histories* are continuously produced. History as a disciplinary practice, as a way of making sense of what came before us here in the present, turns out to have more in common with the humanities than the physical sciences (and perhaps even the social sciences, although some might dispute that claim).[24]

USING DISCIPLINARY STRUCTURE AND PRACTICES TO DEVELOP THE INDIAN-REMOVAL LESSONS

Historical Questions

If we re-examine the way Becker arranged the lessons he was designing, we see how crucial that structure was to his decision-making process. The practice of history involves thinking historically. Thinking historically— that is, employing background organizing concepts in concert with specific analytic strategic processes—results in coming to understand the past— that is, being able to produce a coherent story about that past, or a history. This was a principal goal Becker was attempting to achieve with his students: The process begins with questions: Who were these southeastern Natives? Why did Andrew Jackson want them removed? What were his policies? Where did they originate? How did the Indians respond to the threat of forcible dispossession from the lands they inhabited? What was the Trail of Tears and how significant was it and in which ways? As noted, because Becker's students were still novices when it came to asking rich historical questions—largely as a result of a schooling process that gave them virtually no experience in doing so (recall Brinton's teaching-as-telling, collective-memory approach and its persistence in history courses)—Becker engaged in generating the questions in an effort to model them.

Significance, Change, and Causation

Asking powerful historical questions requires that the interlocutor know something about *historical significance*. Within the practice of historical study, some questions are thought to be more important than others, in part, because answering them is construed to be more generative in helping those who read the results understand the past about which those questions ask. Generativity is linked to various communities of inquirers. For example, in Becker's school-history community, students are presumed to know far less about the past of the Jacksonian period, for instance, than are those historians who have devoted a good measure of their careers to studying Jackson's presidency or the history of U.S. government–Native American relations. As a consequence, the types of questions Becker was asking his students to address might seem rather pedestrian to such historians who practice within a different, more professional community of inquiry. Determining significance, then, is related to what investigators assume they need to know, which in turn is connected to what they already know, what has been investigated by others before them, and the kinds of questions those investigators had asked.[25]

A sense of judgment is implicated in the process, and judgment depends on the historiographical record, ideas about *change over time* (e.g. progress, decline, and the colligatory thematic terms used to describe them) and *causation*, the community of practice in which an investigator is working, and how criteria for judgment are employed in that community. To a degree, an investigator's own historicized positionality also plays a role. As a result, judgments vary. Becker's students, for instance, may find his questions less compelling and therefore less significant than Becker does. This would require Becker to mount an argument about why his questions are important in order to persuade his students to explore them. Professional historians likewise must convince their community of peers about the significance of the questions they ask and attempt to address. In either case, judgments about what counts as historically significant play a fundamental role in adjudicating the kinds of questions that are tendered and investigated.

Becker understands these distinctions and builds his questions around them, drawing on both his sense of what he thinks his students know (and do not know) and on what generative questions investigators have already asked and deemed significant. In this way, he situates the interrogative process within his high-school learning community, but remains carefully mindful of historiographical referents to and antecedents existing within the guild or community of professional historians.

Evidence

Asking questions also necessitates digging about for *evidence* (from the past's archival and historiographical residue) that can be used to address the questions. The concept of evidence is crucial to answering historical questions. If investigators are wont to make claims about what the past means as a way of answering their questions, they need to possess a well-honed sense of what counts as evidence to support those claims. Because histories are fundamentally arguments about what the past means, investigators often rely on argument structures in producing historical accounts and interpretations. This necessitates (a) stating a thesis, (b) introducing claims, (c) providing a warrant for the significance of the claim, and then (d) supporting both with evidence drawn from the *residua* of the past.

Becker's lesson structures are attempts to teach students about how to state theses, make historical claims, establish defensible warrants, and support them with appropriate evidence. History, rather than falling from the sky ready made or someone's more-or-less substantiated opinion about what the past means, is a carefully constructed set of claims and warrants undergirded by evidentiary support. The test of the argument's robustness is established in a community of peer review, in which the argument is made public and then critiqued by those who also have examined the evidence. Becker makes a practice of inviting his students to act as those peer reviewers in order to hone their sense of the criteria used in evaluating historical claims. As the more-knowledgeable other in the classroom, Becker occasionally acts as an arbiter, mediating disagreements and assessing his students' historical claims against the supporting evidence they provided. In this way, he again models how such practices work in coming to make sense of a complex, often unruly and perplexing past.

Contextualization

One difficult aspect of this process for Becker is teaching his students to *historically contextualize* their claims, a primary criterion used in peer reviewing to judge the worthiness of an account of the past. As he teaches them to address the questions he poses, he has noticed that the students tend to judge the actions of the historical agents they were studying using contemporary standards of morality, by present-day assumptions about what people should know, and how that knowledge should then influence how they would behave, rather than by the standards governing choices and actions common to the period in which those agents lived. Professional investigators have long faced this problem. One might argue that this concern inspired Voltaire's dictum that history is merely a pack of tricks the living play on the dead. It is difficult for investigators to rein in the contemporary sociocultural, normative moorings that serve as crucial sociological guides for living. Abandoning those guides, to the extent that one could even imagine doing so, erases the temporal positioning anchors that make present-day life possible. At one level or another, existing temporal, normative bearings intrude on interpretations of the past.[26] Therefore, a moral dimension to historical analysis and interpretation remains unavoidable as investigators—professional historians and student novices alike—cannot help but interpret the past in ways that implicitly or explicitly relate to their present lives. However, more expert investigators do try to temper their presentist judgments (i.e., presentism), attempting instead to read the past as much as is possible on its own terms.

Becker initially found the problem of presentism to be deeply acute among his high school students. They thought historical actors they were studying were alternately stupid, naïve, gullible, dim witted, uncharacteristically brilliant (by present standards), or just plain unbelievable. Such judgments would creep into their historical claims. When he caught them, Becker took great pains during peer-review sessions to critique students' interpretations on grounds that they had wandered too far from the evidence they had gathered and had resorted to making historically de-contextualized, and therefore unfair judgments. He would use these moments to gently prod students to imagine as best they could how different life was during the time period they were investigating, to attempt to understand the lives, thoughts, and actions of those past historical agents on their own temporal terms. Embedded in these critiques was Becker's effort to teach about the idea of *change over time*, how the evolution of intellectual understandings, technological developments, and sociocultural commitments influenced how agents thought about their worlds and made decisions, how historical context shaped agents' lives for better or worse.

Strategic/Analytical Practices

Becker is keenly aware that background, second-order concepts and ideas are necessary but insufficient to understanding that protean past his students were interrogating. They also needed specific investigative tools and practice in using them effectively to answer the questions posed, much the way a carpenter needs saws, nails, and hammers, and an understanding of how to employ each one, and to what specific ends in order to construct a house. Without a combination of investigative tools, experience deploying them, and organizing concepts and ideas, Becker theorizes, students will remain (a) susceptible to believing doggedly almost any historical account they meet, (b) cognitively helpless in the face of conflicting accounts, and therefore, (c) by being unable to reconcile oppositional testimonies and/or incompatible historical claims, prone to adopting a form of naïve but corrosive relativism about how we understand the past. Finding these outcomes to be unacceptable in a democratic culture that required citizens to know how to weigh evidence before participating in democratic decision making, he uses history as a school subject matter to provide his students tools and ideas for doing so.

Becker builds his lessons around giving his students opportunities to learn about and employ analytic tools that were necessary to advance their historical-thinking capacities. Since sources and artifacts (letters, diaries, newspaper accounts, paintings and photographs, relics) offer primary access to the past, Becker identified a cluster of history-specific "reading strategies," printed them out in chart form, and pinned it to the classroom wall early in the school year so he and his students could consult it whenever necessary. He hopes that eventually "reading the past" as described in the three-part chart would become so second nature or automatic to his charges that they would no longer need to consult it.

At the chart's top, he wrote How to Read Sources and Build Interpretations. Just beneath that heading, he noted A. Assessing the Status of Sources after the British history education researchers he had read in his graduate program.[27] Below it he listed out three initial steps:

(1) identify the source and attribute a historical author(s) to it;
(2) assess the author's perspective given the context in which the author(s) lived; and
(3) evaluate the reliability of the source as evidence for addressing the historical questions you are asking.[28]

Following these reading strategies, Becker identified four additional analytic moves he wanted students to make under the heading: B. Constructing an Interpretation. The four moves included:

(1) build a mental map or model for how you can address the questions;
(2) refine the map/model as you read and assess each additional evidentiary source;
(3) use your imagination to fill in gaps in the evidence trail (but stay within the historical context!); and
(4) sketch out an argument that uses the evidence to address the question you are answering.

Finally, Becker added the final point: C. Write up the argument in essay form using the structure: Overall thesis statement → warrant → claims → evidence (with footnote citations) → conclusion.

Becker believes that it is crucial for his students to learn how to write coherently about their interpretations, rather than simply present and debate them orally in class. Here again, he seeks to model practices within the discipline in which the gold standard for interpretive success is measured in well-crafted, published essays and books that have survived rigorous peer scrutiny. Pivotal to this writing practice was relying on the footnote to establish the evidentiary sources on the basis of which historical claims are made, long an unassailable requirement in meeting the guild's gold standard. The historical essays Becker has his students write are a centerpiece of his assessment strategy. He employs them regularly—just as he will as a result of the Indian-Removal lessons he will teach—to gauge the progress students make in learning to think historically as they come to understand the past the questions they investigate are designed to address.

ANTICIPATING A THEORY OF LEARNING HISTORY

If no more than tacitly we can see in Becker's deployment of the structure of domain knowledge and disciplinary-practice modeling a theory of how students learn and come to understand history as a school subject. It works off the assumption that deep historical understanding is possessed by those who are experts in the field. Demonstrations of that expertise can be understood by dissecting the practices and knowledge structures of its principle purveyors—professional historical investigators. If one critical goal of studying history in school is to assist students in *developing deep understandings of the past*, then it makes sense to work from research studies that teach us about how experts think and practice their craft and then, in turn, utilize these ideas as a means of structuring learning opportunities for novice historical thinkers. Manifestations of expertise can serve as targets of achievement to which those novices can be taught to aspire.

However, we also need to consult research studies to give us some idea where novices begin, of what their baseline understandings and thinking capabilities consist. From those baseline positions, teachers such as Becker can plot out how to use the structure of knowledge and practices within the community of expert historical investigators to move novices closer to that knowledge and practice. Possessing a sense of this academic-developmental trajectory (or what some call progression) presupposes a theory of learning.[29] The theory that animates Becker's teaching effort and its relationship specifically to history as a domain of learning is the subject of the next chapter.

CHAPTER 4

Learning History

What Do Students Know and What Can They Do with that Knowledge?

Above Becker's desk at home hung two framed statements that he looked at regularly. The one on the left said, "To teach is to learn twice." He was unsure where that statement originated, but he thought it had come from Joseph Joubert, the eighteenth-century French essayist. As he was planning his unit on Indian removal policies of the Jackson period, his gaze turned to the second statement, which actually was formed as a question: "Who are my students and what do they know?" He often turned to this question as he thought about how to design and order his investigative questions. Knowing who his students were—their sociocultural backgrounds, race, ethnicity, and the like—helped him imagine how they would take to what he was trying to accomplish with them. Understanding—or at least hypothesizing—what they knew about history and what they could do with what they knew was also crucial to his pedagogical decision making.

He stared at the question often because during his four-year tenure at Sentinel High School he had come to realize, perhaps too slowly, that no two classes of students were alike. It was helpful to remind himself to take stock of who these 16-year-olds he taught were, how their ideas about history had progressed, what enabled them to do so, and how this in turned affected the dynamics of their classroom interactions. It also assisted him in focusing on the academic differences among them and therefore where he needed to direct additional attention.

KNOWING STUDENTS

About 40 percent of the students in each of Becker's classes were white, of European ancestry. Another 30 percent were African-American.

Twenty-five percent were Latinos/as and the remainder were Asian-Americans. This distribution mirrored the larger student population at Sentinel. Becker knew from studying the research in history education that non-white students tended to work from different stories of the American past. Common cultural and home life experiences shaped their ideas in ways that sometimes varied considerably from the white students he taught.[1]

Latino/a students at Sentinel, many of them born in the United States, but to first generation immigrants from Central America (most from Mexico), still thought of their pasts in terms framed by histories of that part of the world. They were less accepting of key elements of the freedom-quest narrative because they had not defined their historical trajectory from east to west, but rather by the other way around (as they knew, much of the western U.S. had been home to Hispanics first, and before that, indigenous Americans). The quest for freedom shaped by the promise of work in America had brought their parents to the U.S. but, beyond this, the path of that quest had little in common with the European, Anglo progenitors of the idea of Manifest Destiny and westerly progress across the North American landscape from Atlantic to Pacific. Language also played a key role. Less eager to give up their native Spanish tongue, Latinos/as in U.S. schools had been stigmatized for decades for that reason.[2]

African-American students, the research indicated, were for good reason likewise suspicious of the freedom-quest narrative. As involuntary, forced immigrants, their ancestors came to America in chains and at least figuratively remained in them for hundreds of years. The progressive, Whiggish narrative arc of the standard U.S. history textbook, populated mostly by the exploits of Anglo leaders (capitalists and generals, presidents and pioneers), was one in which these students had difficulty locating themselves. Freedom for the ancestors of these students had been decidedly elusive. The elusiveness of freedom, the hard fought struggle to gain that so-called American birthright, and the continued battle to overturn lingering opportunity-suffocating racism and discrimination were ideas reinforced in the African-American community, at home, and at church, and ideas Becker knew from experience that his African-American students brought—sometimes case-hardened—to school with them.[3] With respect to both his Latino/a and African-American students, Becker could anticipate some resistance to a story focused on the historical machinations of those whites of European stock who so frequently populated the freedom-quest narrative register.

Becker's white students, most if not all of them, could much more easily identify with, appropriate, and master the freedom-quest narrative.[4]

Their own ancestral histories tended to cohere more specifically with that narrative. The pasts of these students more closely paralleled the origins of the United States as traced out on the pages of the textbook. Their sociocultural advantages were to a large degree tied up in believing that storyline. The Asian–American students, about whom Becker had read in the research literature, more quickly and intentionally assimilated to white, mainstream American cultural and normative structures and therefore were generally quicker to identify with and master the freedom-quest, nation-building narrative. They would tend to be more like their white counterparts in school contexts than they would be to the other groups of students. Yet, even these Asian–American students would trace ancestral roots to other shores and therefore other histories not shared by the Anglos of the freedom-quest narrative.

Becker knew from experience teaching such culturally and ethnically diverse students and from reading the research that teaching United States history as a celebratory nation-state freedom quest was a challenging, quixotic, perhaps even impossible undertaking. Resistance to it would mark the reactions of some of his students while others would be quicker to appropriate and master such a narrative. If he were to press on the narrative, it would advantage some of his charges while potentially inspiring a more perverse, but understandably cynical reaction to it by others. As he stared at the framed question above his desk, he was reminded of historian Eric Foner's observation in the book, *Who Owns History?* Foner pointed out that "when [we] seek [a] narrative emphasizing the glories of American development, [we] ignore the fact that . . . it is no longer possible to treat American history as an unalloyed saga of national progress toward liberty and equality." This in turn spurred him to remember another of Foner's incisive observations about efforts to pursue textbook-like, nation-building glorification rituals: "The problem with [such] histories [is] not simply that they [are] incomplete, but that they [leave] students utterly unprepared to confront American reality. The civil rights revolution, divisions over Vietnam, Watergate—these [seem] to spring from nowhere, without discernable roots in the American past."[5] The phrase "leav[ing] students utterly unprepared" haunted Becker when he first read it five years earlier and even more so now. It pushed him to continually reflect on how he could transform his history-teaching practices in ways that better prepared his students—*all of them*—for intersections with an uneven, bumpy, and often contradiction-laden American experience, both past and present.

To accomplish such a transformation, Becker believed, would be a more academically respectable and transparent way of dealing with this school subject. It would serve to acknowledge legitimately competing (vernacular, in Bodnar's vocabulary[6]) histories of the sort his students already possessed to one degree or another. It would render visible the machinery of how *History* and *histories* are shaped and allow students to develop the capacity to render smart, thoughtful, independent interpretations of those histories. In the process, Becker would teach them that, as a result of opening up the landscape, it did not mean that any story would then be acceptable. Rather, the way humans go about remembering the past is fraught with difficulty, and that evidence-supported, defensible histories can reside legitimately side-by-side if a skillful investigator understands that perspective is a powerful and justifiable shaping force in how histories are constructed. Working from a solid core of such ideas, Becker hoped, would leave his students more prepared to confront that smudges-and-all American reality they traversed each day.[7]

UNDERSTANDING WHAT STUDENTS KNOW AND CAN DO

During his graduate school matriculation, Becker was introduced to a heavy dose of the research literature in history education. This literature—much of it on student-learning processes and understandings—served to underpin the development of a research-based approach to teaching history in school. It was rooted in a sociocultural, constructivist-oriented theory of learning spawned by what some called the cognitive revolution in educational psychology.[8] It also flowed from antecedents in the kinds of subject-specific research that animated scholarship in education from about 1980 onward, first in Great Britain and about a decade later in North America.[9] What most interested Becker was the apprenticeship model of learning, in which researchers began to identify what experts in a given field knew and did with what they knew, and then used those understandings as benchmarks to measure where novices fell along a continuum toward expertise.[10] In this sense, researchers began the lengthy and complex (and yet incomplete) process of charting the academic development, or progression, of ideas along the novice-expert range.

Four clusters of results characterized this research scholarship concerning how students learned history: On (a) epistemological understandings; (b) foreground (first-order) ideas; (c) background (second-order ideas); and (d) strategic, analytical capabilities of learners.[11] As we have seen, Becker began using these ideas and their referents to disciplinary expertise as ingredients in a small-t learning theory on which he could rely to make pedagogical decisions. At first uncertain, he later embraced the idea forwarded by one his professors that, if a pivotal goal of history education was to develop in students deep understandings of the past, teachers needed to look to those whose efforts epitomized the zenith of that understanding—the experts. How those experts—historians in this case—went about building their deep knowledge could then serve as an exemplar for how students could learn the subject.[12] Becker augmented this idea with his belief that all students could benefit by possessing the capability to test claims against evidence, a practice common to what the experts did and something they needed for life in an information-rich, digitized, consumption-driven world, one in which claims to truth were everywhere, yet evidentiary support was often flimsily manufactured, if present at all.

Epistemological Understandings

Becker knew from reading the research and from experience that many, if not most of his high school students would enter his history courses as naïve realists.[13] That is, they would subscribe to the epistemic idea that the historical accounts they read—especially if those accounts seemed authoritative and were written in authorless, omniscient prose—were real, beyond question, and therefore eminently believable. Students of color in his classes might harbor reservations about some of the accounts' claims, but generally would hold those misgivings close, partly because, in class where authority was rarely on their side, they were seldom sure what to do with what they perceived as conflicts between their understandings of the past and the versions narrated in the accounts. The more official looking and sounding the accounts were (e.g., the thick, hard-bound U.S. history textbook), the more closely they held their reservations.

Becker had puzzled over why his students seemed so steadfast in their realist epistemic stances until he realized that he too had for a long period relied heavily on a similar epistemic position. The more he thought about it, he understood that school history's mission was primarily designed to shape socio-political allegiance to the nation state, not engender questions about how historical accounts get generated and why.[14] The structure and orientation of United States' history courses in school rested on the school's socialization mission, to build understandings of national development, to champion particular American values, and traffic in officialized collective memories as a means of shaping nationalist-citizen identities. Being a nation of immigrants—voluntary and otherwise—put pressure on schools to use courses such as U.S. history to ameliorate the sociocultural *pluribus* wrought by successive waves of "outsiders" and "others."

As we have seen, a subtext of the narrative register of official textbooks with their embedded celebrations of nation-state collective memories involves conveying a message designed to wrench a measure of national *unum* from a potentially excessive and divisive *pluribus*. Being a good history student, therefore, means getting the right story down and being able to recall it at will and claim it as one's own. Challenging the official account by juxtaposing it against competing others, raising questions, and trying to address those questions by submitting claims to evidentiary support disrupts efforts to secure nation-state *unum* in the face of a threatening degree of sociocultural *pluribus*.

Becker was all too aware, however, that many of his students encountered competing accounts of the American past everyday, in the wider culture, at home, and in school itself. He knew by talking to them personally, when they trusted him enough to be open, that they possessed some not altogether inchoate doubts about the veracity of, say, the textbook's storyline. He also knew from experience in class teaching his charges to question accounts and develop a deeper sense of how they were constructed that the next location in their epistemological transformation was perhaps as equally untenable as their naïve realist stance.

What he had observed them do—and it matched his own experience to some degree—involved a shift to what might be termed a naïve relativist position.[15] That move was accompanied by such statements as, "History is based on opinions, and one opinion is pretty much as good as another because we are all entitled to our opinion about what the past means." Sizing up such observations, Becker realized, left his students incapable of dealing with conflicting accounts. As with the naïve realist position, they remained handcuffed in the face of alternate conceptions of the past told from different angles or perspectives. History reduced to opinions, left his students with little recourse but to believe or reject one over another on the grounds that they "sounded good," "presented a lot of information," or "seemed convincing." Students at this developmental point still lacked powerful, discipline-honored criteria for deciding which accounts possessed greater justified warrants and were therefore more plausible and defensible.

Becker's goal, epistemically speaking, involved imbuing his students' cognitive apparatus with criteria-based tools for getting beyond the naïve realist and/or relativist stances. The key concept here was the idea of evidence. It was deployed in response to asking questions of the past, questions of historical agents who left residue behind in the form of letters, diaries, speeches, newspaper editorials, pictures, relics, and the like. Even though these agents perhaps never intended to address the questions investigating students might ask, the *residua* they deposited, Becker knew, could be harnessed to that end as long as investigative tools and sound criteria were up to the task. Here he was following Collingwood, that to understand the past one needed to understand how people thought in that past.[16] Becker imagined that, by stressing among other things the role of

BECKER'S THREE EPISTEMOLOGICAL STANCES USED TO UNDERSTAND STUDENTS

Naïve realism (aka "copier")	The belief that history effectively falls out of the sky ready made; the past and historical accounts about that past are isomorphic; multiple histories of the same events are just different ways of telling the story; if multiple versions are in conflict, someone has to have made mistakes and got the story wrong; there is a correct story and the task is to get to it. In the face of such conflicting histories, of which it turns out there are many, naïve realists confront an intellectual impasse and struggle to learn history. If pressed, some begin to shift to a naïve relativist position (the other side of the naïve realist coin) in the face of this impasse.
Naïve relativism (aka "borrower")	The belief that history is all about someone's perspective (not an altogether unfounded position), that it is fundamentally a result of people conveying their opinions in the way they decide to tell stories. Even though some people's opinions may be misguided because they got the facts wrong, were biased, or were not present to record what "actually happened," holding opinions is a given human right, so must be tolerated. Conflicting accounts can result from different kinds of testimony offered and/or cut-and-paste operations of storytellers, all a result of reporters' biases. Relativists possess few strategies or tools for discerning better histories from others because they lack criteria for deciding and hold a weak concept of evidence, making learning history difficult. It tends to be "anything goes."
Critical pragmatism (aka "criterialist")	The belief that it is in the nature of historical investigation for accounts that result to vary because of the different perspectives people hold, even those who witnessed and reported on the same events (testimony), that history is possible because we can develop and employ tools (e.g., judging historical claims against evidence) to determine better from less strong histories. In the end, criterialists accept that historical accounts will vary but can still be legitimate if they measure up to judgments about what people agree to believe (criteria) constitute good accounts. Criteria-laden tools (e.g., use of evidence, analyzing/describing within historical context) allow investigators to decide poorer from better accounts. Perspective matters deeply as part of reading and assessing the subtext of an author's/cartoonist's/painter's intentions, but it is not all wanton bias and opinion as naïve relativists tend to think.

evidence (what agents thought) to claim (what that thought meant), he could move naïve realists and relativists to become what he called critical pragmatists, the sort epitomized by many working historians.[17] Having an idea of this developmental trajectory, difficult as it often was to traverse, enabled Becker to know how to listen to his students (or read their writing), make sense of what they were saying, and adjust teaching decisions accordingly.[18]

Foreground, First-Order Ideas

If the research work on college students' understandings of the freedom-quest narrative was any indication, and Becker knew from previous teaching experience even among his pre-collegiate charges that it was, his 16-year-olds would know very little about Andrew Jackson, his military career and "peoples' presidency," and particularly his battle to remove southeastern indigenous Americans westward. Students might have heard of the Trail of Tears, for example, but would have difficulty recalling specific details about it or placing it accurately in the chronological sweep of the nineteenth century. At best they might remember from eighth grade that Jackson was President, that he had some sort of "fight with the bank," was a hero of the War of 1812, and maybe that he hailed from Tennessee. Additional details would escape them. For some of the more astute students, Jackson might appear as a lesser hero in the larger struggle to widen democratic participation in the new nation, as a military man who fought Indians and kept the British at bay in New Orleans in 1814, and as a pro-Indian removal advocate. But such students would likely be few.

In the end, Becker could count on his students remembering very little about Jackson from their eighth-grade U.S. History course. Jackson might be recalled as fitting nicely but very generally into the progressive, westerly sweep of the freedom-quest narrative. This would occur—if it did—on the strength of his reputation as one who did much to widen the franchise for property-less Americans. But the nuance of the cost to Native Americans of this widening would be lost on them. If anything, Jackson would be cast as a participant in a long line of Anglo, military, and business leaders who led the nation ever closer to realizing the freedom-quest ideal. Quite where he fit and how exactly would remain vague. Students of color, if they knew this much about Jackson, would perceive him as simply another in the press of the textbook white, U.S. cultural-leader mold—Washington, Franklin, Jefferson, Hamilton, Jackson.

Becker also knew from talking to other history teachers and especially his colleagues that these assumptions about what students knew and therefore had to work with regarding Jackson and his Presidency were reasonably accurate. Becker would be building upon a variety of loosely generalized ideas germane to the progressive, freedom-quest narrative arc of which students believed Jackson to be a part. However, they would also possess a series of naïve conceptions, a weak sense of chronological sweep, and a presentist-driven tendency to see a president hero such as Jackson as pedestrian and second class compared to Washington, Jefferson, or Lincoln. Their sense of the Trail of Tears and the policy contexts and military environments in which it took place would be thin, under-developed, and oddly strange and sad simultaneously. Mostly, many of them, experience reasoned, would think the Trail of Tears "just happened," a decontextualized historical event, untethered to Manifest Destiny and the anti-Indian policies that it fostered, ones existing before Jackson marched the southeastern natives to Oklahoma territory and certainly ones that persisted through the end of the nineteenth century.

Becker often wondered whether the African-American students in his classes, upon learning more about Jackson and his views toward indigenous Americans, thought Jackson a racist, one of a long line of Anglo leaders so dispositioned. That—should they read the textbook carefully and discover that Jackson was also a slave owner and therefore have their judgments of him reinforced—was also of interest to Becker. He was deeply curious about what his black and brown students did with such thoroughly American contradictions when they encountered such brash examples in school history classes. Perhaps the relentlessness of the upbeat narrative arc and the fact that students rarely read the textbook carefully, and/or such details were so thoroughly glossed by the textbook authors, they never fully noticed. Part of Becker's purpose hinged on helping all his charges notice such contradictions so as to learn how to deal with them, understand their lineage, and as a consequence pay serious allegiance to Foner's idea that it is simply no longer possible to teach American history as an untroubled story of relentless progress toward liberty and equality. History teachers, Becker was mindful, need to do better preparing students to understand the multiple contradictory impulses, intractable struggles, and blemished trajectories embedded in who Americans were, have become, and, in the case of his students, still are becoming.

Background, Second-Order Ideas

Becker knew from the research literature that second-order historical ideas, such as historical significance, change over time, progress and decline, causation, evidence, and colligatory concepts (e.g., the "American Revolution Era," "Jacksonian Democracy") that frame historical narratives and textbook accounts, remain typically opaque to students. These organizing ideas historical investigators impose on an unruly past to bring order to it and structure their narrative choices and judgments are seldom made plain in accounts, functioning in the background, behind the proverbial curtain, the sources of their uses and appearances remaining a mystery. These ideas and concepts are the interpretive, intellectual ropes and pulleys that animate the ways in which investigators craft interpretations. Without them, there would be no History or histories. But most investigators, following perhaps in a guild-respected, von Rankean ideal of letting the past speak in its own words, seem reluctant to share how they manipulate the machinery of ropes and pulleys, how their interpretive judgments develop in the process. They appear, Becker thought, much more concerned about telling stories about the past rather than making visible the choices and organizing the ideas and concepts that guided their efforts. How those stories were selected and on what basis remained the province of the investigator's grey matter.[19]

This investigative opacity tended to reinforce in students' the idea that history falls out of the sky ready made, that authors are simply conduits of a transparent past that indeed speaks in its own language. Becker had come to understand that the process of shaping this sort of epistemological fundamentalism (i.e., naïve realism) regarding history began already in elementary school. Textbooks that students were asked to consume and whose stories they would repeat were perhaps the most guilty of obscuring the author–investigator and the second-order choices and judgments he/she made in crafting an account. This was why Becker leaned heavily in the direction of using a variety of accounts and source materials; doing so helped him make the interpretive machinery more transparent on his way toward developing his students' investigative criteria.

In the lessons that would commence on the Jackson and Indian-removal policies, Becker was deeply interested in second-order ideas such as significance, change over time, and causation. He wanted to illustrate how Jackson—very much a man of his times—carried on a legacy and set of attitudes regarding Indians that could be traced to early British colonizing activity, back even farther to a sense of cultural superiority European colonizers held over the "savages" who were unlike them, and forward to policies such as Manifest Destiny and its role in the "conquest of the west." He also wanted his students to understand that the systematic anti-Indian attitudes and policies that followed Jackson, in part, could be linked to measures such as the Trail of Tears. Although the ways in which U.S. cultural leaders such as Jackson would enact policies saturated by Manifest Destiny and cultural—and by Jackson's time, racial —superiority would change, the policies themselves and their intellectual rationality would remain the same.

However, thinking such thoughts caused Becker to realize that, in pushing an agenda so defined, he was resting on a series of judgments, many of them shaped by his readings of the historiographic literature. This realization—one not new, only revisited again here—helped him to appreciate that the ideas of historical significance, change over time, and causation he was interested in most in this unit were the result of investigators making serious decisions about what counted as each. One could agree to disagree for example, that the Trail of Tears was a significant defining event. Thoughtful investigators looking at the same historical evidence could argue over how much change or sameness followed in the wake of such episodes in American history, or what policies, positions, or beliefs caused which circumstances to unfold. These also were important lessons he hoped to teach his students, that the past does not simply speak in its own words. Historical investigators must render a series of judgments about these matters and not everyone would subsequently agree with them. Human judgments would be in play at almost very turn (a position that would make his naïve realist "copiers" cringe). But there were accepted criteria and strategies for managing those judgments, for preventing the evaluative stage from becoming an opinion-fueled free-for-all in which it all devolved into a matter of believing that any old story one could tell was as good as any other (a direct challenge to his naïve relativist "borrowers").

Even though Becker had been working to reshape his students' epistemological stances since the beginning of the semester (some six weeks now), he was reasonably certain at least three-quarters of them were still clinging to a naïve realist copier position, one reinforced by experiences in school for 12 years and in other school subjects. The other quarter might have moved into that naïve relativist borrower stance as a result of his ministrations. This latter move was not something he sought. But in his four years of teaching, he had come to think of the movement from copier to borrower as a developmental passage rite. One was much like the flip side of the same epistemic coin: giving up being a copier seemed to inevitably push students to flip the coin and move into a borrower stance, in which a cut-and-paste, anything-goes approach seemed to cohere nicely with the realization that the investigator needed to make judgments about significance, change, and causation. Without ample, well-defined and practice-honed criteria and strategies for making sound judgments, it was like, "Hey, it turns out it's just all opinions and it's a free country, so any opinion is as good as a another (except if I just don't agree with it for whatever reason). And besides, who says I can't believe this (or that) about history anyway?"

Similar to all the units he would teach, Becker's task was to use such Jackson and Indian-dislocation lessons to provide robust learning opportunities to build and shape criteria and strategies for making such judgments, to put them on a higher plane in which those judgments could be defended via the historical record—the *residua* emanating out of the past, not a call to some relativistic principle or appeal to some free-market idea that it's simply my choice to like Adidas shoes better than Nikes. In short, Becker was determined to move as many of his students toward becoming criterialists as possible. He was reminded of a chart (see Table 4.1) he obtained in his graduate history education program.

As a part of his interest in change (or continuity) over time and its cousin, historical significance upon which its assessment rested, Becker intended to introduce his students to five interdependent criteria for assessing historical significance. The criteria hinged on an event's or series of incidences' importance, relevance, profundity, quantifiability, and durability.[20] He hoped the criteria when applied would assist his students in getting a measure on the influence of Jackson's Indian-removal policies, some of their antecedents (beliefs about Anglo-European cultural and racial superiority), and potentialities to shape future U.S. government policies (change/continuity over time). He also secretly hoped such criteria could find transfer applications in students' lives away from school, but he reassured himself that he'd be content simply seeing those criteria retained and successfully applied in his history classroom. Becker knew that to apply the five criteria in class would most likely require some type of understanding of the historiographic terrain; that is, what other investigators had thought about the significance of Indian removal and the Trail of Tears as manifestations of Indian–government relations in nineteenth-century America. Yet, he was somewhat unsure about how to proceed with providing access to this previous work. More reading might meet with resistance. A lecture might meet with the same. He made a note to himself about this and moved on.

Strategic, Analytical Capabilities

Becker knew all too well that, in tackling the landscape of moving students away from their copier and/or borrower dispositions and on to a criterialist approach, he had to teach them some strategic, analytic tools that would help them get beyond the learning impasses the former dispositions created. He had been slowly working on this effort since the beginning of the year. But he knew from past experiences that it would take time and concerted effort over the entire semester (and likely longer). He also knew that such tools were typically not in most of his students' cognitive repertoire and that they were best taught as explicitly as possible. It was unwise to assume students either already possessed this sort of tool set or

Table 4.1 Epistemology/knowledge/novice–expert level matrix

	LEVELS		
	Novice	*Competent*	*Expert*
Epistemic Stance	*Copier*—no distinction between past and history/ past (what actually happened) comes to us unmediated; or *Borrower*—history consists of cutting and pasting *residua* of the past together, but lacks a rule structure for doing so	*Moderate Criterialist*— history results from mediation by investigators via rule structures, yet needs more knowledge about rule structures in order to apply them fully and effectively	*Strong Criterialist*— investigators mine the past in order to develop historical interpretations via a rule-guided process (criteria for warranted claims) overseen by experts who shape and reshape the rules
Type	Naïve Realist— Naïve Relativist	Relativist—Pragmatist	Strong Critical Pragmatist
Knowledge			
First Order	Little to weak	Moderate/strong in some areas, weak in others	Very deep in areas of expertise
Second Order	None	Moderate to strong	Very strong/deep
Strategic	Little to none	Moderate to strong	Very strong/deep
Reading Approach	Meaning is in the text, in the words and ideas represented there. Reader can "get the main idea" by reading carefully. Reading is unidirectional, from text to reader without mediation. Reader is subservient to the text's authority	Reader engages the text in a transactional approach. Reader interprets the text based on cues and structures provided by the author. Assessing and evaluating text are crucial but other interpretation development strategies can be more limited	Transactional reading approach. Reader and author engage in "conversation." Deep strategic capability and knowledge reservoirs assist in reading. Expert reader assumes power over the text and uses the text for his/her purposes
Who?	• Most K-16 learners who have received a strong content– knowledge focus • Some history teachers	• Some college students who have taken historiography and research-methods courses • Some history teachers	• Some history graduate students • Some history teachers • Most historians

that they would develop it through occasional and casual mention. The best pedagogical approach Becker had undertaken was to plunge his students directly into investigations of the past, such as a close examination of Jackson, his actual policy statements and positions toward the south-eastern natives, and their reactions and positions to being forcibly disposed of their land and homes and moved to Oklahoma territory.

Critical Reading. From experience Becker knew that in presenting his students with original accounts from Jackson and the southeastern Indian leaders, the contrast between the positions immediately opened up the landscape on which he could work. However, he also knew that many students would find such accounts difficult to read and this would conspire to create challenges for his less strategic readers. His task then was twofold: He would need to teach some strategic reading capabilities of the sort reading researchers suggested were helpful in getting less-accomplished readers beyond the impasses that such original accounts engendered. But Becker also knew that such reading strategies (e.g., repeatedly monitoring comprehension and using repair procedures when comprehension broke down, checking fit of new ideas with previous knowledge by being metacognitive, assessing and evaluating new ideas[21]), would not be enough. He would need to consistently and persistently engage his students in learning to read such accounts in a history-specific manner, something about which the content-area-reading textbook he encountered in his graduate education program seemed frequently vague, if not exactly silent. He was pressed to look into the history education research literature in order to find support for these history-specific reading strategies.[22] Teaching them as explicitly as possible was then his second task.

Because understanding the past involves studying the past's *residua*, that this *residua* comes mainly in the form of a variety of texts, the set of history-specific reading capabilities students would need to learn involved coming to grips with the fact that texts must be read and assessed relative to other related texts (i.e., intertextually). Doing so creates additional cognitive complexities and amplifies the reading load. Add to this the fact that Becker wanted to teach his students to hold a broad view of what constituted a text, one in which an artist's depiction of a historical event or a political cartoon needed to be "read" just as a diary account or a political address. Becker reminded himself to renew his stress on the idea that the past, beyond the material pottery shard or the paper on which a speech was written or newspaper printed, comes to us via texts that must be read and interpreted, from the "visual text" of a film or the "oral text" of an ex-slave narrative to the printed word. "Reading the past" was therefore the principal preoccupation of historical investigators.

Becker heard himself say, "It's all about accounts of the past, from the student's textbook treatment and Jackson's 'errand in the wilderness' address to Congress rationalizing his efforts to remove the southeastern Indian tribes to Cherokee leader John Ross's response." Students would need to be taught explicitly to read, assess, and make sense of these various accounts *inter-textually*. They would need to learn a reading approach replete with powerful strategies for accomplishing it and much guided practice before such efforts became cognitively automatic. That reading approach and many of the strategies that accompanied it would be foreign to most of his students, if not all of them, and would sometimes clash with their common copier or borrower epistemic stances (see Table 4.1).

Becker had come to understand that the reading approach most of his students had adopted had been honed in elementary school. That approach made students subservient to the text and the author (with the possible exception of some of his more astute black and brown students who could be counted on to be more skeptical readers). Most of his students appeared to believe that the putative meaning of any text or account was "in the text," that the author wrote in a way so as to make the meaning clear for everyone, that any group of readers would (and should) draw the same meaning from any given text. Typically, a few of his students had learned the idea that texts might have multiple meanings depending on what questions you asked of it and who did the asking. This was an important first step, but as his classroom experience had taught him, it led these students to reason that they could interpret texts in whatever way they chose in a heady effort to release themselves from the perceived force of the text over them. Those efforts, no doubt, also seemed consistent with the adolescent angst they sometimes demonstrated and the desire among some of them to shed the power of the authority structures that they reasoned were dominating them. Such angst nonetheless provided a cognitive opening on which Becker could teach a more powerful strategic reading approach, one consistent with a strong criterial and pragmatic reading process.

The PAIR^e Toolkit. There were four specific, interrelated strategies Becker thought students needed to learn in order to read and analyze accounts successfully. He drew these four from his graduate history education program and the reading he did in it.[23] The four included perspective assessment, attribution, identification, and reliability judgment. He studied a chart he had created that he had pinned to the bulletin board above his desk. He had labeled the chart the "PAIR^e Toolkit," an acronym-based title drawn from the first letters of each of the four strategies (see Becker's "PAIR^e Toolkit" for Reading and Analyzing Historical Accounts). He thought the label was fairly clever, although he

BECKER'S "PAIR^E TOOLKIT" FOR READING AND ANALYZING HISTORICAL ACCOUNTS[24]

Perspective assessment: It involves the investigator in a careful analysis of an account followed by a set of assessments as to an author's social, cultural, political positioning. Making these kinds of judgments can be difficult because the author is absent, unavailable for direct questioning about her position or authorial intent. To engage this strategy well means investigators must study the context in which the source was authored and wait to complete assessments until a variety of related accounts have been read. Making sense of an author's perspective or positionality[25] often takes the form of reading between the lines, or below the surface of the text.[26] Understanding something about the historical context also helps in this effort.

Attribution: It involves a fundamental recognition that an account is constructed by a human being for particular purposes. It also requires locating an author/artist within her historical context. Recognizing that an author with a historically contextualized position constructed an account for a purpose and that it can function as evidence in making claims about what the past means is a crucial cognitive step that makes helpful attributions possible.

Identification: It involves knowing what an account is. This requires a series of moves in which an account is interrogated by questions such as: What type of account is this—a journal, a diary, an image, a newspaper article? What is its appearance—does it seem older or newer; is the handwriting or print clear, is the drawing faded? When was it created? What is the grammar, spelling, and syntax like? Knowing what an account is helps an investigator determine what questions can be asked of it and what sorts of evidence claims and interpretations can be drawn.[27]

Reliability judgment: It involves investigators in corroborating evidence (the superscript e in R^e stands for evidence). Related accounts are assessed for their relative value as evidence used in making claims about what occurred in the past. Judging the reliability of an account involves comparing it to other accounts from the period (see perspective assessment). An investigator attempts to understand if an author's claims can be corroborated elsewhere among related accounts. An account has no innate reliability; it is established by the investigator. Because accounts are reliable (in that they provide evidence for claims) only in relation to the questions that are asked of them, and because an account's reliability cannot be fixed definitively (because it can also be used to justify other claims as well), judging reliability is a necessary but almost always a relative and partial accomplishment.

also realized from his own account-analysis practices that readers using these strategies would not necessarily follow P-A-I-R^e in the order he had listed the strategies. Rather, he customarily taught his students to begin by (1) identifying and (2) attributing the account, then (3) assessing the perspective(s) it contained, and ending by (4) judging its reliability against other related accounts and with respect to their ability to provide evidence for addressing the historical questions being posed. That I-A-P-R^e order, however, produced no memorable acronymal mnemonic device he could impress upon his high school students. He further reasoned that PAIR^e was a good title because it served as a reminder to him to pair this history-specific strategic-reading toolkit with the more general reading strategies such as comprehension monitoring he knew his students would need in order to read accounts well.

Becker found in previous classes that his students took rather well to the PAIR^e approach. It appeared to work for them. Initially his treatment of it would be met with wrinkled brows and general confusion. Some students would ask why they had to learn it; could Becker just tell them what the right answer was so they could move on and skip all this expended energy on learning "new reading strategies." Other forms of resistance would surface (e.g., refusing to read at all). But Becker would insist and then persist until he had them using the approach consistently. This often took weeks and sometimes months because he was trying to get his charges to shed unproductive ideas they had learned in previous schooling experiences, to give up the idea that the text was always right about everything. Becker theorized that if he persisted long enough—and used the power of the "red pen" to grade them on their applications of the approach—students would eventually come to realize that finding some freedom from the text's/author's control would be attractive. In his informal conversations with students who came to trust him, they would reinforce his theorizing. They would mutter something about how it helped them become more independent readers and thinkers able to read between the lines and form strong arguments rooted in solid evidence-backed claims. They especially liked how it enabled them to argue convincingly with parents over contested issues and concerns at home.

THEORIZING ABOUT LEARNING IN HISTORY

Experience has taught Becker how crucial knowing something about students and working from a theory of how they learn history are to his pedagogical decision making. Studying the research literature on student learning in graduate school were critical first steps on the path to growing his teaching expertise. Repeatedly testing ideas from that literature in his classroom helped in sharpen his capabilities. As he likes to say to himself, practice helps him refine those ideas; but it does not make him perfect. Practice only gives rise to additional insights into how his students learn. Practice helps him strengthen his theoretical framework. However, as he has come to understand, it's an ongoing process that he must persist at in order to improve what his students learn from him and his courses in American history. Becker would like his charges to become competent historical thinkers who are capable of serious historical analysis and reasoning, the sort that helps them understand American history more deeply. He believes with historian Margaret MacMillan that, without deeper knowledge of the American past, his kids will succumb to collective memories that that are designed merely to "strengthen group solidarity, often at the expense of the individual, to justify treating others badly, and to bolster arguments for particular policies and courses of action." Becker believes, like MacMillan, that deep knowledge of past will help his 16-year-olds ". . . challenge dogmatic statements and sweeping generalizations. It [will help them] all think more clearly."[28]

To get there, Becker knows he needs to continue sharpening his learning theorizations. Where is he with them at the moment? First, he understands that his students come to the history that he teaches with different sociocultural frames of reference. His white, European students will note (more or less consciously) that the traditional textbook iterations of America's past align more readily to their typical middle-class Eurocentric-oriented value systems and normative structures, largely because the history those students encounter in school has historiographically been dominated by historians who share their sociocultural, and often privileged frameworks. In other words, the "fit will feel right" to them. African-American and Latino/a students will understandably be more suspicious of such versions even if they cannot exactly explain why when they enter his course. Asian students may either resist or adapt to standard school history depending on a number of factors aligned to cultural expectations, family life, and peer relations.

Despite variations, of course, both across *and* within these characterizations, the point for Becker is knowing something about what he might expect rather generally from them. It provides him purchase on how to initially hear what his students are saying as they engage the sort of historical reasoning, reading, and researching practices he will ask them to undertake. What students tell him—about what *they* find historically significant, for example—provide building blocks on which he can (re)construct his practices. Yet he knows more experience will continue to reshape his thinking as long as he remains open and thoughtful about his students and how their sociocultural frames of reference intersect with their understandings of the American past.

Second, Becker has tried to make an art out of sorting through students' epistemological commitments. Here again, knowing whether a student is attempting to understand the past from a copier or a borrower stance is extraordinarily valuable in making sense of the struggles they have in coming to understand what he attempts to teach them. Copier and borrower sensibilities, as we have seen, create intellectual impasses for students that make deeper understandings impossible.[29] Knowing what these sensibilities "sound like" when students put their reasoning on display in class enables Becker to hear where his kids are and then allow him to pedagogically strategize about what to do to unstick the cognitive roadblocks. Absent the capability to characterize various features of epistemological stances, impasses remain, and deepening reasoning and understanding is arrested. Harnessing the power to characterize unhelpful epistemic thinking and know where and how to move students past it is crucial to Becker's theorizing about his student's learning. Yet, he realizes that there is still much he can learn here. He thinks that the epistemic categorizing he draws from is still rather crude and could benefit by further refinement.

Third, Becker has honed what he thinks of as a reasonably powerful theory of the interaction between the three different types of historical knowledge: first order, foreground knowledge; second-order background knowledge; and strategic, tool-like knowledge. In practice, second-order ideas work in concert with strategic tools to produce first-order knowledge, or more pointedly, evidence-based interpretations of the past developed on the basis of rich historical questions. Without the former two types, the acquisition of the latter becomes nearly impossible save for rote memorization. However, as Becker's work with his students has convinced him, memorization of someone else's interpretations rarely constitutes the deep understanding MacMillan writes about and believes all Americans must possess.

Fourth, Becker knows that these types of knowledge need to be put to use. Learning them independently of one another or in isolation simply reverts to the trite and unproductive content-skills division and the "new" lists-of-things-to-memorize regime that plagues much of public schooling. Those rich historical questions must be posed to animate the use of the three forms of knowledge. In other words, Collingwood was right, Becker thinks, when he asked, What were our ancestors thinking?[30] Such questions form the pivotal entrée into Becker's treatment of the Indian-removal unit: That is, what were Jackson and the Choctaw, Cherokee, and Seminole thinking at the time?

To pursue knowledge-in-use, Becker uses the exemplar of the apprenticeship approach to structure his theorizing. He construes himself as the more-knowledgeable other and operates as a guide. At the early point in the semester, he selects the historical questions as a model for students about how to ask them. He later gradually releases responsibility for setting these questions to his students as they become more astute at asking them; likewise with the application and structuring of the three forms of knowledge. Initially, he models the investigative process explicitly, noting each step in considerable detail until students become more comfortable with their rather arcane features (arcane in the sense that students rarely have much experience working with them before they encounter Becker's course). He uses charts and models of the investigative process (e.g., PAIR^e) frequently as we shall see in the next chapter.

Fifth, Becker follows the typical periodization schemes found in the U.S. history textbook the school system's curriculum policies charge him to use. However, rather than accept the storyline the textbook contains and the school system's curriculum officializes as an apparent *fait accompli*, he searches that narrative for historiographic controversies and conflicting viewpoints among key historical agents and what he considers pivotal events in the saga of American democratic experimentation. He employs them as a means to promote investigation into the American past, a practice that his experience has taught him deepens understanding. The Indian-removal unit is simply one case in point. All of his units contain that investigative focus. It is as though he turns the curriculum upside down metaphorically speaking: Instead of accepting the standard, Whiggish narrative arc of the textbook treatment at face value, he problematizes the script by turning it into a running series of investigative questions around which he creates curriculum units (i.e., opportunities to learn). This allows him enough pedagogical room to consistently (a) engage his learning theory, (b) animate the three forms of knowledge in concert with one another, (c) listen for epistemological impasses that crop up and stop progress so that he can work to move his students beyond them, and (d) construct assessments aligned with these practices and goals. Because building coherent and diagnostic assessments has been one of his largest challenges, a separate, upcoming chapter is devoted to that process and thinking it has entailed for Becker.

★ ★ ★ ★ ★

As Becker well knows, this complex endeavor has been hard work, consuming almost as much planning as actual teaching time. Nonetheless, over four years, he has amassed potent investigative units for many topics about which he wishes his students to learn. He has added them one at a time. He has built an archive of source and account materials and can efficiently draw from them to help students address the investigative questions he poses. The Internet has been one of his closest curricular friends. Just as his precursors had file folders filled with lecture acetates aligned with the textbook chapters, he has digital files filled with accounts and charts and investigative units allied with his selection of rich historical questions. He has also built a small archive of DVD sources he uses to augment his digital print sources, considering them merely as additional accounts rather than anything resembling definitive declarations of what the past means.[31] Because his students often have difficulty with the language of many accounts, he has taken to "translating" many of the more difficult ones into more modern English (and occasionally Spanish for his Latino/a students with the help of the ESOL office at his school).

Of course, as Becker will freely admit, working from such a learning theory and investigative approach takes precious time, making teachers' busy lives even more so. However, as he has found, the benefits for his students of working at it steadily has paid him powerful dividends in the ways they come to learn and in how much more deeply they know American history compared with their counterparts who receive no such opportunities to learn.

CHAPTER 5

Teaching about Indian Removal

Describing and Unpacking the Investigative Approach

Becker sat at his laptop examining a file folder filled with documents and images he had amassed on Indian removal, Jacksonian-era Indian policies, and Native American positions and reactions prior to and during the process. The images and documents spanned the period from the late eighteenth century through about 1840. It was time to make some decisions about what he would teach in the Indian removal unit.

PLANNING OUT DETAILS FOR THE UNIT

Becker never taught a unit or series of lessons the same way twice. He continued to experiment with new ways of presenting them, attempting to increase their investigative power in order to accelerate the way his students acclimatized to the process and developed the thoughtful, strategic capabilities he wanted them to learn. In all his units, he was trying to deepen their understandings, not only of the details of a particular episode in American history, but the larger import of what had occurred, as well as the investigative machinations inquirers needed to more fully make sense of it.

Indian removal, especially in the southeastern states in the early nation, turned on many complex stories that one could tell depending on perspective. Historians still debated how events unfolded and stewed particularly on the motivations that drove the agents involved, from cultural leaders such as President Andrew Jackson and John Ross and John Ridge of the Cherokee nation, for example, to northern anti-Indian removal protestors and women's groups, to embedded Protestant missionaries and the larger membership of Creek, Choctaw, Cherokee, and Seminole nations themselves. Becker sat pondering how to teach this level of complexity to his 16-year-olds. His previous experiences had taught him that, in the short time he had to teach the unit (about 5–6 class periods), the complexity and number of stories was too great to do justice to any one of them alone. He had to sharpen and narrow the focus. To do so, he needed to pay attention to his specific goals for the unit and sort out how, perhaps, to use one of the particular episodes of removal that was rich enough to satisfy all or most of those goals. He began perusing the key investigative questions he had posed in preliminary planning:

(a) What were Jackson's Indian-removal policies and what insight do they provide us into the mind of the man (as an embodiment of Anglo-cultural leaders of his time)?

(b) In considering his treatment of the Native Americans, can we fairly call Jackson the "people's President?" If so, which people are we speaking about, and what does this tell us about how leaders such as Jackson conceptualized what it meant to be an American in the early nineteenth century?

(c) How did the Cherokee, Choctaw, and Seminole tribes, for example, respond to efforts at removing them from their homelands? What were their positions? How did they communicate them?

(d) What exactly was the Trail of Tears and what were its consequences for white settlers in the southeast and for the natives moved to the west?

(e) In what ways were Jackson's Indian removal policies and tactics a historically precedent setting and how can we tell? How did the idea of Manifest Destiny relate to such possible precedents?

He seized for a moment on question (c). He realized that what he wanted was *one* historical exemplar of Indian removal practice during the period, if one could be found. Did he need to teach about all the southeastern tribal removals? Could he concentrate on just one, have his students investigate it more deeply in the class periods allotted (five), and still achieve deepening understanding of both Indian removal and its relationship to Manifest Destiny, while further developing the nature of investigative historical practice? Would studying one tribe's removal process provide fecund, authentic investigative questions that students could address and therefore continue learning how to participate in the ongoing arguments about what the past means?[1]

Becker had recently rediscovered a book he had bought a year or so ago, one he never quite found time to read. It was one of those Bedford

"Series in History and Culture" books sometimes used in college history courses. Becker had several of these in his collection. The one he now took in his hand was Theda Perdue and Michael Green's, *The Cherokee Removal: A Brief History with Documents*.[2] He remembered that had cited the first edition in his master's thesis. Becker had read and studied the book carefully over the previous summer and found it fascinating. Drawing from it heavily seemed like the perfect antidote to the perennial history-teacher dilemma of too much past and not enough time to teach it adequately. This led him on a momentary intellectual tangent.

Curricular planning—as in the architecture of opportunities you provide students to learn—was a tricky endeavor in history education, he ruminated. What seemed to reinforce persistent instruction in school history, and in learning and curriculum approaches were those requirements to cover the entire textbook, a chapter a week, semester after semester. Students reacted to what they perceived as an incessant bombardment of historical details (images of carpet-bombing drifted across his mind) in an effort to jam "other people's facts" into their heads with disengagement and occasional resistance.[3] And, as he had learned in his master's program, there was nary a shred of evidence that the march of all those details produced much cognitive "stick." Because arranging the history curriculum any other way seemed so foreign to many history teachers and assumed to be such hard work initially, many history teachers preferred to follow the traditional script and remain in denial about its learning impact on kids. They seemed to be working off the principle that if they talked about a textbook topic in class, the kids would know it, or else, in the face of the perceived pressure to cover the curriculum, take some cold comfort in believing the idea.

School history curricular policies and assessment practices reinforced and sanctioned persistent instruction, making it more difficult to face up to its feckless results. He was attempting to weave a thin line between pursuing his investigative approach and hoeing to elements of the common curricular approach and the sanctions that supported it. He had to show evidence that he was following the general contours of the nation-building script, but instead of presenting it as a *fait accompli*, he would turn it into an investigation of that script's past, one that would allow him to teach his students how to mine it and thereby enhance their engagement and understanding because the investigative result then became about "their facts," not someone else's. Careful curricular and pedagogical planning aligned with powerful investigative goals were the key. "Okay," he thought, "enough for the tangent—back to work."

Focusing on the Cherokee tribe as an illustration of removal, as the Perdue and Green volume made clear, was complex enough. Becker would need to streamline even this storyline somewhat.[4] The book followed a structure that he could appropriate and adapt to his goal framework. He also could see where the streamlining could occur. But he would have to be cautious; it was easy to overplan and overpopulate the ideas with which he wanted to have his students wrestle. He reminded himself that he would allow for no more than five class periods to investigate Cherokee removal, followed by a sixth class in which he would more formally assess their gains in understanding.[5]

Becker opened a new text document on his laptop and began sketching out the key investigative questions that would headline each of the five classes' activities. He did this sort of thing for each unit. Once done, he would reshape it into an advance organizer that he would share with his students in order for them to see a general roadmap of where he wanted them to go.

Conveniently enough, the Perdue and Green book was divided into five chapters. He would use them to generate his investigative questions. What he found so attractive about the book was that the authors, as is common to these Bedford-series books, included a vast array of original sources from which he could in turn draw excerpts to use in class with students as they investigated the removal of the Cherokee tribe to Oklahoma.[6] Many of these sources he already possessed in digitized form after a number of excavations through the Internet to digital archives and repositories. Many were merely three mouse clicks away and easily downloadable; others were a bit more difficult to locate. Because most were time-period specific (1770s through 1840), they were not copyrighted. He had accumulated these sources one by one over the years and especially the preceding summer until his own archive contained over 30 images, maps, and documents on this one topic, some document excerpts of which he had typed himself from books. He had such personal archives on his laptop on all the topics he taught. Some were more extensive than the items in his Indian-removal folder, others less so. He simply kept building each of them little by little, year by year.

He began typing key questions organized around headings that roughly paralleled the structure of the Perdue and Green volume. Using such questions was Becker's attempt to model strong versions with authentic characteristics, ones that reflected the types of questions historians ask in their investigations into the past. He was working off the assumption that, because it was still early in the school year and with respect to the students' time with him, they needed guidance in knowing what good investigative questions looked like. Within a couple of minutes, the document looked like the following:

FIVE INVESTIGATIVE LESSONS ON CHEROKEE INDIAN REMOVAL, 1770–1840

(1) Introduction and Setting Context:
   - Who were the Cherokee Indians?
   - Where did they live and how did they live?
   - Who were their leaders? And how did they lead?
   - What early arrangements (e.g., treaties) had they made to coexist with a rapidly growing European population?
   - What was that population's attitude toward them?

(2) States and Federal Rights and Responsibilities in the Early 19th Century:
   - How did the state of Georgia interpret them and how did the federal government respond? Why these responses?

(3) Cherokee (and Others') Reactions to Removal Policies:
   - What was the Cherokee response to talk of removal?
   - How did other non-Cherokees respond?

(4) Final Cherokee Removal:
   - What happened? And why?

(5) Making Sense of Indian Removal?
   - How might we interpret removal policies and practice?
   - What does it teach us about life, attitudes, and change in America at the time?
   - What could we say about its connections to history before and after it?

Becker moved to the next page in his planning document and began aligning the accounts he had in his archive to each question. This would serve as a preliminary list of the source material he wanted students to investigate on their way to addressing the question(s) on each of the five sections posed. Based on past efforts to teach the unit and with the current modifications coming into view, he reasoned that the general lesson sequence would follow this cycle:

- *Class 1*: His initial, oral introduction to the unit and explanation of the advance organizer to students. His setting of the overall context of the period in question, although it would be a brief process since students had just finished investigating Andrew Jackson's background, election, presidency, his political approach, sentiments and policies, and the degree to which the term "People's President" was an apt description and by whose perspective. He would follow this by explaining (a) how small groups would pursue addressing the first section (Context) and its cluster of questions during the remainder of Class 1 followed by a discussion of what their investigations turned up, (b) how six groups of approximately four students each would then assume the process of investigating the middle three sections (State and Federal Rights and Responsibilities, Cherokee Reactions, and Cherokee Removal, two independent groups per section), during Classes 2 and 3, (c) how they would talk about what their researches turned up during Classes 4 and 5 on their way to addressing the fifth and final section (Making Sense?) and the questions raised there, and (d) how there would be a test during Class 6.

- *Classes 2 and 3*: Small-group investigations of the three middle sets of queries ending with preparations for presenting the results of that research.
- *Classes 4 and 5*: Presentations and discussions of what these researches produced followed by efforts to address section five's (Making Sense?) questions.
- *Class 6*: Assessment.

He would build his advance organizer around this layout. Given the order and structure, he had to efficiently connect the documents he was going to use into section clusters and align them with each day's planned activity. This would allow him to create "packets" of documents and accounts that he could distribute to each of the investigative groups. As always about this point, he lamented not having a fully wired classroom and laptop capabilities for each student. It would allow him to post documents (or their URLs) to course website "folders" by section focus (or to build the unit into a "Blackboard" site). Students then could enter and read the documents digitally without him having to photocopy them each time. He was resigned to the fact that he would have to wait for this scenario to come to fruition, imagining how comical his digital-native charges found his digitally non-native approach to be. Photocopy he would—again.

His spirits were buoyed, however, by the prospect of talking his department chair into purchasing classroom copies of the Perdue and Green book, with its myriad original sources, should this unit produce solid results on the assessment. He was a bit concerned about this move, though, because Perdue and Green present their own interpretation of Cherokee removal. If he used the book *in toto*, he was afraid his students might accept their version as singularly authoritative, largely because they had been repeatedly taught in school to privilege and accept synthetic treatments (i.e., Histories, with a capital-H such as the textbook) without criticism or question.

The alignment of accounts from his archive with each section of the series of class sessions was a bit tricky. Becker needed to be careful not get too far ahead of himself with accounts in Class 2's investigation process. He needed to be mindful that Class 1 was context setting and not designed to address subsequent questions students would pursue. Accounts needed to be aligned with that idea closely in mind. He kept needling himself as he assembled the number of accounts that less was more. Yet he wanted to be sure to include at least a few images for their visual impact and mapping characteristics that could allow an extra layer of cognitive support for his less-accomplished readers. His pass at the alignment process looked like this:

(1) INTRODUCTION AND SETTING CONTEXT

Images

"Original Extent of Cherokee Lands" (map)
"Cherokee Lands, 1791" (map)
"Cherokee Nation, 1838" (map)
"Treaty of New Ochota" (original image)
"Andrew Jackson Portrait"
"Painting of John Ridge"

Documents

"Chronology of Cherokee Removal"
"Treaty of New Ochota, 1835"
"Andrew Jackson speech excerpts, 1814"
"John Ridge Letter to Albert Gallatin, 1826"
"Young Wolf, 'Last Will and Testament, 1814'"
"Excerpts from Cherokee Constitution, 1827"
"Andrew Jackson, letter to General Coffee, 1832"
"Andrew Jackson, Address, 1829" (excerpts on Indian removal)

(2) STATES AND FEDERAL RIGHTS AND RESPONSIBILITIES IN THE EARLY 19th CENTURY

Images

"Survey of John Ross' Plantation, 1832" (From Perdue and Green, 2005, p. 85)

Documents

"Treaty of New Ochota, 1835"

"*Worcester v. Georgia*, 1832" (excerpts)

"Georgia State Assembly, 'Laws Extending Jurisdiction Over the Cherokees,' 1829, 1832" (excerpts from Perdue and Green, pp. 76–79)

"Memorial of Protest of the Cherokee Nation, 1836" (excerpts from Perdue and Green, pp. 87–92)

"Zillah Haynie Brandon, 'Memoir,' 1830–1838" (excerpts from Perdue and Green, pp. 95–100)

"U.S. Senate and House of Representatives: 'Speeches on Indian Removal,' 1830" (excerpts)

"Andrew Jackson, 'Seventh Annual Message to Congress,' 1835" (excerpts on removal)

(3) CHEROKEE (AND OTHERS') REACTIONS TO REMOVAL POLICIES

Images

"*Cherokee Phoenix*, front pages (2)" (see Elias Boudinot document)

Documents

"Indian Removal Act, 1830" (excerpts)

"Lewis Cass, on Indian removal, 1830" (excerpts)

"Memorial of Protest of the Cherokee Nation, 1836" (excerpts from Perdue and Green, pp. 87–92)

"William Penn [Jeremiah Evarts] Essays, 1829" (excerpts from Perdue and Green, pp. 105–110)

"Cherokee Women, 'Petitions,' 1817, 1818, 1831" (excerpts from Perdue and Green, pp. 131–134)

"Elias Boudinot, 'Editorial in the Cherokee Phoenix,' 1829 and 'Letters and Other Papers Relating to Cherokee Affairs,' 1837" (the latter in excerpts from Perdue and Green, pp. 161–166)

"John Ross, 'Letter in Answer to Inquiries from a Friend,' 1836" (excerpts from Perdue and Green, pp. 154–159)

"Treaty of New Ochota, 1835" (excerpts)

(4) FINAL CHEROKEE REMOVAL

Images

"Two Artistic Renderings of Indians on the Trail of Tears"

Documents

"Memorial of Protest of the Cherokee Nation, 1836" (excerpts from Perdue and Green, pp. 87–92)

"Evan Jones, 'Letters,' 1838" (excerpts from Perdue and Green, pp. 171–176)

"George Hicks, 'Letters From the Trail of Tears,' 1839"

"Rebecca Neugin, 'Recollections on Removal,' 1932" (from Perdue and Green, p. 179)

Another key feature Becker wanted to keep in mind as he built up these collections of documents and images was to retain a sense of tension or conflict between the perspectives of the key historical agents. In this case, Becker smiled, because the task was not difficult. The Cherokee leaders were divided among themselves about whether to resist removal or capitulate, giving rise to much tension among themselves. Anglo populations were similarly divided. Many Georgia policymakers and their land-hungry constituents sought to roust the Cherokee by due force, sometimes in any way they sought fit. The federal government, whose task it was to attend to Indian affairs by Constitutional provision, had to deal with the Georgians' desire to take the law into their own hands. Anglo religious groups (e.g., Moravians) had missionaries embedded with the Cherokee and frequently held sympathetic views toward the Cherokee desire to maintain their homelands. White, often northern, anti-removal advocates (not unlike abolitionists) frequently weighed in on the conflict. And then there was, of course, Andrew Jackson, the Indian fighter, pro-removalist, and erstwhile "Imperial President," who came to power with a marked tendency to have his way against the natives, even if it meant completely disregarding rulings of the United States Supreme Court.

What made Becker smile was that he found such tensions and their consequences a key fuel that fed the historian's desire to understand the past, and simultaneously, the raw material that could repeatedly pique his students' curiosity. In the latters' case, they sat there waiting to be entertained (as their visual media-driven culture had trained so many of them), and conflict and tension—so often central to their pubescent vitiations and adolescent gyrations—rarely failed to spark interest. It was a productive recipe: A potent, focusing investigative question or two, a cauldron of stoked historical tempest rife with discord, and an opportunity to dig in. Prurient? Maybe. Fascinating? Certainly. But then so is history if we don't completely whitewash it or turn it into a *fait accompli* to be memorized, Becker thought.

In under an hour of planning and rumination, Becker had pulled together the underpinnings of his version of the removal unit. Now he had to create an organizer for his students based on his 6-part class scheduling, print and reproduce the question guide, make decisions about the exact documents and images he would use (again reminding himself that less can be more) and package them together, and develop lists of which student groups would work on which questions. He thought he could accomplish these tasks rather quickly.

He began work on the organizer. After ten minutes he had produced the following (see p. 90), drawing rather seamlessly from the sequencing he had already established.

Class 1: Introduction to the Question of Cherokee Indian Removal, 1770–1840 (Becker)

Understanding the Historical Context of Removal: Five Questions (student groups)

Group A: Who were the Cherokee Indians? (Where did they live? Extent of tribal lands about 1700? 1791? 1838?)

Group B: How did they live? What was their culture like by about 1800? In what ways had it changed over the course of the 1700s?

Group C: Who were the Cherokee leaders? And how did they lead?

Group D: What early arrangements (e.g., treaties) had the Cherokee made in order to coexist with a rapidly growing European population close on their borders?

Group E: What was the Cherokee population's attitude toward them?

Discussion of Investigation Results (to conclude at the beginning of Class 2 as necessary)

Classes 2 and 3: Investigating the Politics, Economics, and Consequences of Removal

Group A (and D[7]): States and Federal Rights and Responsibilities in the Early 19th Century: Investigative Guiding Questions—How did the state of Georgia interpret state and federal rights and responsibilities? How did the federal government respond? Why these responses? How did Georgia citizens react?

Group B (and E): Cherokee (and Other's) Reactions to Removal Policies: Investigative Guiding Questions—What was the Cherokee response to talk of removal? Was there a unified response? Why or why not? How did other non-Cherokees respond, particular those sympathetic to the Cherokee? What were pro-removalists saying at the same time (e.g. Lewis Cass)? Why?

Group C (and F): Final Cherokee Removal: Investigative Guiding Questions—So in the end, what happened exactly? And why this outcome? What became of the Cherokee? What happened to their historic homeland? Why?

Classes 4 and 5: Part 1: Presentations and discussions of investigative results (see attached guidelines for formats and procedures)

Part 2: Making Sense of the Past?

How might we interpret removal policies and practices?

What does it teach us about life, attitudes, and change in America at the time?

What do we learn about the idea of Manifest Destiny?

What could we say about its connections to history before and after it?

Class 6: Assessment (details to be explained in class at the beginning of Class 5)

Becker had developed a template outlining his expectations for address-ing investigative questions, working with organizing ideas, reading and analyzing sources, considering them as evidence for making claims, and crafting historical arguments that addressed the questions he posed. He used it with each of his units. It was framed around his understanding of the interpenetrating relationship between *background, second-order organizing concepts* and the application of *procedural, strategic knowledge* needed to develop evidence-based arguments and interpretations that constituted *first-order knowledge* of the past, knowledge that could withstand the scrutiny of peer analysis and critique.[8]

Akin to past years, as students became more proficient following these practices, Becker would slightly tweak the template, offering guide-lines for making them responsible for crafting questions; adding in addi-tional, more complex second-order ideas, and/or sharpening the focus of the strategic knowledge capabilities he expected to see. The purpose of the template was twofold: It was designed to (a) guide students' investi-gations into the questions he posed by offering explicit structures and practices he wished to see followed (to short circuit an "anything-goes" approach) and (b) focus their attention on how to build historical arguments that addressed the questions (orally or in writing) that would underpin classroom discussions, peer analysis, and essay writing. In many ways, this template served as the centerpiece of Becker's pedagogical practice because it represented the heart of what he was attempting to teach his students: Historical thinking, the *sine qua non* of historical understanding on his view.

At this early juncture in the school year at which point his students were still rather raw at these practices and procedures, Becker's template looked like the following, printed on two sides of the same page (see Becker's Investigations Template). The template's guidelines seemed to him quite formalized for young high school students, but he rationalized the formality on the idea that he wanted his students to take the guide-lines seriously, with the eventual hope that they would become more automatized in thinking and doing practices as the semester progressed. The degree of formality also put students on explicit notice about what he expected and therefore about how they effectively would be graded in his class. His experience had been that students generally appreciated his clarity, even if they did not initially understand why he was teaching history under such different expectations from what they had become accustomed.[9]

BECKER'S INVESTIGATIONS TEMPLATE

Part 1: A Guide for Investigating Historical Research Questions

Goal: To carefully address the question(s) to which you (and/or your group) are assigned.

Strategies to Accomplish the Goal

(1) **Read and study all the documents and images** (accounts) before drawing any firm conclusions. Accounts can conflict with and contradict each other because of differing perspectives that guide those who authored/created them. They were not necessarily originally meant to answer your questions. "Buyer beware!"

(2) **Engage in PAIR^e.** *Identify* the account/source (When was it created? Why? What sort of account is it—text, image, relic?). *Attribute* it to an author/creator. Make an effort to understand the creator's purpose by assessing the *perspective* it contains. After you have examined all the accounts/sources, begin to make judgments about their *reliability* in addressing your question; that is, is this account better or worse than that account in supplying me with solid evidence for answering my question(s)?

(3) As you engage PAIR^e, for each account/image, try to **assume that you were the author/creator**—what would you have been thinking? Be careful here! . . .

(4) . . . **Try to put yourself into the context of the period** you are trying to understand. People back then didn't always think the way we do now because things were different for them. Try to understand authors/creators *on their own terms* in *their* historical context! And try to understand them as active agents, working to solve problems and make their lives better, just like you and I do today just under different circumstances.

(5) Now **organize.** Based on your assessments of source reliability and understandings of authors/creators, try to cluster documents and images together that are more or less useful in helping you answer your question(s).

(6) **Crafting an initial interpretative answer/argument** to your question, using the documents and images (as sources) to support your reasoning. You must account for all the evidence, even if it does not support the line of your argument. Your interpretation should include (a) an initial claim that addresses your question(s) and then reasoning that supports that claim using the evidence provided by the documents/images (as sources). This will be what you present in class and your classmates will be asking you questions about your interpretation. Be prepared to defend your reasoning!

(7) **Discussing the interpretation**: In class, we will discuss, analyze, and critique your interpretation. You will have to defend your work and practices, to show that you carefully analyzed all the available materials as evidence for addressing your question (see procedures on the back side of this paper). This discussion can help you revise and sharpen your interpretation.

Part 2: A Guide for Presenting, Discussing, and Writing Up Results of Your Research

Researching Together: Several heads are often better than one here, so you will be researching your questions in groups that I have assigned. Everyone needs to read all the documents/accounts/ images. Use a round-robin strategy of choosing, for example, one document, reading it carefully, taking notes, then passing it on to another member of your group until all materials are read and studied by everyone in your group.

Assigning Roles: Before you begin, collectively assign roles to group members: Who will be the primary speaker for the group during the whole-class discussion? Who will take notes of the inter-group discussion points before the presentation? Who will lead this inter-group discussion? Who will write up the interpretation? And so on.

Discussing Your Interpretation in Your Group

(1)   As soon as you all have examined and studied all the materials, talk with others in your group and try to reach consensus (agreement) about what you think happened and how you want to address your question(s).
(2)   Assuming you reach consensus, state a clear concise answer to your question (claim).
(3)   Now use all the materials (even the accounts or images that don't fit your answer) as evidence to argue and support your claim (e.g., tell a story).
(4)   Follow the practice of citing the evidence as I have showed you how to do.

Presenting Your Interpretation

(1)   State the question(s) your group was to address.
(2)   Indicate your claim(s) (or thesis) in a way that clearly addresses your question(s).
(3)   Now support your claim(s) with the evidence drawn from the documents/images/accounts. Cite them specifically as necessary.
(4)   Respond carefully and respectfully to others' questions about your research work and claim. That is, be prepared to defend your claim(s) with evidence.
(5)   Use the results from this discussion and critique to refine your interpretation as necessary.

Refining and Writing Up the Interpretation: Following the steps in Presenting Your Interpretation above, collectively write up your final response. Be sure that you state your claim in ways that it answers your question, and provide support with the evidence.

With source materials and guides and organizers in place, Becker was now ready to begin teaching the unit. Every year, Becker attempted to focus on one of his more problematic classes and take notes—a sort of journal or teaching log—about his impressions of how the class proceeded through the investigative process. His idea of "problematic" had no nefarious undertones. It was his attempt to learn better how to teach particular groups of students who posed particular challenges to his investigative approach. He figured that if he kept some kind of record, he could better understand the difficulties they experienced and use those understandings to improve what he was doing.

FOURTH PERIOD U.S. HISTORY

This year, his fourth-period class was the focus of his record keeping. Although the students interacted well enough with each other, they had some difficulty to this point sorting out how to read the materials he provided in such a way as to provide evidence-grounded interpretations of the questions they were assigned. Rather, they were prone to generating interpretations that served more as personal opinions of what was going on in the nineteenth-century past and had a tendency to simply disregard accounts or sources that did not square with the sorts of opinions or ideas they thought adequately addressed the questions he had posed to them. Often, they engaged in a sort of presentism, that is, using their own contemporaneous cultural assumptions and normative anchors to judge the actions and perceived intentions of past historical agents. In other words, teaching them to exercise a restrained interpretative imagination that hoed to the line of the historical context of the period under investigation was challenging, more so than in his other classes.

A group of "overachievers" in this class also had a laser-like tendency to search for what they thought was that sole correct answer to a question posed, one they thought was in Becker's head and the one that he wanted to hear. Becker assumed that such tendencies were powerful artifacts of the way students had been groomed to do school in the preceding 10 years, the details of which he wished to document more thoroughly. It was an idea he was working hard to disabuse them of on the way to helping them understand that history, at least, was not so easily reduced to single, unequivocal answers. Rather, history was a discipline and practice that invited debate and thrived on argument. These concerns prompted his fourth-period note-taking focus and the thread that we follow here.

There were 22 students in Becker's fourth-period class, his smallest group by some five students.[10] They were almost evenly divided by males and females, and no one ethno-racial group dominated (almost even numbers of African-American, Anglo, and Latino/a students with no students of Asian background). Two students were on Individualized Education Plans (IEPs; James and Juan) and were pulled out occasionally to receive specialized support. A quick check of the students' reading levels as determined by state standardized tests indicated that 16 of them were reading on or above grade level, two were reading well below grade level (the same two who were on IEPs), and the other four were reading just below grade level. Becker had some misgivings about putting too much stock in these ratings since they had not always proved accurate, at least in his classes.

TEACHING ABOUT INDIAN REMOVAL

Class 1

As was his frequent custom, Becker greeted his students in fourth period as they entered the door. Noisy and chattering, they slowly took their seats. He typically had to call them to order after he had taken roll. Today was no different. He had to ask several students to sit down in their assigned seats as he began the roll process, telling them that if they were not in the assigned seat, they were counted absent. This resulted in quick compliance. He took roll quickly and then lit up the screen with a projection of the graphic unit organizer. Students slowly attuned themselves to the graphic while Becker handed out paper copies of what they were seeing on the screen. By the time he had finished and returned to the front of the room, the students had settled in. They had come to expect some intriguing things from Becker and getting their attention typically was not especially difficult, at least at this relatively early part of the year.

Becker took them step by step, but quickly, through each item on the organizer, stressing his expectations for investigations they would launch. A bit to his surprise, no one asked any questions; the students followed along fairly attentively. Somewhere along his rather rapid trips through the organizers he typically relied on, one of his overachievers would ask about the test at the end and what would be on it. Not today. Good, he thought.

With the image still on the screen, he began orally situating the unit within its historical context. He reminded them that they had just finished exploring the initial years of the Jackson Presidency, had sized him up as the "people's President," studied what that meant, investigated his policies toward "expanding the franchise" so to speak, and dug into his "war with the bank." He also noted how they had looked into his appropriation of the idea of Manifest Destiny generally. In this small unit on relations with the southeastern Indian tribes, they would pick up that thread of Manifest Destiny, coupled with the idea of the meaning of a "people's President," and further explore each in the context of those relations. Jonathan raised his hand. Becker acknowledged him by name and Jonathan asked, "Mr. Becker, you say 'Indians' and we've learned from other teachers that the right way to say it is 'Native Americans.' So are you saying it's okay to say 'Indians'?" Becker, ever mindful of the time, responded politely but curtly that, in recent years, there had been some push by Native Americans to return to and accept the term Indians. He was following that lead.

Moving on, Becker called the students' attention to what he specifically wanted them to do in this first class period. He noted on the guide the five questions that constituted the frames for exploring the historical context of Anglo-Southeastern Indian relations in the late eighteenth and early nineteenth centuries. He noted that the class would focus, as the organizer indicated, on the stories of what happened to the Cherokee tribe. He paused and then asked if they knew anything about the Cherokees. He waited. After about six long seconds, Abby raised her hand. She said that she had heard somewhere about these big casinos that the Cherokee— or so she thought she remembered it was the Cherokee—were running, "like in the west or something," that they were making huge amounts of money. Becker thanked her and asked for other ideas. Javon noted in his typical way of coupling a question with a statement by turning the inflection up at the end of his sentence that he had heard, "like, there was some sort of legal thing where the Cherokees, or some Indian group, like in Wisconsin, was tryin' to fight to get their land back(?)." "Interesting," Becker responded without comment. "Today, we're going to dig some deeper into this story of the Cherokee. It's a crazy story, filled with curious interactions between whites and the Cherokee and among the Cherokees themselves. Like many stories of the American past, it was a battle over land, as we will see. And I hope it'll tell us more about who we Americans were back then and how it may contribute to who we are today."

With this brief introduction, he went over each context-setting question on Class 1 of the organizer and began assigning the questions to groups of four or five students each. Because Becker typically insisted on assigning group members, rather than letting students choose their own group mates, an undercurrent of grumbling would occur. Today was no different. Becker dispensed with the task quickly using a group assignment sheet he projected on the screen off his laptop, one that also noted where in the room groups would cluster (back right, back left, center, etc.). He then handed out the "Investigations Template." Although students had seen the template before, Becker was in the process of continually modifying it from unit to unit, and as noted, adding to its complexity slightly (based on what he learned from its application among students in preceding unit investigations) and tweaking it to fit each new unit topic and its attendant ideas. The template always needed re-explanation, Becker thought.

When they saw it, a couple of students (two of his underachievers—Salvator and Paul—who could be counted on to have such reactions) muttered, "Oh, this thing again," with a thinly disguised sense of incipient resistance. Becker quickly assured them that it had changed since they last saw it, that, as always, it contained in crystal clear terms his expectations for them concerning what was about to ensue, and that he wanted to take them through it quickly before they launched into efforts to address their investigative, context-setting questions. Becker added with a smile on his face, that if it wasn't on this sheet, it was not something he could grade them on in this unit. So they should be thanking him for giving them an edge in how to do well in his class. He then took them through the template step by step.

At this early stage in their experience with him, Becker knew how critical this template was in helping students come to understand the set of practices he was trying to teach them. Becker explicitly stressed the importance of carefully considering each document and image contained in the folders he would provide them for addressing the sets of questions he was asking them to consider. He then emphasized the value of relying on the PAIR^e strategies, going over each one on the template carefully. He then momentarily switched the image on the screen to the "PAIR^e Guide" sheet (see Guide Becker Provided Students for Engaging in PAIR^e), multiple copies of which he had included in each folder. Students were to use these guide sheets to take notes on the documents. He noted that the last item—the R^e, or Reliability/Evidence—was to be reserved for taking notes once everyone in a given group had taken the opportunity to study each document, account, or image. Judging the reliability of the accounts in question was to be a collective activity, one in which they made an effort to arrive at some consensus about how each of the documents could be used to address their question(s). Becker noted that he would return to this point in a minute, as he switched back to project the template itself back on the screen.

At this point, he stopped to ask if there were any questions. Angie raised her hand and asked, because she had been wondering since the beginning of the semester, how group members were to know *for sure* which documents were reliable or not. Becker responded by observing that this was a superb question and that the answer was complicated. First,

GUIDE BECKER PROVIDED STUDENTS FOR ENGAGING IN PAIR[E]

The P-A-I-R[e] Guide

Research Question: _____

Name of Account or Image: _____

Identify? What is this document or image? (Examples: A diary excerpt? An artist's depiction of events or a portrait? A photograph? A newspaper account? A letter? Other?) When was it made or written?

_____
_____
_____

Attribute? Who is the "author"? What do you know about the "author"? Why might the "author" create this account or image?

_____
_____
_____

Perspective? What's the author's perspective? What is he/she trying to communicate? To whom? Why?

_____
_____
_____
_____
_____
_____

Reliability? How might this account or image and the perspective it contains be used to address the question(s) you are asking? Would it be reliable evidence for answering your question(s)? Why or why not?

_____
_____
_____
_____
_____

he explained that a good measure of what he was asking them to do is develop some capacity over time to learn to judge various accounts' reliability. Second, that engaging in this practice was tricky, because often accounts like the ones they would work with were never written or recorded or generated to answer the kinds of questions they would be asking. As such, judging reliability was always more-or-less partial and therefore successful. And third, he smiled, and told them that part of his job as their teacher was to help them get better at doing so, something these investigative exercises were designed to do.

At this point and despite noting how quickly the clock was ticking down, he could not resist explaining that the broader value of knowing how to judge the reliability of accounts as evidence for making claims and addressing questions was tied up in being able to assess "what people they would encounter in their world were selling," so to speak. Michael asked, "Well, like what do mean—what's an example?" Becker explained that, say, in an election for public office, candidates often made claims about what they would do for their constituents if elected, or about the credibility of their opponents. Being able to judge those claims against available evidence used to support them was crucial to assessing the qualities and capabilities of those candidates. In other words, being able to ask, "What's the evidence for that claim or promise?" and then judging it was a powerful piece of strategic knowledge and life competence.

Becker glanced at the clock and moved quickly through the remaining sections of the first page of the template (Becker's Investigations Template, Part 1), stressing the importance of how to build an interpretation (item 5) and noting that such interpretations need to be evidence based and defensible because they would be scrutinized in class by him and classmates (item 6). He turned to the flip side and went over procedures for engaging the tasks he had set out for them (Becker's Investigations Template, Part 2). Because of their prior experience following these sets of procedures, Becker moved through them without stopping. At the end, he asked if students had questions. He waited, but there were none, so he asked students to rapidly cluster themselves into groups (despite worrying a bit that they were questionless). As soon as they had done so, he gave each group a folder filled with printed documents, images, and PAIR^e Guide sheets and told them to begin. Each group (A through E) received the same set of documents and images. Becker was curious how they would use them to address their questions, how they would variously judge their reliability in addressing their different questions. He would give them 20 minutes and see how far they had progressed. With a teacher's knowing cringe, he could already see that this initial context-setting activity might spill over into Class 2.

Students in Becker's fourth-period class had become accustomed to these transitions and quickly moved into the task without much difficulty. As students began pouring over the documents in their assigned groups, Becker circulated. He would stop at each group, kneel and listen in, usually without saying anything, but intently listening to the process by which documents, images, and PAIRᵉ Guides were distributed and students undertook the task. Occasionally, he would need to intervene to speed the process along, particularly if a group was off task, but more often when they would be fussing over who would get which document first. In such cases, he would simply assign each student one from the cluster and recommend that the group distribute the PAIRᵉ guides. However, such interventions were rare.

A gentle quietness slowly descended over the class as students began reading and studying the documents and scribbling notes on their guides. Soft conversations would pop up here and there as students exchanged materials. Becker continued to circulate as he attempted to gauge progress, while frequently checking how much time remained before class ended. With about 20 minutes of class left, he called attention to the time and suggested that each group soon begin the process of discussing the ways in which they would attend to the several questions they needed to address. In short order, such conversations began. Becker continued to visit the groups, interested now in listening in on how they were verbalizing their thinking about the documents and images vis-à-vis their questions. Such talk served as a key window on the types of historical reasoning and cognition they had developed. To date, it remained rather novice-like. Because he was interested in honing their capacities, hearing what they were saying to each other was crucial to his goal.

After ten minutes, Becker put them all on notice that he would be asking Group A to address their questions publicly in about one minute, followed by each of the other groups in succession. Members of Groups C and D protested, noting that they were not yet done. Becker insisted on his timeline nonetheless. At the one-minute mark, he called on Group A, asking the person they selected as their spokesperson to begin addressing their questions (Who were the Cherokee Indians? Where did they live? Extent of tribal lands about 1700? 1791? 1838?). Amanda addressed him as he simultaneously motioned her to turn and look at her peers in other groups. She shifted in her seat, and as she did so, Becker stopped her to remind students to remain quiet until Amanda had finished, a classroom rule he insisted on in these discussion/presentation settings.

Amanda noted that the Cherokee were a southeastern tribe of Native Americans who mostly lived in northwestern Georgia, but that their tribal lands actually spread at one point into southern Tennessee and southwestern North Carolina also. Amanda noted that the group had spent most of their time talking about three maps included in the cluster of documents and images. She held them up one at a time, noting that one map, titled "Original Extent of Cherokee Claims," seemed to show that the Cherokee tribe had widespread land claims that included much of Kentucky and Tennessee, northern Georgia, a part of northern Alabama, and sections of western West Virginia, Virginia, and North Carolina, and about half of South Carolina. While she talked, Becker displayed the map image digitally on the screen. Amanda then noted how map images dated 1791 and 1838 (holding them up for the class to see) showed how the Cherokee land claims had slowly shrunk to a much smaller corner of northwestern Georgia, overlapping slightly into North Carolina, Tennessee, and Alabama by 1838 (Becker put these two images up also on the screen as she proceeded). Becker asked her how confident the group was in the reliability of the images they were using to address their questions. Amanda explained that the images looked authentic and showed some detail, but that they were not source-able because no attribution or date of origin was included. The group thought they might be acceptable but remained unsure. As she finished her sentence, the bell rang. Students gathered up their books and PAIR[e] Guides, leaving the documents and images rather loosely stuffed back into the folders. As they departed, Becker told them that they would resume the discussion the following day with Group B.

ANALYZING BECKER'S PEDAGOGY

We can entertain several questions here about what Becker is doing and what accounts for his pedagogical decision making.

First, why did he not say more to correct students' ideas about who they thought the Cherokee were? At this point, Becker is simply attempting to understand the kinds of ideas his students hold about this tribe. It is not his goal, at this initial juncture, to correct those ideas, but only to see what sorts of prior knowledge they bring to the task ahead. His goals are about investigating this period as a means to build new ideas anchored in their investigations, ones he hopes will dislodge their naïve or confused conceptions. As students indicate, their knowledge is thin, uneven, and misguided, something Becker predicted. They do not really know who the Cherokee are or much about their history. Most importantly, their ideas about Indian removal in the early nineteenth century are fundamentally non-existent (or if somewhat evident, at least distorted). This gives him an indicator of the terrain on which his efforts will operate. He listens as a way of hearing where they are developmentally as learners.

Second, why did he not press Group A harder about relying so heavily on those questionable maps? Becker is aware that these were the only source materials of such a nature that they had at their disposal. He is not surprised that they rely on them as much as they do. Again, he is listening to see what they do *with* them. Do they *spontaneously* question the reliability of those maps? Or do they simply take that reliability for granted? In this case, it is the latter, perhaps as an artifact of only having these maps to consult, a consequence of how Becker has arranged the accounts vis-à-vis investigative questions. He is listening to how students function under such circumstances as a means of gathering ideas about what he will need to stress about the importance of engaging in PAIR[e] strategies and to what end (e.g., making reliability judgments as a guide to tendering knowledge claims).

And third, what about his (mis-)sense of how long things would take? As we will see, Becker fights a losing battle with the clock throughout the unit. This is the first time he has arranged this unit. As a result, he can only guess how long each set of segments will take. The clock will repeatedly get the better of his efforts. With only four years of experience, Becker remains a bit of a novice himself when it comes to judging how long his activities will take. But he is learning. It turns out that to deepen students' understandings and capabilities, it takes him longer to deal with the material than if he assumed a more traditional approach and simply narrated the "right story" to his charges. He has learned that, if his goal is to foster deeper historical knowledge and understanding, rapid coverage will almost always be his enemy.

Class 2

Now slightly behind in his timetable, Becker stood at the front of the room, acknowledging students with a smile, but asking them to please sit down so he could undertake roll and commence with where they had left off yesterday. With some feigned begrudging, they complied. As the bell rang in Class 2, Becker was ready to begin. He asked students to return to their groupings quickly, watched and waited for 30 seconds, and then began a quick review of Group A's effort the day before. He noted that, *if* the map images studied by Group A could be believed, the Cherokee land claims by 1838 had shrunk to about an eighth of what they had been "originally," a remarkable reduction in perhaps a 100 years. The question that faced the class was why. Four hands immediately shot up. Becker smiled broadly, but asked for patience for the moment so that they could dig deeper into the story of the Cherokee and build to an evidence-based response to the question, that at this point it probably was too early to say anything definitive in response to his "why" query. He then said,

"I do appreciate your efforts to conjecture—to offer imagined possibilities —regarding my question. It's something historical investigators must do. But we have four groups to hear from yet."

Becker turned and called on Group B to address their cluster of questions, which he was now displaying on the screen (How did the Cherokee live? What was their culture like by about 1800? In what ways had it changed over the course of the 1700s?) Michael spoke for Group B, turning to face his classmates directly and donning an air of teacherly formality in a way that only Michael could pull off. He explained that "in the early days," the Cherokee were just like "regular Indians, hunting and fishing and growing some food, living, like, together in small villages." However, things started to change as the Cherokee came into contact with more Europeans and especially as the Americans fought against the British for independence. "They got, like, way more Americanized and started acting all white and European and stuff to blend into the new country. It's like they wanted to be seen as Americans and not Indians any more. This was like by 1800, or so, said the documents we read." Becker asked him for more specifics. Jumping in, Britney from Group B, held up "Excerpts from the Cherokee Constitution, 1827," noting how much it read like "our Constitution, like they had a very similar type of government, with the exact same three branches of power" (Article II, Sec. 1). "And look at this [holding up a painted portrait of John Ridge]. Does this guy who was a Cherokee leader even look like an Indian of the time? No, he looks like an Englishman. He doesn't even look much different than Andrew Jackson [holding up a Jackson portrait for comparison] except for his, like, a little bit darker skin."

Becker thanked both of them for their interpretations. He pointed to the whiteboard where he had written a set of sketchy notes about both Group A and B's responses and asked students to copy these notes into their notebooks as a record of what was discussed. He told them to put it under the heading of "Historical Context of Indian Relations in the Early 1800s." He then turned back to Group B and questioned them about how they rated the reliability of the documents they used to address their questions.

Again speaking for Group B, Michael asserted that by looking over the documents and images, it was clear that the Cherokee had become just like the European-Americans right down to copying the U.S. Constitution. Becker walked toward Michael and said, "But you really didn't answer my question. How do you know these documents and images are reliable accounts for making the statements and claims that your group has made?" Jorge, another member of Group B, registered in by noting that they really had not made it that far in their discussion. "We sorta ran out of time." "Okay," Becker said, "but we have to be able to sort this out, to support and defend our claims by assessing the accounts' status and using all the evidence available to us to address our questions. Jorge, did any of the accounts contradict what Michael and Britney are claiming?" Jorge shook his head as did Michael and Britney and two other Group B members. "All right for the moment. Moving on to Group C and their questions" (Who were the Cherokee leaders? And how did they lead?)

Serena, one of the stronger, more articulate students in the class, spoke for Group C.[11] "Well, after looking over all the sources, we decided as a group to concentrate on two documents, Young Wolf's, 'Last Will and Testament, 1814' and John Ridge's, 'Letter to Albert Gallatin, 1826.'" She then added:

> We think these two give us the best picture of how the Cherokee
> governed. We weren't quite sure about who the Cherokee leaders
> were, but we think that John Ridge was a key leader for the
> Cherokee, because in his letter to Gallatin it shows that he knew
> a lot about the tribe, the ways they grew crops, sold things, and
> the laws they had. Like, on one page [holding it up] he gives a list
> of 13 Cherokee laws. Most of them look like laws we have today.
> So the Cherokee, like Group B said, were pretty modernized and
> like white Americans at the time. Young Wolf's will also helped us
> look into how the Cherokee worked. He owned property and was
> a farmer. We were surprised because he had black slaves just
> like southern, white plantation owners. And it was interesting that
> even back then he had a real will so he could give his property
> and stuff to his family after he died. And both Young Wolf and
> John Ridge could speak and write good English, like it was their
> first language or something.

Without saying anything, Becker thought, "Now this is the sort of investigative practice results I'm looking for. She handles this so well for being such a novice."

After Serena finished, he asked, "None of the other documents were especially helpful?" She shook her head. He noted how well he thought she represented her questions and offered evidentiary support, but he found himself compelled to ask her the source-reliability question he had asked the previous two groups. Serena explained that the two documents they relied on appeared to be original sources that allowed a direct window on Cherokee culture of the time. Both shed light on who the Cherokees were, how they governed themselves, and how surprisingly "American" they seemed. The group had agreed that they should be given a high score for reliability.

At this point, Max, from Group D, stuck his hand up and Becker acknowledged him. Max wanted to know why they had not come up with more evidence about who the Cherokee leaders were. Serena explained that the documents simply were not very clear about this. Max then held up the document with excerpts from the 1835 "Treaty of New Echota." He pointed out that at the end of the document, there was a list of 20 Cherokee who signed the treaty for the tribe, including Major John Ridge. Max conjectured that those 20 must have been Cherokee leaders if they were important enough to sign a treaty with the U.S. government. Serena, who had been given the proper page in the Treaty document by her group member, Melissa, agreed that this would have been useful, but that they must have overlooked it. Becker thanked both Serena and Max, noting that this was a powerful start to an interesting historical discussion that could continue for the rest of class. But the ticking clock meant they needed to quickly hear from the last two groups.

Group D now had the floor and Max—to no one's surprise because he was bright, energetic, and also articulate—took the lead (What early arrangements, such as treaties, had the Cherokee made in order to coexist with a rapidly growing European population close on their borders?). Following Serena's approach, he described how Group D focused their effort especially on the 1835 "Treaty of New Echota." However, he also added that the document, "The Chronology of Cherokee Removal" was important in helping them understand the different arrangements the Cherokee had constructed to deal with the white Americans' moves to strip the Cherokee of their land. He observed that the chronology source described the Cherokees ceding land to the state of Georgia in 1783, signing the Treaty of Hopewell in 1785 as a means of creating more peaceful relationships with encroaching whites, agreeing to the Treaty of Holston in 1791 in which the Cherokee arranged to become more "civilized," and that there even was a Supreme Court case, *Cherokee Nation v. Georgia*, in 1831, that granted the Cherokee control over their own lands.

Max continued, "This shows like a history of the Cherokee trying to live peacefully while white Americans kept trying to take their land. Maybe this is why their territory shrunk to such a small size by 1838, like Group A said. They kept having to give their land away to hang on to smaller and smaller parts of it." He then added, "But it all ended in 1835 with that treaty, because the Cherokee agreed to move to the west and give up what little land they had left." Becker thanked him and turned immediately to call on Group E (What was the Cherokee population's attitude toward white Americans and their desire to take Cherokee land?).

Salvator spoke for Group E. He started off rather sheepishly, declaring that his group really had no good answer to their question. He explained that the documents, though interesting, really did not describe the nature of the attitudes of the Cherokee toward the white man. So they were a bit lost and perplexed. He said that they had to "kinda like read between the lines." Salvator observed that in the John Ridge letter (1826), Ridge explains to Gallatin that the Cherokees were trying to be very loyal to U.S. laws and customs, that the chronology document showed the Cherokees trying to keep their land and live in peace but slowly giving it away, apparently to keep the whites "off their backs." In conclusion, he maintained that when they finally agreed to move west rather than fight to keep their land (Treaty of New Echota, 1835), his group thought that that showed how the Cherokees' attitude had sunk to the bottom, and escape westward was their only hope. As he had done with Group D, he thanked Salvator and, pointing again to the whiteboard where he had continuously scribbled notes about what each group speaker had said, he asked students to be sure to copy the ideas into their notebooks if they had not already done so.

Becker then took 90 seconds to summarize what he had thought the groups had concluded about the context of the Cherokee situation from 1700 to about 1835. He quickly synopsized that context by running down each group's question responses. When he had finished, he said, "I expect that you'll have these ideas written down in your notebooks because we'll be coming back to these issues of historical context as we move on through our investigations. In order to address the next cluster of questions I'm asking you to dig into, know that these ideas about context will be crucial." He asked a member of each group to bring him the packet of materials and sources he had given them.

He then moved swiftly into he next phase of his plan, announcing new group formations by displaying them on the screen. There were six new groups with three to four members each, two groups per topic/ question cluster (Cluster 1, Groups A and D: States and Federal Rights and Responsibilities; Cluster 2, Groups B and E: Cherokee Reactions to Removal Policies; Cluster 3, Groups C and F: Cherokee Removal). A few audible groans erupted after students saw who they would be work-ing with, something common among all his classes. Otherwise, the quick transition occurred smoothly, as Becker pointed to the places in the classroom where he wanted the various groups to conjoin.

After watching the students shifting about and once they seemed settled, he called their attention back to him. He reminded them of the need to establish a role structure within the group, and called their focus to the set of questions the groups would address by re-displaying the organizer on the screen. He also mentioned that he wanted them to diversify group role arrangements so that the group presenters, in particular, were different than for the last series. As he talked, he began giving each group a packet of documents and images that were germane to the questions they needed to address. In the packets were new sets of blank PAIR[e] guides. Becker directed their eyes to them. He observed:

> I watched you during the first round of investigations, and I noticed that many of you—and you know who you are— were pretty slack in filling out your PAIR[e] guides. These guides are critical in helping you to become better readers and analysts of the documents and images I give you to address your questions. I'm requesting—well no, I guess you could say that I'm demanding that you carefully fill these guides out—all of you! I'll be watching for this as I visit in on your groups.

He asked if there were any questions, and seeing no raised hands, told them to commence assigning group roles and digging about in the materials.

As the students did so, talk ensued among the groups. It steadily died down as the groups began exploring the packets. Again, Becker circulated among the groups, stopping to listen in and keeping a wary eye open for the application of the PAIR[e] Guides. As the bell rang to end Class 2, students quickly shuffled the materials back into the packet folders and put guide sheets into their notebooks. Heading for the door, Abby asked if they were going to continue the process the next day because, she noted, her group had not made much progress. He assured her (and others who might be listening in) that they would.

ANALYZING BECKER'S PEDAGOGY

Again, any number of questions present themselves. Two seem especially critical here.

First, Group D's Max makes a raft of knowledge claims regarding the question his group investigated (How did the Cherokees manage to coexist and maintain their culture and land holdings in the face of encroaching Anglos?). He supports them with references to a number of documents Group D analyzed. Yet, like other groups, he does not spontaneously offer any discussion of how reliable his group thinks these sources/accounts are for addressing their question. Becker, rather than pressing him, as he had done with previous speakers, calls immediately on Group E. Why? This is another case of Becker trading off a deeper discussion and an effort to hold Group D accountable to the PAIR[e] Guide's strategic practices and principles to a ticking clock. He is hoping that as the unit proceeds he will get additional opportunities to press students. But at that point in Class 2, he opts for shortchanging the discussion in favor of pressing on to Group E. Becker has already made it clear to previous groups that he will question them about assessing sources and using them to make claims, that reliability judgments cannot be dismissed as unimportant, or unwarranted simply because Becker—the ostensible historical authority in the classroom—chose them. At the same time Becker continues to listen and observe—without always commenting—how students appear to be engaging historical practice, as a means of gauging where they are and what, therefore, he will need to emphasize next.

And second, in the race against the clock, why not assign much of this investigative effort as homework? Becker reasons that doing so would deprive him of this eye-opening opportunity to observe how his students attend to the investigative work. He also appreciates the group effort students put in for two reasons: (a) Such arrangements offer students a chance to debate the nature of how to address the questions they are assigned, which in turn can potentially mimic a type of peer engagement and critique that animates work within the discipline; and (b) Becker has deliberately assigned group memberships to stratify who works with whom. That is, he arranges group membership structures so as to mix less- with more-accomplished students, stronger- with less-strong readers on the assumption (borne out in some research literature he remembers reading) that such stratification will serve to benefit all his charges. Do students complain? Yes, sometimes. But he remains undeterred for the reasons just noted.

Class 3

After taking the roll, Becker asked students to quickly move to their group arrangements (he had the group assignments up again on the screen), after which he returned the requisite packets to each group. He asked them to settle in and return to where they had left off the day prior. He told them that they needed to explore the materials diligently today to avoid running out of time. In the event of the latter, what they had not completed might well become their overnight homework assignment. The next day, they would certainly be discussing the results of the research process and each group needed to be ready. He asked them to find their "Investigations Template" and look with him on page two, Part Two.

He reviewed the four points under "Discussing Your Interpretation in Your Group," the five points under "Presenting Your Interpretation," and the final injunction under "Refining and Writing Up the Interpretation." He stressed the importance of the latter for these groups of research efforts, pointing out that because two groups were addressing each of the three topics/questions, there might be disputes between different interpretations offered. They needed to be able to arbitrate between these interpretations, attempting to decide on which best cohered with the evidence available. "Given the personalities in this class, it could get pretty dicey," he asserted to a murmur of laughter from several corners of the room. "You need to be ready. Be sure to have your Organizers in front of you as you research the materials. Then lay out your guiding investigative questions. You will be building your interpretations around those key questions."

Silence gradually fell over the room as students began where they had stopped the day before. Again, Becker circulated, looking over shoulders. He did not stop at any of the groups because students were reading individually and applying the heuristics of the PAIR^e Guides. He simply walked around the room slowly, watching. Occasionally, soft conversation could be overheard among different groups of students as documents and images were exchanged. Overall, Becker was reasonably satisfied with the focus of their efforts. Chances were, he thought, that they had hunkered down to their interpretive tasks to avoid the exercise becoming their homework.

After approximately two-thirds of the class period had expired, two groups began discussing the sources, comparing notes on their PAIR^e Guides, and hammering out interpretative responses to their guiding questions. Becker began sitting in on groups and listening to their conversations. He rolled his wheeled desk chair around as he went. Other groups eventually began their discussions. Only Group C remained intent on reading and writing throughout what was left of class time.

After one circulation through the groups, Becker returned to Group E (Cherokee Reactions to Removal Policies) to listen in because he found them having one of the more intriguing conversations. It was a debate between two pairs of students comprising Group E. Jonathan and Amanda were arrayed in interpretive opposition to Zenith and Melissa. The latter two were intent on arguing that, from what they could tell, there was a general unified position among the Cherokee against an array of removal policies and practices. Indeed, they acknowledged, there were differences among the Cherokee, but the leadership and overall position that dominated Cherokee reaction was linked to John Ross and his fervent opposition toward relinquishing Cherokee land to encroaching Anglo-Americans.

Jonathan and Amanda pressed against their argument by noting the shifting position of Elias Boudinot ("Letters and Other Papers Relating to Cherokee Affairs," 1837), who at first was deeply opposed to removal forces but later feared that whites would overrun the Cherokee by force and kill them all. As a result, he threw his support toward agreeing to removal. They also noted how the Treaty of New Echota (1835) showed that the Cherokee were willing to give up their lands and move west. Zenith and Melissa protested, arguing that it was only a small number of Cherokee who were really behind Boudinot and the signers of the Treaty of New Echota, that leader John Ross never signed (holding up the last page of the Treaty document), and as the Cherokee women's "Petitions" (especially the 1831 petition) showed, average Cherokees passionately opposed removal. They also pointed out how John Ross, in his "Letter in Answer to Inquiries From a Friend" (1836), made it clear that most Cherokees thought that they had been deceived and shortchanged in the Treaty of New Echota. Jonathan and Amanda countered by asking, "So why did all those Cherokee leaders sign the Treaty then?" Zenith retorted, "But Ross says right here [holding up the 'Letter' document] that those Cherokee who signed were [quoting] 'unauthorized individuals.' And not that many signed anyway." And on the debate went until the bell rang. The four of them kept at it as they left the classroom.

ANALYZING BECKER'S PEDAGOGY

Why doesn't Becker intervene in this dispute to set the record straight and end the interpretive battle in Group E?

Effectively, there is no surefire way to set the record straight, so to speak. The dispute is legitimate, a counterpoised set of arguments about what the past means with both sides drawing off available accounts to maintain different positions. The past and what it means turn out to be ambiguous in this case (and many others). One can mount a successful, evidence-based argument that differs from another successful argument, both drawing from the same accounts. This *is* history, like it or not. Students in Group E put this truism in play in Becker's fourth-period class.

If Becker attempts to use his authority to intervene, he only adds another interpretation (or account) to the swirl of interpretations. At best, he simply would be using his teacher authority to trump either or both groups. He would be under the same obligation to offer the very best evidenced-based argument in order to "succeed." And then other investigators could still disagree with him on evidentiary or other grounds. It would be classroom as trial; may the best argument win.

Most importantly, this sort of exchange is exactly what Becker is looking for. By not intervening and trumping the debate by teacher authority, he has a wonderful opportunity to hear how his students think, how they use remnants from the past to build and argue interpretations. If he were to invoke his authority, he would abort student engagement in the past, short circuit discussion, and his opportunity to understand his students and how they think historically would disappear (see Chapter 4). This is what textbooks do. In the hands of many more traditional history teachers and via the sanctioning power they hold in school curricula, they "work" to silence students (as fellow inquirers) because they offer up an unwieldy, unstable past on the artificially ordered plate of *fait accompli*. Becker's entire investigative approach is designed to avoid this outcome. Therefore, he listens, observes, gauges, and uses what he learns for making decisions about where to go next in his bid to deepen student understanding. Without such debates, there would be very little to listen to, observe, or gauge. A broader and deeper understanding, Becker is convinced, would suffer.

Class 4

Becker knew that in order to consider each of the groups' interpretations, he would need to use this class period efficiently. He also knew that Group C had only just begun to discuss their interpretation to the guiding investigative question in the previous class session. Following roll and the transition back to group clusters, he began class by telling the students that they had 15 minutes to arrive at an interpretation to their question. He noted that, given what he had overheard yesterday, there could be split ideas within groups, that this was certainly acceptable, and that a group, upon taking their turn, could announce divided interpretations before commencing their presentation. He asked for questions. Paul, a member of Group C, raised his hand and simply stated that he didn't think his group would be ready in 15 minutes. Becker maintained that, though he was sorry to press them, each group had to be ready, that he was going to be querying them at that point.

Called again to task, groups moved directly into discussing and ironing out their interpretations to the guiding questions. Having left their interpretation unresolved since the day prior, Group E picked up where they had left off. Becker circulated on foot this time, attempting to gauge progress in each group while occasionally measuring it off against the clock. At the 15-minute mark, he felt reasonably assured that the groups were generally ready, even though Group C still lagged behind. He was most interested in how pairs of groups might respond to each other since his intention was to address the topics and their guiding questions in group pairs (A then D, B then E, C then F).

In his strongest teacherly voice, Becker called attention to the front of the room where he was now standing. "OK, Group A [States and Federal Rights and Responsibilities regarding the Indians], you're up first even if you're not quite ready. We have to move on. I'll be curious to hear how each pair of groups assigned to the same topic and investigative question responds with their interpretation, whether you agree with each other or not. Group A? Who's speaking for you?" Jorge raised his hand. "Hold up a second," said Becker, motioning with a hand raised. "I'm going to be writing down each group's interpretation on the whiteboard. I expect you to do the same in your notebooks. I'm ready for you, Jorge."

"Well, we found out that since, like, the Revolutionary War or the Constitution times, the national government was supposed to be in charge of dealing with the Native groups like the Cherokee," Jorge began. "But problems kept coming up because, like, the Georgia people kept trying to take Cherokee lands even though they weren't supposed to. The federal government had like treaties with the Cherokee that let them keep their land. The Georgia people and other white people in North Carolina and stuff just kinda ignored the government. They said that states' rights made it okay to take Cherokee land because it belonged to the states." Becker prodded, "So what happened with that?" Jorge continued:

> Georgia leaders just kept passing laws that said they had control over the Cherokee and so they could do what they wanted to with the land. People, like representatives in the federal government—we read about this on one of the documents [holds up "U.S. Senate and House of Representatives: Speeches on Indian Removal," 1830]—seemed like they agreed that it was okay for Georgia to do that. And Jackson, you know, the President, also wanted the Cherokee to leave so that whites, like in Georgia, could take the land. But the Cherokee weren't cool with that. Then there was like a Supreme Court case, Wor-cess-tur [trying to pronounce it phonetically] against Georgia. It said that the Cherokee had a right over their own land and that nobody could take it away if the Cherokee didn't agree to it. But the Georgia people really didn't care. They just tried to claim Cherokee land anyway. They tried to figure out ways to maybe like scare the Indians into giving their land away.

Becker was writing on the whiteboard as Jorge was talking, attempting to record the nuances of his group's interpretation. He asked if all Group A's four members agreed with this set of claims as a response to their guiding questions. Heads nodded.

Becker then asked Jorge to defend his group's interpretation by supporting it more extensively with evidence from the materials they studied. Jorge noted that his group thought that the documents generally fell into two groups: (a) those that supported positions of the white people trying to get at the Cherokee land, and (b) those that defended the Cherokee's right to hold onto the land they had. He said that the group thought all these documents were reliable in helping to show the way the sides were drawn up opposing one another. Jorge said that the group thought that documents and materials made it fairly clear that the whites thought that the Cherokee held valuable land and the whites wanted it because they thought it should be theirs as Anglos who now controlled the country. The Cherokee were angry about this and protested again and again. As he talked, he held up clusters of documents, one supporting what his group thought the whites were doing and the other demonstrating how the Cherokee were resisting. He put the *Worcester v. Georgia* case excerpts on the Cherokee side.

Becker asked him what his group had done with the "Treaty of New Echota" (1835), since that document showed the Cherokee agreeing to give up their land claims in the east in exchange for support to move west. Jorge said that the group was stumped a bit with the Treaty. It did not fall neatly into the "two piles." Becker explained that they had to account for all the evidence, and so, what would they do with this piece of it. Serena, another Group A member, interjected, "We think that all that pressure by the Georgians just wore down the Cherokee. By 1835, they were tired and just wanted to live in peace. So they signed the Treaty because they thought it would be the safest way for their people to survive—you know, by leaving for the west to new land." Smiling wryly, Becker responded by noting that Groups B and E might have something to say about that particular interpretation. He thanked the group and called on Group D. Sonia spoke up, "Mr. Becker, we don't mean to bail on answering, but our interpretation is pretty much like what Jorge said. I mean like we have notes here that pretty much say the same thing. We can't really say anything to make Group A's presentation any better." One of the students from Group A said, "Yeah, you better believe it girl," as though engaged in a form of interpretive competition. Becker shot a look at Group A, then asked Sonia for her notes, adding that he wanted to look them over. While retrieving them from her, he called on Group B (Cherokee Reactions to Removal Policies).[12]

Regina responded for Group B. "Well see, the Cherokee were kinda split. But most of the Cherokee were angry about all these policies to try to get them to leave their homelands. They even protested. They said they weren't going to move anywhere, that the land belonged to them and they were staying."

Becker interjected, "How do you know they were split and how do you know that most of the Cherokee were against being removed?" Regina responded primarily to the second question, noting that, even though some Cherokee had signed the Treaty of New Echota which stated that they would move west, this was but a small group of Cherokee that felt that way. She then added:

> And John Ross, a big Cherokee leader like we found out earlier, said in his "Letter . . ." [holding it up] that those Cherokee who signed the Treaty were not authorized signers. Our group thought that he meant that they weren't really speaking for all the Cherokee. John Ross said that the Cherokee were not going to go with the Treaty of New Echota. The Cherokee also protested against the people of Georgia trying to take their land [holding up "Memorial of Protest of the Cherokee Nation, 1836"]. And the Supreme Court said that the Cherokee had a right to stay on their land. We didn't have that source, but like I'm talking about what Group A said about it.

Sensing that this might be a good place to let Group E offer their divided interpretations to the conversation, he called on them without pressing Regina any further.

A bit of a verbal scuffle ensued between Jonathan and Zenith, each attempting to speak first and drown out the other. Becker told them to stop talking; then he called on Jonathan because his (and Amanda's) position offered an immediate contrast to Group B's. Jonathan reiterated much of what Becker had overheard him arguing about the previous day. The Cherokee were more or less evenly divided in their response to the pressure to remove coming from people such as President Jackson, Lewis Cass, Elias Boudinot, and the Indian Removal Act of 1830. John Ridge, a key Cherokee leader, signed the Treaty of New Echota along with others who wanted the Cherokee to save themselves by moving out west as the government promised they could do. But other leaders, such as John Ross objected, arguing that the Treaty of New Echota was wrong and was signed by people who did not really represent the wishes of all the Cherokee people. As he talked, Amanda nodded in agreement and held up the documents Jonathan referred to as he offered their interpretation. Becker thanked them and called on Zenith, who restlessly twitched about in her chair, waiting to talk.

Zenith said that she and Melissa could see why Jonathan and Amanda could come to the sort of interpretation they did, but that they were just plain wrong. Jonathan retorted, "No way!" He started to interject, but Becker stopped him by walking toward him and gesturing for him to cease. Zenith continued. He noted that she and Melissa agreed exactly with Group B. Yes, it was complicated and the Cherokee were divided, but that their research showed that John Ridge and Elias Boudinot did not speak for all the Cherokee. In fact, reading the documents—especially the "Letter" by John Ross made it clear that most of the Cherokee were against the Treaty of New Echota and moving west. She and Melissa thought they could see evidence of a conspiracy in the Treaty, a scare strategy that would allow whites to steal more Cherokee land by using threats of disaster if the Cherokee refused to go. Becker asked her, "But how do you know that Ross' position was shared by the majority of the Cherokee? What's the evidence?" Zenith replied, "It just makes sense. Why would a whole bunch of Cherokee want to give up their land for some unknown place out west. I wouldn't." "Neither would I," Melissa chimed in. Jonathan growled audibly.

Becker found this exchange fascinating for a host of different reasons, but particularly because of the issue of evidentiary support, something at this stage of the learning process he was anxious to teach. But the clock continued to tick. He observed that, although the "It just makes sense" argument was interesting and certainly plausible, he was unsatisfied with it. He asked Zenith and Melissa, and by extension Group B, to dig deeper into the materials and come up with stronger support for the argument. That was their homework assignment—to see him after class to check out the packet of materials in order to take them home. Jonathan smiled in apparent vindication just as Becker caught his eye. "And to you Jonathan and Amanda, you have the same task. See me after class for the materials you'll need," Becker ordered. He then called on Group C (In the end, what happened to the Cherokee? Why?).

Javon addressed the class. He said that their investigative question was pretty easy to answer: "The Cherokee got screwed and so they had to bump on a long trail hike to, like, Oklahoma territory. On the way, a bunch of them died, like almost half of them or something. That was it. They got rounded up and pushed out west by the U.S Army." "When did this happen?" asked Becker. Javon turned to his group, fumbled around in the documents, looked up at Becker and said he thought it was 1838. Just as he uttered the date, the bell rang. Students started packing up. Over the din, Becker shouted, "I want to see your PAIR^e Guides. Put your names on each copy and put them in a pile on my desk before you leave. That's ALL of you!"

ANALYZING BECKER'S PEDAGOGY

Three related questions concern us here: Why doesn't Becker press on the subtext issue regarding Ridge and Ross? Why didn't Becker challenge Zenith's comment, "It just makes sense?" Were Zenith and Melissa engaged in a bit of unwarranted conspiracy theorizing with regard to the Treaty of New Echota?

First, it seems quite clear that the students may have missed considering the subtext of a power dispute going on among Cherokee leaders in the 1830s. Ross and Ridge were vying for control over the direction of the Cherokee tribe. Ross favored a strong stand of resistance toward efforts to dislocate the Cherokee, while Ridge had come to believe that capitulation and relocation was the only way the Cherokee could save themselves from sure destruction at the hands of the Georgians. Ridge had garnered friends in Washington. One could argue that politicians there who championed removal used Ridge in a divide-conquer strategy. However, the accounts students studied did not provide any such clear picture. It would have required them to more fully understand the leadership subtext and use it to engage in a form of conjectural logic to arrive at that conclusion. In short, they would have needed more evidence to make such claims. As a result, Becker avoids pressing the issue. He also realizes that at this point in the year, students have acquired few strategies for reading subtexts of this sort. He understands from this exchange how important it will be for him to use subsequent units to stress this idea and help students to read for it.

Second, regarding Zenith's comment, "It just makes sense," Becker does note his dissatisfaction with it, putting students on notice that a historical claim cannot be fully justified simply because it makes sense to someone. Conversely, one could argue that Zenith is engaging in that form of conjectural logic. Having read the accounts and attempting to refine an interpretation over two class periods, and in the absence of definitive evidence, Zenith is trying to read between the lines. This practice is common for historical investigators especially when evidence is thin. Becker calls her comment unsatisfactory, but he does not want to fully disabuse her or her classmates from engaging in it. Becker confronts a difficult challenge here. That relentless clock is ticking, he has much to do, and a rather intriguing historical-thinking issue confronts him. He effectively punts, choosing to save the issue for a future discussion, when this question of subtext reappears.

And third, what is Becker to do with this hint of a conspiracy theory offered up by Zenith and Melissa regarding the Treaty of New Echota. Is it warranted? Should he intervene with a cautionary note? Here again, these student novices are broaching the issue of subtext, but without adequate evidentiary traces to attempt verification one way or another. As we have seen, this is a complex issue for Becker. On one hand, students are prone to making unsubstantiated claims on the grounds that they have yet to learn a significant distinction between an evidence-based position and a personal opinion, thinking that the latter is an entitlement because it is after all a free country (recall "the borrower/subjectivist"). On the other hand, investigators attempting to make sense of the past at least a portion of the time must engage in conjectural logic that transcends available evidence. The boundaries separating conjectural logic from opinion are fuzzy. What reigns in mere opinion occurs in the context of peer questioning, critique, and arbitration. Again, Becker punts on this issue, preferring to save its consideration for a future date with historical indeterminacy. But he does make special mental note of this opening the debate has generated, knowing that there will be future opportunities to consider it as his investigative units unfold across the semester. As part of his broader plan, he will teach them to read and think in such terms. Again, these early investigations serve to reveal clearly how students think and therefore provide superlative educational fodder that in more traditional history classrooms would remain inaccessible because of its invisibility.

Class 5

As students filed in, Becker stood at his desktop computer, leaning over it, ready to take roll. He knew there was much to accomplish in this class session. He needed to hear from Group F, to check on whether they had anything to add to what Javon and Group C had said the day before (he was hoping they did). He needed to return the PAIR^e Guides first.[13] He also had to bring the short unit to a close by holding a discussion of the set of questions he had posed on the organizer under the heading, "Making Sense of the Past?" However, before undertaking this heady schedule, he needed to explain to students the structure of the test they would write in Class 6, as he had promised. He had do to so succinctly.

As the bell rang, Becker asked students to take their seats as he quickly finished taking roll. He began introducing the test, accompanied by a number of audible groans. He paused a moment, stared down the grumblers, and then proceeded. He noted that there would be a handful (15 or so) multiple-choice items that dealt with their understandings built up from reading and analyzing the documents. Focal prompts for those items would derive directly from the "Guiding Questions" on the organizer along with the questions they would discuss in today's class under the heading "Making Sense of the Past?" He reminded students about his practice for constructing multiple-choice items: A prompt followed by four options, three of which could be construed as generally acceptable, depending on how students interpreted evidence they obtained from the documents and images they analyzed. A fourth option would be inappropriate given the item's prompt. He would weight the appropriate responses. The most evidence-defensible choice would receive 3 points, the next most 2 points, and the least defensible 1 point. The inappropriate response would garner 0 points.

Max immediately registered a complaint: "But Mr Becker, those kind of questions are so hard!" Becker smiled somewhat wryly and noted that he understood. But he wanted students to remember two things. First, historical study, especially the sort that involved asking questions and analyzing evidence in order to address them, was a tricky undertaking because reasonable investigators could dispute what that evidence meant and the degree to which it could be amassed to support and interpretation. "We saw that with Jonathan and Amanda, and with Zenith and Melissa—different interpretations of Cherokee reactions to removal attempts, now didn't we?" Becker added, "I'm trying to construct items that allow for reasonable people to disagree about the evidence and still earn points on the question. I'm weighting the responses based on my analysis of where the most evidence points. You'll need to take a look at this carefully based on your notes. Our final discussion today should help I think."

"And the second point," Becker continued, "is that, hey, even if you aren't quite sure of the 'best' answer, you still have a good chance—like 75 percent—of earning some points. And as you've seen in earlier tests, I encourage you to argue items with me afterward as long as you see me in person. Would you prefer to have only one shot at "the correct" answer, like in typical multiple-choice items? That kind of approach isn't really aligned with the sort of good historical study I'm trying to teach you in my class." "Ok, I hear you," retorted Max. "I just think these kinds of questions are really hard. I have to study each one really carefully. It takes a long time." Several heads nodded in support of Max. "That's why I'm only giving you maybe about 15 of them," Becker observed.

Becker then broached the essay question he wanted them to write. He told them to look at their organizers and examine the questions under the heading, "Making Sense of the Past?" "The essay question, like the ones you've seen from me on other tests, will be drawn around that cluster of questions, and especially the one about Manifest Destiny," Becker asserted:

As you can see by those questions, I'll be asking you to make an interpretive argument that's supported by evidence we discuss

today and what you've been reading about and taking notes on
the last several days. I'll be grading you basically on two things:
How well you make your case in writing, that is, clear and concise
argument, and two, how well you draw from the evidence to
support your line of thinking. I'll be using the scoring rubric you
all have.

Britney interjected, "So like before, there really won't be, like, a right or
wrong answer? It's how good we make an argument and support it?" Yes,
exactly," Becker responded. "Any other questions or comments?" Many
students stared at him rather blankly, something that made Becker nervous.
But seeing no hands and glancing at the clock, he resolved to press on
even though he would have preferred to spend more time discussing the
test because he sensed that they would not be ready for it.

Becker called on Group F to discuss the final act of Cherokee removal,
referred to by the Cherokee as the "Trail of Tears." Reggie spoke for
Group F. He reiterated what Javon had said the preceding day, that the
Cherokee finally relinquished to the pressure and more or less agreed
to be moved west to Oklahoma territory. They were rounded up by the
U.S. Calvary with bad weather coming on and marched west. Reggie said
that their group would dispute the "half died" figure offered by Javon and
reduce it to about a quarter, based on their group's reading of the documents. "It still was, like, pretty brutal and stuff. The Indians got marched
out there in the winter. The sources we read said that the Cherokee
were already hungry before they left because the white people had
been starvin' them, tryin' to force them to move." Reggie continued,
"So, they were, like, really weak and so it was like no big surprise that
so many died. What our group found kinda hard to believe was that, even
though the U.S government said they'd take care of the Cherokee on the
trip, they really didn't do much to help them at all. Well, at least that's
what the Hicks and Neugin documents said. And Hicks was, like, there
when it happened."

Javon raised his hand and Becker called on him. He noted that his
group had reassessed their claim of how many Cherokee had died and
they wanted to simply say that they agreed with Reggie and Group F that
it was more likely to be about a quarter of the Cherokee. His group, too,
was a little surprised that even that many died on the "Trail of Tears,"
especially since the government had offered their support for and protection
of the Cherokee on the move. Becker thanked him and turned back to
Reggie to ask, "Why does your group think the Cavalry offered so little
help to the Cherokee on the trail?" Reggie said that their group had not
actually discussed that question, but that he had an opinion. "And?" Becker

queried. Reggie offered that he thought it was racism and discrimination against the Indians in general that probably caused the mistreatment, that the government probably did not care at all how many Cherokee died on the march. They were just happy to get them to move to the west and end the trouble in Georgia. Becker wondered if anyone in either Group C or F could provide some evidence to support Reggie's conjecture. Following a momentary silence, Javon noted that the groups would need to go back through the documents and sources to check, but that Becker had already collected them the day before. Becker said, "Good point. And we really don't have time to do that today. But as all of you prepare for test, it might be good if you went online and checked for some sources—hopefully reliable ones—that could shed some light on this question."

Becker knew he needed to press onward with the discussion of the final set of questions, the "Making Sense of the Past?" section. He observed this need out loud to the class and added that he wished there was more time also to consider the debate that had arisen between Groups B and E about how the Cherokee responded to the pressure to move west. However, the class needed to continue onward. He told Zenith, Melissa, Jonathan, and Amanda to see him for a minute after class to discuss their collective homework assignment. "Right now, I want you to turn to your Organizer and the last section, "Making Sense of the Past?" and the questions there. I also want you all to open your notebooks to your notes, assuming of course you've been taking them," he quipped with a slight air of sarcasm because he knew some would have been remiss in this regard.

"Let's take up these four questions in sequence. I want to hear from as many of you as possible across our discussion of the questions," Becker ordered. "And let's not forget to do what we can to support our positions with evidence from the accounts we've considered as well as from the notes you've all dutifully put down in your notebooks," again with a bit of veiled chagrin, but also signaling his expectations. "The first question: How might we interpret removal policies and practices?" Becker asked. Silence. Becker waited. Finally, Max raised his hand:

> Well, it's kinda complicated. It seems like, at first anyway, that the federal government was trying to protect the Cherokee. You know, like honor their claims to the land and honor the treaties they had made. I mean, that was like their job. But white people in Georgia kept saying that they were a state, and states had land rights, and the Cherokee had to go because they needed the land for farming and business. Then when Jackson got elected, he supported the white people in Georgia and was for removal, as we saw in a couple of the documents—you know, his speeches.

> That made the Georgia people feel better about taking Cherokee
> land. So it's sort of conflicting. Some whites, and part of the time
> the federal government, were trying to protect the Cherokee. But
> later it started to change. And eventually the Cherokee got
> bumped.

Cynthia raised her hand. "I agree with Max that it's sort of conflicting. It's hard to follow. Like, what caused the policies to change, first from protection of the Indians, like in that Supreme Court case [*Worcester v. Georgia*], and then to removal like only a few years later?"

Serena raised her hand. "I think the pressure was just building and building to force out the Cherokee. I think, based on some of the documents, that the white people especially in Georgia—no matter what the U.S. government did—would have just worn down and harassed the Cherokee until they felt like they had to move. I think that's exactly what happened no matter what the policy was. White people wanted that land. They thought they had a right to it." Jonathan followed immediately, as if to press his group's earlier position: "Yeah, it is complicated. That's why there were disagreements in the Cherokee people's leadership. It was hard for them to tell if the policy of the government was gonna be followed or if the Georgia people were just gonna over run them." Jonathan was talking rapidly. He paused to catch his breath and then continued. "So some of them signed the Treaty of New Echota because they were scared and wanted to save the tribe." Several additional hands were now up. Becker surveyed the class, held up his hand, palm forward, and asked a minute's forbearance from those who wished to speak because he wanted to go back to a point Serena had made. Looking straight at her, he wondered what she meant by her statement that the white people thought that they had a right to Cherokee land.

Serena initially offered that she just said it and had not really thought it through, but she continued, "Isn't this like Manifest Destiny stuff. The white Georgians thought that they had a right—like a God-given right—to take over all the land, grow crops on it, raise families, you know, populate America. They fought for that right in the American Revolution, at least that's what they were thinking. A bunch of like Senators and stuff said that in those documents we saw about those Congress hearings [referring to the source, 'U.S. Senate and House of Representatives: Speeches on Indian Removal, 1830']." Jorge, who had spoken for Group A, one of the two groups who had studied federal rights and responsibilities, interjected, "But Serena, what do you do with that Worcester versus Georgia case, when the U.S. Supreme Court [putting considerable emphasis here] said that the Cherokee were entitled to their land, like they had sover . . . sovereign-ti-ty over it [struggling to pronounce the word sovereignty]? What do you do with that? That doesn't really sound like that Manifest Destiny thing to me." "Yeah, but look what happened in the end," Serena retorted.

Becker stopped the discussion at this point to raise an issue about being careful when it came to overgeneralizing. He wanted them to understand that when it came to policies and practices regarding taking Indian homelands, not all white Americans believed in the same thing, or in many cases, had even heard of such high-minded ideas as Manifest Destiny. He asked them to think about present-day divisions across the country concerning social and cultural policies, that some Americans held deeply conservative views, say, on abortion, whereas others argued much more liberal views. "We still are a conflicted country. Is it so hard to think that in the 1830s, we'd all be on the same page about Indian removal, or, as we will see later, on the institution of slavery, or even later still on civil rights policy? " he asked rhetorically. "This is what makes history so interesting—all these conflicts over ideas. And I really like how you're digging into this stuff! Let's think a minute about the next question. It's related. What does this all teach us about life, attitudes, and change in America during this early-nation period? James, I haven't heard from you. What do you think?"

James, a quiet student and one of two in the room on an Individualized Education Plan, stared at his notes. Becker waited as several hands went up. "I'm really kinda not sure, Mr. Becker," James replied. "But I think it's like people are saying. As a country at that time, we were, like, not all agreed about what to do about the Indians. Some people wanted them gone, but like there were missionaries in with the Cherokee who were trying to convert them. They wanted to help the Indians, not see them get pushed off their land." Thomas jumped in, "It looks like the white Georgians were pretty greedy. They saw value in the land and wanted it. But not everyone in the country agreed, like even the Supreme Court. But when the President says he wants the Indians out, it's kinda hard to stop that attitude from winning." Becker thanked both of them and then asked, "What does this teach us about the idea of Manifest Destiny in the country?" Javon replied immediately without being called on: "It's really strong; it's like off the hook—a powerful idea affecting a lot of people. I think the Georgia people used it as, like, an excuse to take Indian land, like they thought God was saying they had a right to it, or something." Several heads nodded. Becker queried, "What's the evidence for that?"

Ever the astute student and reader of source material, Serena jumped back in: "Well, if you look at those Senate speeches and read President Jackson closely, they seemed to be saying exactly that, that the Indians are in the way of America achieving its greatness. They are blocking the right to the land, so they gotta go. I'm not saying, like, I agree with that or anything. I'm just saying. There's evidence to show it." "But how influential were these speeches and the view of Jackson?" Becker followed. Abby, who had raised her hand periodically, had it up again. Becker called to her:

> I think that, you know, based on what we read, that it was like somebody said: white people in Georgia wanted the land and thought they had a right to take it, that the Indians were blocking progress. If anything, they kinda used that whole idea of Manifest Destiny to, like, justify what they were doing. And they thought the Indians were like second-class people anyway. So it was all pretty easy to push them out and not really care that much what happened to them.

Becker glanced at the clock and mentally cringed. He had about five minutes remaining and he had not yet dealt with the question about continuity and change: What could we say about Manifest Destiny's connections to history before and especially after this period of Cherokee removal? Becker had to choose: Push on Abby's statement in an effort to test it within the class, or press on to the final question. He opted for the former, but hoped that he could simultaneously invoke comments that spoke to the latter. He asked the class, "So, Abby is making a pretty profound claim and others have said the same sort of thing. The idea of Manifest Destiny was powerful, but it was used more as an excuse to justify actions of the Anglos than as a policy that pushed people to act in particular ways? Yes? Carlita, I haven't heard from you at all."

Carlita, a generally thoughtful but shy Latina, who always appeared to be paying only half attention, but who also could offer up the occasional jewel, did not let Becker down. "I mostly agree with what you just said. But I was thinking about that thing, you know, during Jefferson's time, when the Anglos bought up like half the country. I can't remember what it's called." "You mean the Louisiana Purchase?" Becker interjected. "Yeah," Carlita continued. "Didn't we find out after studying it that like Jefferson thought the country had a right to all that land and that we should buy it from the French or the Spanish—I can't exactly remember. But that's what we did, even though there were all these Indians who lived on that land. You know, and some of them are like my people too. Did the government even ask them? No! So it was like a powerful idea that also made leader people do stuff like the Louisiana thing."

As she finished, the bell rang and the scuffle to leave the room began. As students departed, Becker called after them that he would review these ideas before the test tomorrow. "Study hard!" he charged as they filed out. Jonathan, Amanda, Zenith and Melissa stayed behind as Becker had asked. He wondered if they had reached any evidence-based agreement about how the Cherokee had responded to policies that threatened to exile them. Zenith said, "No!" immediately, shooting a wicked glance at Jonathan. "We still disagree. We think there's evidence to support both sides!" added Melissa. "Okay then," Becker smiled, sensing the still simmering dispute. "Good historical investigators often disagree about how to interpret the evidence," Becker observed. "Off you all go. But if I ask you about this tomorrow on the test, you have to be ready to provide a solid evidenced-based case for your interpretation." And out they went.

ANALYZING BECKER'S PEDAGOGY

Three concerns appear in Class 5 that raise pedagogical issues

First, in the discussion about why, after pledging such support in the Treaty of New Echota, the U.S. Cavalry provided so little help to the Cherokee on their cold-weather march across the country, Becker presses Groups C and F to offer more evidentiary support for their position. This follows Reggie's reasonable but generally unsupported conjecture. Javon points out that students would need to study the accounts more carefully and Becker has already collected them. Becker chooses to move past Reggie's conjecture and on to the "Making Sense?" discussion. Why not call up some of these documents digitally on the classroom screen and parse them more closely? Becker opts to move on in deference to the time that remains and press instead on his concern about adequately dealing with the complex questions in the "Making Sense?" portion of the unit. Again, he practices trading off one important aspect for another—a chronic teacher's dilemma.

Second, Becker questions Serena about her comment concerning how she was of the mind that the white Georgians, regardless of Federal policy, would simply have forced the Cherokee off their lands one way or another. He asks her to defend her idea that the Georgians believed they had a right to Cherokee land. Her response regarding the use of Manifest Destiny as a rationale to defend removal aggression that, at the time was considered by some as highly objectionable, was exactly what Becker was hoping to hear. Because Serena was African-American, he also was interested in the degree to which she understood white Georgians' aggressiveness to be rooted in racism. What he receives from this line of questioning involves getting the idea of Manifest Destiny on the table for discussion. He, however, receives little opportunity to pursue the issue of racism because he turns to focus students' attention on a pressing worry about overgeneralizing.

Third, the issue of underlying racism reappears in comments by Carlita (a Latina) several minutes later. Becker receives a second opportunity to consider the question of the role of racism in Manifest Destiny. Yet, his efforts to explore it are foiled by the ringing of the bell. Should he begin class 6 with a pointed discussion of it? Becker knew this was an important concern among his non-white students, as evidenced by both Serena's and Carlita's expressions. He also knew that the chances were very high that, should they wade into it, it could easily consume much of class 6 in heated debate, and he had designated it as a time to review the "Making Sense?" cluster of questions and also provide time for them to complete the first section of the assessment. As we will see, Becker chose not to press on it directly, to follow his plan, and save this discussion for a forthcoming unit.

Here we have another example of a history teacher's dilemma, one that investigative approaches to studying the past will inevitably unearth. Students approach their investigations from particularistic sociocultural anchors (positionalities). Those anchors differ, the results of which, when interpretations are invited and honored, will surface repeatedly. They must be addressed. But when? This remains a difficult question to answer with any precision. As we have seen, judgments about historical significance, issues of empathy, contextualization, agency, and moral judgment are all deeply implicated by the sociocultural positionalities of investigators (Chapters 3 and 4). History teachers ignore these relationships at their own peril. Timing is crucial if the goal is to optimize what students will learn about how their own positionalities influence the ways in which they interpret the past. This may have been one of those moments, and Becker missed it. His only hope is that he will witness future opportunities that he will need to plumb.

Class 6

Test day. Overnight, as he assembled the assessment, Becker had decided to split the test into two parts, the multiple choice section that students would complete in class, and the essay, which he would assign as a homework exercise due the following day.[14] This, he reasoned, would allow him to do some review of the questions in the "Making Sense of the Past?" portion of the organizer. That section and its questions were deeply important to Becker's goals for the unit. He wanted time in class to touch on them again, to press students about their culminating understandings.

As he began the sixth class, Becker explained his strategy. As soon as students heard about the essay homework exercise, a predictable collective groan erupted. Becker explained that such a homework essay worked to their advantage for it allowed them to use their notes to write the essay. This, he assumed, would benefit them. And besides, they could take more time to craft strong, evidenced-based positions. This rationale seemed to provide momentary comfort. But he knew this also could invite trouble for him, because there would likely be one or two students who would come to class that following day empty handed.

The essay hinged on a weaving together of the three final questions on the organizer's "Making Sense" section: What do we learn about life, attitudes, and change in America (for whites *and* Indians) based on our exploration of the Cherokee removal process? What role does evidence suggest the idea of Manifest Destiny played in this Indian land-taking episode? And does that idea relate (or not) to policies and practices exercised by Anglo-Americans before it, and after it, in the shaping of a nation called the United States of America? Becker wanted to spend about half the class revisiting this historical landscape, being careful to review the ideas without foreclosing on one particular interpretation that might influence the essay-writing exercise in a particular direction. He wanted students to struggle some—as he thought good historical investigators do— with questions of what the past means.

As it turned out, Jackson and his pro-removal views had become more of a sidebar in their examinations of Cherokee removal. This was not as he initially intended it. But he was generally pleased with the path his fourth-period class had traversed. The review he conducted showed as near as he could tell that students generally had come to appreciate the Cherokee and their plight, how they had "Americanized" themselves and assimilated into Anglo culture of the time as a means of protecting remnants of their most cherished cultural beliefs and ideals. Some students also came to agree (as we have seen) that this assimilation process and the constant pressure to relocate divided the Cherokee people, and may have led them in the end to an almost inevitable "Trail of Tears."

Students also seemed to understand (if not altogether appreciate) white Georgians and their desire to expand and acquire land. They came to see that acquisition mentality as fitting into overall American culture of the early nineteenth-century definition of an expanding republic. They understood Manifest Destiny largely as a handy rationalizing script, that Congressional leaders, powerful Georgians, and President Jackson would use to justify their pro-removal policies and efforts. Finally, some students— and certainly not enough of them, unfortunately, as far as Becker was concerned—could comprehend the notion that the Anglo idea of Manifest

Destiny had origins that preceded Cherokee removal and also antedated it. But the latter remained a fuzzy understanding, largely because students had not yet investigated enough about what followed to fully grip its growing role in nineteenth-century American history.

At about the halfway mark in Class 6, Becker brought the discussion/review to a close and moved to pass out the test. Hands kept popping up as students tried to game him by stalling the onset of test taking. Undeterred, Becker pressed on. By the end of the period, all 22 had finished the multiple-choice section, turned it in, and copied down the essay question Becker had posted digitally using the projector and screen. Becker felt generally pleased with the way the unit had unfolded. However, he had yet to grade the multiple-choice items and it remained to be seen how many essays he would get the next day, not to mention the degree of quality they would demonstrate.

To Becker, these assessments provided some prima facie evidence of his success (or lack thereof) at garnering understanding, not only of his first-order knowledge-enhancement goals, but also how well (or not) students were taking to the second-order and strategic knowledge development process, the latter being the *sine qua non* of the former by Becker's lights. These assessments also provided diagnostic power in that he could use the results to gauge where individual students were on a developmental trajectory in learning history. These gauges could in turn help his future planning and portend ways of working with certain students to enhance their cognitive capabilities and historical understandings.

CHAPTER 6

Assessing Student Learning

The night before the sixth class of his Indian removal unit, Becker sat at his desk, pondering the multiple-choice items that would appear on the assessment the next day. He needed approximately 15 items, although several fewer might do, but probably no more. He looked over the assessments that he had used in the past. But he possessed few items, largely because this was his first time teaching the unit and he was embarking on a close investigation of the Cherokee tribe's experience alone. He needed to develop a fresh cluster.

CONSTRUCTING AN ASSESSMENT

Decisions about Multiple-Choice Items

Developing these multiple-choice items with weighted distracters was a difficult undertaking, but not insurmountable given some concerted effort his previous experiences had taught him. A different matter made constructing this year's items seem more arduous. Each of his five classes of American history had handled the investigations somewhat idiosyncratically and therefore produced somewhat different interpretations to the questions they addressed. To Becker, this occasioned little surprise. In fact, the result reflected the sorts of outcomes that occur in the discipline all the time, he ruminated. But choices now confronted him. He could either develop items that would appear common to all five sections, or he could intersperse common items with those that were specific to interpretations generated within each section. He opted for the latter approach.

As was his habit, he began by simply brainstorming items derived from the organizer he had given students. He would generate as many items that he could from that organizer. Then he would draw from the list to tailor final assessments to fit each class. He sought to balance the number of items from the list of five headings on the organizer (Context, State and Federal Rights and Policy, Cherokee Reaction, Cherokee Removal, Making Sense?). If he was fortunate, he would generate perhaps four items for each heading for a total of 20 from which he could shape the final tailored assessments. But he knew that he might need to construct one or possibly two very specific items for each class, given their varying interpretations.

The most complex portion of shaping items involved creating weighted distracters, the sort that would represent the types of interpretive disagreement possible given the questions, but yet yield one defensible, top-weighted item (3 points) that could be identified by those who listened and participated in class discussions, took detailed notes, and read with care and diligence. He comforted himself as he began with the reminder that he made a practice of encouraging students to see him if they thought they could mount a successful challenge to his weighting system on any given item. He was open to the idea that, since history is an argument, they were certainly capable of presenting cases for a different weighting structure for an item they chose to debate. However, as he had done in the past, Becker would warn students that if they undertook what he considered frivolous cases, ones in which they had failed to do their homework and built an evidence-based argument for changing a weighting structure, he would take points away from them as a penalty. Finally, Becker reminded himself that he needed to consider how his less-accomplished readers and achievers would deal with how the items read. He resolved to broach this concern through an editorial process after he had generated the items.

He began sketching items out rapidly on his laptop. After ten minutes, he had hammered out four items, two on context and two on states and federal rights/responsibilities. He noted his first attempt at weightings after each distracter (e.g., W3, W0).

---

1. By the 1820s, the Cherokee had made some progress in "Americanizing" themselves. They had adopted a number of Anglo-white customs and laws. The best explanation for why they did this would be that they
   - Wanted to blend invisibly into white, Anglo society (W1)
   - Wanted to prove that they could be just like whites (W2)
   - Thought white, Anglo culture was better than their own (W0)
   - Thought it would better protect them and their land holdings (W3)

2. From about 1700 to 1838, Cherokee land holdings in the southeastern part of America appeared to shrink by about 85 percent. The best evidence **we studied** that seems to verify this change is:
   - The three maps showing changes in the boundaries of Cherokee lands (W3)
   - The front pages of two editions of the *Cherokee Phoenix* newspaper (W0)
   - The document that explained the "Chronology of Cherokee Removal" (W2)
   - The document that provided excerpts from the Treaty of New Echota (W1)

3. The U.S. government and state governments, especially Georgia, were not always in agreement about what the policy should be regarding the Cherokee people. Two of the strongest pieces of evidence showing this would be:
   - Georgia State Assembly, "Laws Extending Jurisdiction Over the Cherokee" (1829, 1832) and *Worcester v. Georgia* (1832) (W3)
   - Survey of John Ross's Plantation (1832) and *Worcester v. Georgia* (1832) (W0)
   - Zillah Brandon's "Memoir" (1830–1838) and "Memorial of Protest of the Cherokee Nation" (1836) (W0)
   - Andrew Jackson's "Seventh Annual Address to Congress" (1835) and U.S. Congress, "Speeches on Indian Removal" (1830) (W2)

4. The evidence we studied suggested that many U.S. Anglo leaders were not in agreement about what to do with the Cherokee tribe. As we saw, some were convinced that the Cherokee should be removed right away and sent to Oklahoma. Others thought that the Cherokee had a right to remain on their homelands. Which of the following accounts do you think **best shows support for the SECOND of these two positions?**
   - The Indian Removal Act (1830) (W0)
   - William Penn (Jeremiah Evarts) Essays (1829) (W3)
   - Cherokee Women's Petitions (1817, 1818, 1831) (W2)
   - Elias Boudinot's "Editorial in the *Cherokee Phoenix*" (1829) (W1)

Becker paused for a minute and reread each item, slightly tweaking the wording and distracter ordering. He then noticed that he was focusing student attention heavily in three of these items on specific types of accounts they had encountered in the unit. He needed better balance among the types of items. He studied the organizer's questions and began again to brainstorm items. After another 15–20 minutes, he developed seven more.

5. What do the accounts we studied suggest is the most important reason whites, for example in Georgia, wanted to take Cherokee land?
    - They were land hungry and just plain greedy (W1)
    - They thought the land was under their control as a part of State's rights (W2)
    - They saw economic advantages of the rich land held by the Cherokee (W3)
    - They were supported by Supreme Court cases (W0)
6. The accounts we read show that treaties between whites and the Cherokee made before 1830 had at least one important influence on them. This was
    - Cherokee stayed on their homelands while they decided to Americanize (W1)
    - Cherokee stayed on their homelands but those land holdings got much smaller (W2)
    - For protection the Cherokee gave away some of their land with each treaty signing (W3)
    - To defend themselves the Cherokee fought a number of wars against the U.S. Army (W0)
7. The most likely reason the U.S. Cavalry offered the Cherokee so little support and protection on the march to Oklahoma was
    - They did not have enough resources to help the sick and dying (W1)
    - The soldiers were white and did not like Indians in general (W2)
    - Many soldiers had fought against Indian tribes and were happy to see them removed (W3)
    - The cavalry was ordered by the U.S. government not to help the Cherokee at all (W0)
8. According to our investigations, the accounts we read, and discussions we had, which of the following statements best describes U.S government policy toward the Cherokee **in the early 1830s**?
    - Leaders were opposed to allowing the Cherokee to remain on their lands (W1)
    - Policy was mixed with some leaders in favor of removal and some opposed (W1)
    - Leaders were in favor of allowing the Cherokee to keep their land (W3)
    - U.S. government had no policy and let states handle Indian affairs (W0)
9. As talk of Cherokee removal increased and Georgians continued to make claims on their land, the Cherokees responded in different ways.

According to our study of the evidence about how they responded, which of the following statements **best** describes what happened?

- The Cherokee were stumped about what to do and waited to see what would happen (W0)
- The Cherokee eventually packed up their belongings and headed to Oklahoma (W2)
- Cherokee leaders became divided about what to do, leave or stay and fight (W3)
- Cherokee leaders finally gave in to the pressure and signed the Treaty of New Echota (W1)

10. It is possible to argue that white, Anglo leaders thought they were superior to and more important than the Cherokee. Which of the following documents would help support that argument.
    - Georgia State Assembly, "Laws Extending Jurisdiction [Control] Over Cherokees" (W1)
    - U.S. Congress, "Speeches on Indian Removal" (W1)
    - Andrew Jackson, "Seventh Annual Address to Congress" (W1)
    - All of these documents support the argument (W3)

11. In 1817, Cherokee women wrote to the Cherokee male leadership in the form of a petition. Here is part of what they said in that 1817 petition:

    > Your mothers, your sisters ask and beg of you not to part with any more land. We say ours. You are our descendants; take pity on our request. But keep it [the land] for your growing children, for it was the good will of our creator to place us here, and you know our father, the great president [James Monroe] will not allow his white children to take our country away. (From Perdue and Green, 2005)

    The evidence from this quote and what you know about what had been happening to the Cherokee by 1817 suggest that they are making their voices heard because they fear that Cherokee male leaders:
    - May sell off too much Cherokee lands in order to hold whites back (W3)
    - Will make a habit of ignoring important women in the tribe (W1)
    - Never listen to the women in the tribe and make all the decisions (W0)
    - Did not understand that President Monroe would protect the tribe (W2)

At this point, Becker again paused to reread the items he had just generated. He reflected on the weighting system, noticing that he had departed from his 3-2-1-0 weighting procedure for three items, "U.S government policy in the 1830s," "U.S. government policy toward the Cherokee," and the question concerning which document best supported a case for the attitude of "white superiority." He reminded himself that adjusting the weighting procedure was necessary for some items. He would need to explain this to students for these three items—if he used them—when he returned their graded tests. The item that drew from the Cherokee women's petition of 1817 involved using a quote to elicit responses. It was different than the preceding ones, reminding Becker that he had used such items before with generally good success. He liked the item and resolved to generate a few more and weave them into the assessment.

---

12. In 1836, John Ross, an important leader of the Cherokee tribe, wrote a letter to a journalist named Howard Payne. Payne thought that the Cherokee should fight against the Treaty of New Echota (1835) because it did not reflect the support of all the Cherokee people. Ross never signed the Treaty. Payne asked Ross to use the letter to show why the Treaty should not be followed. In the letter, Chief Ross states:

> My name is not, by mistake, omitted among the signers [of the Treaty], and the reasons . . . are the following: Neither myself nor any other member of the regular delegation [Cherokee leaders] to Washington, can, without violating our [Cherokee's] most sacred [rules] ever recognize that paper as a [real] Treaty. [The Treaty] is entirely inconsistent with the views of the Cherokee people. Three times have the Cherokee people . . . rejected the [removal] conditions [described in the Treaty].

Ross is arguing that the Treaty of New Echota is not valid because
- The Cherokee people would never support their removal to the west (W2)
- The majority of Cherokee would see that the Treaty goes against their will (W3)
- The Cherokee leaders disagreed among themselves about what to do (W0)
- As Cherokee chief, he did not sign or support the Treaty of New Echota (W1)

13. In late December, 1838, a white Baptist missionary named Evan Jones, who was traveling with the Cherokee on the "Trail of Tears" because he supported them, reported the following (an excerpt) to a Baptist magazine back east.

> We have now been on the road in Arkansas 75 days and traveled 529 miles. We are still 300 miles short of our destination. It has

... been [very] cold for sometime past, which [makes] the condition of those who are thinly [dressed] very uncomfortable. I am afraid that, with all care that can be [given to] the various [groups], there will be immense suffering, and loss of life [with this] removal.

Which of the following statements **best describes** what reliable evidence we can draw about the Trail of Tears from Jones report?

- Just as it says, that many Cherokee will most likely die on the "Trail of Tears" (W0)
- We do not know if this report is reliable unless we can compare it to other accounts (W3)
- Jones was probably giving an accurate report because he was a Christian missionary (W1)
- Jones is stretching the truth because he does not favor Cherokee removal westward (W1)

14. In 1830, President Andrew Jackson gave his *State of The Union Address* on December 6. He talked about a number of things, including Indian removal. He begins this part of his address by announcing that the "benevolent [kind and supporting] policies of the Government" toward the Indians were about to come to a happy conclusion. Jackson like to used big, complex words. So the following excerpt is a translation of some of the things he said to help you better understand him.

We Americans should not want our country to be restored to how we found it, covered in forests and filled with a few thousand savages. We should want cities, towns, and prosperous farms occupied by 12 million happy American people who know the blessings of liberty, civilization, and religion. Our current policies of Indian removal are but more of the progress of these good changes only by a milder process than killing the savages. It is painful for them to leave the lands of their fathers. But our ancestors did the same when they came to America. Should we weep because of these painful separations? Far from it. It is more a source of joy that we give our people a chance now to go out to new lands, opened up because of the removal of the Indians, so that they can develop their powers to the highest perfection.

Jackson seems to be justifying Indian removal on the grounds that it is

- Not that bad an experience for the Indians to have to move west even if they are forced (W1)
- Better for Americans to have the land so they can have more freedom and follow their religion (W3)

- As good a policy as one that forces the government to use the army to kill the Indians (W0)
- Not good for Americans to be kept from building towns and successful farms on Indian land (W2)

Becker quickly counted. He had 14 items and his quick review noted that a number of them were quite complex and might handcuff even a few of his best students. He worried about that, especially because, if they were difficult for the most accomplished readers and thinkers, they might be simply impossible for his less-accomplished kids. He decided to choose 12 items, and to attempt some balance between what he considered the difficult ones and those less so. He would make that set of decisions momentarily. First, he needed to sketch out short rationales for each item's weighting procedure. This move would serve him if students wished to challenge his structures. He was certain he would receive at least a few of those. Becker quickly printed out the 14 test items, then opened a new document and began sketching out rationales for each as he ran down the list.

BECKER'S RATIONALES AND NOTES FOR MULTIPLE-CHOICE ITEM WEIGHTING[1]

Item 1. A. W=1: Partially accurate, but "blending invisibly" too strong. B. W=2: Partially accurate; evidence suggested that many Cherokee thought that their longevity depended on acquiring Anglo customs and government systems; other evidence suggested that they still wished to retain some aspects of their culture. C. W=0: no evidence for this perspective. D. W=3: Strongest evidence supporting this position.

Item 2. A. W=3: Of the four choices this is most directly linked to evidence students examined. B. W=0: Not relevant, inappropriate. C. W=2: This document was partially helpful in that it implied decreases in land holdings but did so imprecisely. D. W=1: Partially helpful, but only in that it indicated that some Cherokees were willing to give up their land holdings.

[The original **Item 3** dropped from the final assessment.]

Item 4. A. W=0: Not relevant to the prompt. B, C, and D. Weighting here is related to the relative clarity by which each account speaks to the prompt, with the Penn essays being the clearest.

Item 5. Of A, B, and C, the clearest evidence students studied points to C. D. W=0: Inappropriate given the prompt.

Item 6. Of A, B, and C, the clearest evidence points to C. D. W=0: Inappropriate; no evidence.

[The original **Item 7** dropped from the final assessment.]

Item 8. A and B (W=1): Both partially accurate, however they ignore the Supreme Court order of *Worcester v. Georgia* (1832) as the leading definition of U.S. policy. C. W=3: Defining policy as described in *Worcester v. Georgia*. D. W=0: Inaccurate based on evidence.

Item 9. C. W=3 is the best response based on the evidence studied. A. W=0 is inaccurate. B. W=2: Technically accurate, but Cherokee were forced out and did not choose to respond this way. D. W=1: Not all Cherokee signed the Treaty, so it did not represent a consensual response.

Item 10. A, B, and C, all W=1: All reflect accounts that address the prompt, but from different perspectives. D. W=3 represents an evidentiary conjunction, indicating knowledge that the three accounts listed in A, B, and C address the prompt.

Item 11. A. W=3: This is the most appropriate response, especially given the opening line. B. W=1: This is a possible subtext, but remains only an impression. C. W=0: Not defensible given the quote. D. W=2: A defensible conjecture given the last clause, but is secondary to and part of the justification for the first sentence.

Item 12. A. W=2: Part of the argument but secondary to B. B. W=3: The most defensible distracter given the quote. C. W=0: Inappropriate. D. W=1: True, but a weak distracter given A and B.

Item 13. A. W=0: Inappropriate; does not make this claim. B. W=3: The most appropriate response given that the prompt asks about the account's reliability. C and D. Both W=1: Plausible choices but both make claims that cannot be rendered reliable without additional evidence.

Item 14. A. W=1: Partly defensible, but Jackson says many other things as well. B. W=3: Goes to the heart of Jackson's defense of Indian removal on the grounds that doing so supports Anglo destiny in the New World. C. W=0: Inappropriate; no evidence in the quote. D. W=2: Similar to B, but B states Jackson's position more clearly based on the quote used.

Becker looked over what he had done. The more he examined the items and their rationales, the more he realized that he had done a reasonable job of creating items that he could use across his five sections of American history. He paused, studied the items again, and then asked himself how he could justify that decision, particularly if some items favored certain classes over others. He assessed the items one-by-one yet again. He heard his mind say that he needed to remember that these multiple-choice items served a much richer purpose than as some type of definitive indicator of what students did or did not know. In many ways, they were a reflection of his ability to engage thinking and induce understanding. In that sense, the outcomes they produced served more as a verdict on him, rather than on his charges. Grading would need to become negotiable once he saw how students scored.

Second, and perhaps more importantly, such items provided a window on where his students were in their progression toward becoming more astute historical thinkers. If he was smart, he could continue to study the results in an effort to understand better who his kids were, what each needed, and how to frame future pedagogical decisions that could more aptly serve that goal. In short, these were all formative assessments. To the extent that they were well written, they could generate profound diagnostic power, much the way a physician's tests provide her with powerful diagnostic capabilities. Using the same items in all five classes might provide him rich comparative data and teach him something about the strengths and weaknesses of both his teaching practices and his students. He had used the comparative angle in the past with some success. He would use it again in this unit to see what it yielded. "Ah, classroom as laboratory," he said to himself as visions of the Frankenstein story danced comically across his mind.

Deciding on an Essay Question

Becker next turned his attention to the essay question. Fatigue was setting in. But this question was crucial to several of his goals, the least of which involved teaching his students how to write defensible, evidenced-based historical interpretations.[2] He had to press on with it. He knew it needed to derive from the "Making Sense?" section of the organizer. He had told his students as much. He wanted it to focus on the context of that period and what it can teach us about who "we" were as "Americans," about continuity and change in the so-called "democratic experiment" in particular. He looked at the "Making Sense?" questions and began sketching out the essay prompt. He needed to be careful to produce a prompt that contained no more than one question. Experience and course work on assessment design taught him that multiple-question essay prompts often confused students, who responded frequently by addressing only one of the questions at the expense of the others. This made grading them difficult. His effort to craft the essay prompt produced the following:

> What do we learn about life, attitudes, and change in America (for both white/Anglos and Indians) from our study of the Cherokee removal/dislocation process?
>
> In addressing this question, you are generating an interpretation of what the past means. Be sure to cite evidence from the sources we read to support and defend your interpretation. As I have taught you to do on past essays, it might be helpful to begin by making a claim and then supporting it with evidence. If you make more than one claim (for example, if you talk about life, attitudes, and changes for Anglos and then discuss the same for the Cherokee—and you need to talk about both!), you must support each section with evidence from the sources. You might be tempted to talk about all of this from your perspective in the twenty-first century. But I will be looking for you to pay very close attention to the **context** of the times in which these Indians and Anglos lived, how people thought and lived back then. I will be awarding extra points for those who pay careful attention to that historical context.

Becker chose the question he did (as opposed to, say, one specifically about Manifest Destiny) because he believed it was pivotal to his goal of working with the second-order idea of continuity/change. He thought that the question was broad enough that students could discuss, if they wished, the idea of Manifest Destiny as thematic for Anglos in their attempts to relocate southeastern tribes. Such essays would likely distinguish themselves. Becker was also deeply curious about whether or not students would choose to integrate the idea of Manifest Destiny into their essays without him mentioning it. As he studied what he had written, he wondered if he should try to tie the question more closely to the idea of change and continuity by asking students to deal more specifically with the linkages between what had come before Cherokee dislocation and after it. After thinking about where his classes had ended up, and the general fuzziness of their ideas concerning what had followed this period, he decided against any modifications. Again, he wanted to see what the essays yielded and what the range of responses looked like. He chose to go with what he had.

FINAL UNIT ASSESSMENT GIVEN TO STUDENTS

Unit Assessment on Cherokee Removal/Dislocation

Instructions: Circle the letter of only **one choice** for each multiple-choice item. Remember that possible selections are all weighted, with the best response worth 3 points. There is one response for each item that is clearly not appropriate; it gets 0 points. Think about each item carefully and make a selection even if you are not sure. You have a 75 percent chance of getting at least some points.

(1) By the 1820s, the Cherokee had made some progress in "Americanizing" themselves. They had adopted a number of Anglo-white customs and laws. The best explanation for why they did this would be that they
   (a) Wanted to blend invisibly into white, Anglo society
   (b) Wanted to prove that they could be just like whites
   (c) Thought white, Anglo culture was better than their own
   (d) Thought it would better protect them and their land holdings

(2) From about 1700 to 1838, Cherokee land holdings in the southeastern part of America appeared to shrink by about 85 percent. The best evidence **we studied** that seems to verify this change is:
   (a) The three maps showing changes in the boundaries of Cherokee lands
   (b) The front pages of two editions of the *Cherokee Phoenix* newspaper
   (c) The document that explained the "Chronology of Cherokee Removal"
   (d) The document that provided excerpts from the Treaty of New Echota

(3) The evidence we studied suggested that many U.S. Anglo leaders were not in agreement about what to do with the Cherokee tribe. As we saw, some were convinced that the Cherokee should be removed right away and sent to Oklahoma. Others thought that the Cherokee had a right to remain on their homelands. Which of the following accounts do you think **best shows support for the SECOND of these two positions?**
   (a) The Indian Removal Act (1830)
   (b) William Penn (Jeremiah Evarts) Essays (1829)
   (c) Cherokee Women's Petitions (1817, 1818, 1831)
   (d) Elias Boudinot's "Editorial in the *Cherokee Phoenix*" (1829)

(4) What do the accounts we studied suggest is the most important reason whites, for example in Georgia, wanted to take Cherokee land?
   (a) They were land hungry and just plain greedy
   (b) They thought the land was under their control as a part of State's rights
   (c) They saw economic advantages of the rich land held by the Cherokee
   (d) They were supported by Supreme Court cases

(5) The accounts we read show that treaties between whites and the Cherokee made before 1830 had at least one important influence on them. This was
  (a) Cherokee stayed on their homelands while they decided to Americanize
  (b) Cherokee stayed on their homelands but those land holdings got much smaller
  (c) For protection the Cherokee gave away some of their land with each treaty signing
  (d) To defend themselves the Cherokee fought a number of wars against the U.S. Army

(6) According to our investigations, the accounts we read, and discussions we had, which of the following statements best describes U.S government policy toward the Cherokee **in the early 1830s**?
  (a) Leaders were opposed to allowing the Cherokee to remain on their lands
  (b) Policy was mixed with some leaders in favor of removal and some opposed
  (c) Leaders were in favor of allowing the Cherokee to keep their land
  (d) U.S. government had no policy and let states handle Indian affairs

(7) As talk of Cherokee removal increased and Georgians continued to make claims on their land, the Cherokees responded in different ways. According to our study of the evidence about how they responded, which of the following statements **best** describes what happened?
  (a) The Cherokee were stumped about what to do and waited to see what would happen
  (b) The Cherokee eventually packed up their belongings and headed to Oklahoma
  (c) Cherokee leaders became divided about what to do, leave or stay and fight
  (d) Cherokee leaders finally gave in to the pressure and signed the Treaty of New Echota

(8) It is possible to argue that white, Anglo leaders thought they were superior to and more important than the Cherokee. Which of the following documents would help support that argument.
  (a) Georgia State Assembly, "Laws Extending Jurisdiction [Control] Over Cherokees"
  (b) U.S. Congress, "Speeches on Indian Removal"
  (c) Andrew Jackson, "Seventh Annual Address to Congress"
  (d) All of these documents support the argument

(9) In 1817, Cherokee women wrote to the Cherokee male leadership in the form of a petition. Here is part of what they said in that 1817 petition:

> Your mothers, your sisters ask and beg of you not to part with any more land. We say ours. You are our descendants; take pity on our request. But keep it [the land] for your growing children, for it was the good will of our creator to place us here, and you know our father, the great president [James Monroe] will not allow his white children to take our country away. (From Perdue and Green, 2005)

The evidence from this quote and what you know about what had been happening to the Cherokee by 1817 suggest that they are making their voices heard because they fear that Cherokee male leaders:

(a) May sell off too much Cherokee lands in order to hold whites back
(b) Will make a habit of ignoring important women in the tribe
(c) Never listen to the women in the tribe and make all the decisions
(d) Did not understand that President Monroe would protect the tribe

(10) In 1836, John Ross, an important leader of the Cherokee tribe, wrote a letter to a journalist named Howard Payne. Payne thought that the Cherokee should fight against the Treaty of New Echota (1835) because it did not reflect the support of all the Cherokee people. Ross never signed the Treaty. Payne asked Ross to use the letter to show why the Treaty should not be followed. In the letter, Chief Ross states:

> My name is not, by mistake, omitted among the signers [of the Treaty], and the reasons . . . are the following: Neither myself nor any other member of the regular delegation [Cherokee leaders] to Washington, can, without violating our [Cherokee's] most sacred [rules] ever recognize that paper as a [real] Treaty. [The Treaty] is entirely inconsistent with the views of the Cherokee people. Three times have the Cherokee people . . . rejected the [removal] conditions [described in the Treaty].

Ross is arguing that the Treaty of New Echota is not valid because

(a) The Cherokee people would never support their removal to the west
(b) The majority of Cherokee would see that the Treaty goes against their will
(c) The Cherokee leaders disagreed among themselves about what to do
(d) As Cherokee chief, he did not sign or support the Treaty of New Echota

(11) In late December, 1838, a white Baptist missionary named Evan Jones, who was traveling with the Cherokee on the "Trail of Tears" because he supported them, reported the following (an excerpt) to a Baptist magazine back east.

> We have now been on the road in Arkansas 75 days and traveled 529 miles. We are still 300 miles short of our destination. It has . . . been [very] cold for sometime past, which [makes] the condition of those who are thinly [dressed] very uncomfortable. I am afraid that, with all care that can be [given to] the various [groups], there will be immense suffering, and loss of life [with this] removal.

Which of the following statements **best describes** what reliable evidence we can draw about the "Trail of Tears" from Jones' report?

(a) Just as it says that many Cherokee will most likely die on the "Trail of Tears"

(b) We do not know if this report is reliable unless we can compare it to other accounts

(c) Jones was probably giving an accurate report because he was a Christian missionary

(d) Jones is stretching the truth because he was not in favor of Cherokee removal westward

(12) In 1830, President Andrew Jackson gave his *State of The Union Address* on December 6. He talked about a number of things, including Indian removal. He begins this part of his address by announcing that the "benevolent [kind and supporting] policies of the Government" toward the Indians were about to come to a happy conclusion. Jackson like to used big, complex words. So the following excerpt is a translation of some of the things he said to help you better understand him.

> We Americans should not want our country to be restored to how we found it, covered in forests and filled with a few thousand savages. We should want cities, towns, and prosperous farms occupied by 12 million happy American people who know the blessings of liberty, civilization, and religion. Our current policies of Indian removal are but more of the progress of these good changes only by a milder process than killing the savages. It is painful for them to leave the lands of their fathers. But our ancestors did the same when they came to America. Should we weep because of these painful separations? Far from it. It is more a source of joy that we give our people a chance now to go out to new lands, opened up because of the removal of the Indians, so that they can develop their powers to the highest perfection.

Jackson seems to be justifying Indian removal on the grounds that it is

(a) Not a bad experience for the Indians to have to move west even if they are forced

(b) Better for Americans to get the land to have more freedom and follow their religion

(c) As good a policy as one that forces the government to use the army to kill the Indians

(d) Bad for Americans to be kept from building towns and farms on Indian land

Essay Question

What do we learn about life, attitudes, and change in America—for both white/Anglos and Indians—from our study of the Cherokee removal/ dislocation process?

In addressing this question, you are generating an interpretation of what the past means. Be sure to **cite evidence** from the sources we read to support and defend your interpretation. As I have taught you to do on past essays, it might be helpful to begin by **making a claim** and then **supporting it with evidence**. If you make more than one claim (for example, if you talk about life, attitudes, and changes for Anglos and then discuss the same for the Cherokee—and you need to talk about both!), you must support each section with evidence from the sources. You might be tempted to talk about all of this from your perspective in the twenty-first century. But I will be looking for you to pay **very close attention to the context of the times** in which these Indians and Anglos lived, how people thought and lived back then. I will be awarding points (see the scoring rubric) for those who pay careful attention to that historical context.

Scoring the Assessment

Before classes on the day of the assessment, Becker sketched out the range of possible points students could earn on its 12 items. A maximum score would be 36 (3 points times 12 items) and a minimum score would be zero (0 points times 12). He could calculate percentages from the maximum of 36 to arrive at some possible grade distribution. But he would wait to see what that distribution looked like before making any decisions. For his own purposes, he could calculate the number of 3-point, 2-point, 1-point, and 0-point responses per item to arrive at some sense about where his students' ideas lacked clarity or were deeply confused. His regular post-assessment review in class would involve deploying this distribution to focus attention around those ideas. This was one of the key advantages to working off a weighting system; it gave Becker some diagnostic purchase on which ideas students were struggling with, and how in particular, and what remaining pedagogical moves he still might take to rectify those issues.

Scoring the essay would be a complex process that would require some tweaking in the rubric that Becker used. As the semester proceeded, his essay prompts pressed student ideas more deeply. He would require more as each unit unfolded. In this unit he pushed on the requirement for evidentiary support and added the stress on interpreting within historical context. His rubric would need to reflect these additional elements. He would also need to create a one-page explanatory document students could take home with them and consult as they crafted their interpretations. He typed up the rubric, reminding himself that these rubrics were always works in progress. The rubric for this unit turned out to look like the following:

ESSAY SCORING RUBRIC

Section 1: Addressing the Prompt
> 2 points = Addresses all elements of the essay prompt (in this case, two: interprets life, attitudes, and changes for *both* Cherokee and Anglos)
> 1 point = Addresses only one or two elements (life, attitudes, changes) of the essay prompts and/or only for one of the two groups
> 0 points = Does not address the essay prompt (e.g., mentions one of both groups but makes no claims about life, attitudes, or change)

Section 2: Use of Evidence
> 3 points = Makes a claim and uses a variety of evidence to support that claim, and in this case, does so for both prompt elements (for Cherokee and Anglos)
> 2 points = Makes a claim and uses a variety of evidence to support that claim, but does so for only one element of the prompt
> 1 point = Makes claim(s) but does not support them satisfactorily with a variety evidence
> 0 points = Makes no claim and draws from no evidence for support

Section 3: Historical Context
> 2 points = Constructs an interpretation that remains faithful to the context of the period
> 1 point = Constructs an interpretation that is only partially faithful to the context of the period; some elements of the essay make judgments about the past that relate to current ideas
> 0 point = Makes claims and judges the past based only on current ideas (e.g., that some Georgian leaders should have been arrested for stealing Cherokee land and put in jail)

The maximum points an essay could yield would be seven and the minimum would be zero. Because the multiple-choice section yielded a maximum of 36 points, Becker decided to use a multiplier of two for the essay question, reasoning that if a student managed all 36 points on the multiple-choice section and all seven on the essay, by doubling the essay score, it would total 14. Adding the two totals together would weight this test at 50 points, a number students would understand relative to other assignments and assessments he administered that would be weighted more or less relative to their degree of difficulty and the time they required to complete. He copied the rubric for his classes, delivering copies to each student as they took the multiple-choice portion of the assessment, and reminding them to take it home and consult it carefully as they constructed their interpretive essays.

FOURTH-PERIOD ASSESSMENT RESULTS

Multiple-Choice Items

As Becker anticipated, the range of scores was broad. The high score was 33 (92 percent) (Serena) and the low score was 14 (39 percent) (James, a student with an IEP, who had taken the assessment with support from a para-educator in the counseling office). The mean score for the class was 28 (78 percent), revealing that scores were skewed toward the higher end of the range, something for which Becker was hoping. However, he was anticipating a mean score higher than 80 percent, and therefore emerged somewhat disappointed. Fourth-period students scored second highest among his five classes.

A study of individual item responses for fourth-period students showed that they struggled the most with four key ideas sampled by this section of the assessment: (a) identifying evidence that supported Anglo support for the Cherokee remaining on their homelands, (b) the reason whites in Georgia were after Cherokee land (about 60 percent of the students chose the distracter that described whites as "land hungry and just plain greedy"— suggesting that they reacted to this item more on the basis of opinion than evidence), (c) the issue of the reliability of the Evan Jones report from the Trail of Tears, and (d) Andrew Jackson's effort to justify Indian removal policy in his State of the Union Address. Becker suspected that the last two ideas and the items sampling them, both demanding careful reading capabilities and comprehension strategies, may have hamstrung the 50 percent of students who opted for distracters other than the best ones. Almost a quarter of fourth-period students selected distracters with a weight of zero points. Becker was disheartened by this outcome because he found these items deeply linked to the kinds of strategic reading and thinking goals he was attempting to teach. He tried to comfort himself by observing that it was it was still early in the year and he would need to work harder teaching these capabilities in subsequent units if students were to improve.

Regarding the first two ideas—(a) and (b)—Becker was a bit stumped by the fact that over 40 percent of the students missed these two. He looked at them again, studying them carefully for clues. In the first case (identifying evidence), students tended to select the weight-2 distracter, and so were not far off. He reasoned that because the class as a whole had spent relatively little time with the evidence this item sampled (especially with respect to his other class sections), students were mostly guessing perhaps. He would converse with them about this item. The other item involving the reasons why Anglos were interested on taking Cherokee land, the "land hungry and just plain greedy" distracter was too attractive and aligned too closely with their opinions of Georgians to resist. "Opinion trumps evidence," Becker mumbled to himself. "Something needs to be said about this when we discuss the assessment results in class."

Then he paused and looked at these items more closely. All but four of his students of color opted for the "land hungry and greedy" distracter, but none of his white students. This pattern was not altogether a surprise. Research he had read suggested that the sociocultural positionalities of students of color would predispose them—understandably and perhaps rightly—toward viewing such Indian relocations and land dispossessions as a function of Anglo racist sentiments. Forcing Indians west could be linked to the racist undercurrents of Manifest Destiny and the Anglo cultural leaders who were convicted of it. Land dispossession based on greed might simply be an outward manifestation and likely another "proof" of their existence. Given their inherited sociocultural privilege, white students might simply be predisposed to obliviousness with regard to the racism that underpinned land taking and Anglo policy rationalized by Manifest Destiny. After all, Becker thought, at the core of Manifest Destiny was the religiously imbued notion of "the white-man's burden" in North America. Becker would need to openly confront this phenomenon as well.[3]

Essays

Becker was especially pleased with the results on the take-home essay questions. Although he admittedly assessed them against the rubric rather liberally, he was struck by how generally thoughtful students' responses were. Five students wrote responses to which he awarded all seven points.

Another five students garnered six points, four received five points, six managed four points, while the remaining two students (one James with the IEP and the other Salvator, one of the underachievers) scored three points. The average score was 5.2 or 74 percent, a mean percentage score almost ten points higher than on previous unit essay questions. As he surmised, the most significant difficulty students encountered was constraining themselves when it came to passing judgment on the white leaders for what students thought was their reprehensible policies of removal and the death of so many Cherokee on the Trail of Tears. A number of students chose the exaggerated numbers of deaths on the trail to justify their judgments. Abject "greed" among "land-hungry" Georgians who could "only think of themselves" also were common complaints. Again, opinion weighing out reasoned evidence.

Students who wrote more accomplished essays tended to be more careful, refraining from making exaggerated claims or passing harsh personal judgment on Anglo leaders. They were more apt to describe white Georgians, for example, as men (and women) of their times, those who believed it was their right as victors in the American Revolutionary War to lay stake to lands in the west, or west of their then-present land claims. If Indians, who were "deemed to be in the way of progress" resisted, they had to be moved. However, these students frequently registered difficulty reconciling the end result with the idea of freedom and a growing set of rights for all Americans. As one student (Max) put it, it was hard to figure out why white Americans could not accept Americanized Indians such as the Cherokee as fellow Americans who deserved the same land rights they held. A few of these students (including Max) drew on the theme of Manifest Destiny to show how it could be used to rationalize removal, occasionally dancing too close to the edge of overgeneralizing about how widespread that idea was among average white Americans in the 1830s. Becker awarded these students higher scores on the historical-context section of the rubric. He would also make how he did so clear in class when they discussed the essay-score results.

Becker leaned way back in his chair for a minute and stared at the ceiling. He was reflecting on what he had learned from the test results. "What do these results teach me about what I need to work on more diligently in fourth period?" he asked himself. "Reading! And opinionating, even if legitimately tied to sociocultural positioning," he thought. Becker resolved to press these two key themes with period-four students. "They need to become more astute, accomplished readers and they need to be more careful to check their opinions against the evidence," he said to himself. Becker would resolve to place far more stress in future units on strategic reading, to stop and model it when he could, and to repeatedly insist on the use of the PAIR^e guide and the strategies it entailed. He also heard himself say that, perhaps, using fewer sources and accounts would assist in giving him more time to focus in on those strategies. With regard to the issue of opinion overriding evidence, he decided to be more sensitive to its likelihood, particularly when employing provocative accounts, and more quickly call students out if he sensed they were headed down that path, giving him the opportunity to openly consider the role positionality may play in the process as it competes with thoughtful historical conextualizing.

WHAT DOES BECKER KNOW ABOUT ASSESSMENT IN HISTORY?

Assessing as Becker does is a complex undertaking. However, it is not something that necessarily defies understanding. The key is aligning assessment practices with teaching goals and strategies. How does Becker— or any other U.S. history teacher so disposed—come to this alignment? Here we focus on Becker's understandings, and how they developed, as an exemplar, not necessarily of exquisite expertise, but more as a work in progress that gradually allows him greater degrees of diagnostic power the smarter he becomes about aligning goals to practices to assessment strategy.

Suspicions about Standardized and Pre-Packaged Tests

Early in his teaching career, Becker became rather disenchanted with standardized tests, high- or low-stakes versions. He had grown suspicious of them for a series of fundamental reasons. All dealt primarily with his perception regarding the undesirable consequences such standardized-testing regimes produced. The first, intended or otherwise, dealt with the ways in which such tests had the effect of attempting to standardize both teachers' practices and students themselves. Although he understood the policymakers' impulse to get some reliable indication of student achievement using assessments that could be given to large numbers of students and therefore produce comparative data, he found such efforts as attempts to press everyone they touched into the same mold. His teaching experience had taught him that students in particular were different enough, diverse enough, that such an effort seemed designed to tamp down this sort of variation. Becker was more the proponent of the idea that, despite the difficulties it could create for teachers in classes of 20 to 30 students, there was unbounded strength to be found in all that diversity. Testing policies that had the apparent consequence of pressing everyone toward a common mean ran counter to his sensibility, his respect for student difference, and his appreciation of the diversity in the practices of his colleagues from which he thought he could learn much even if he disagreed with their core approaches.

Linked to the first, the second objection Becker had hinged on was using standardized testing practices and policies as a wrench to drive the educational equity screw. He appreciated the attention generated around this equity issue via standardized-testing outcomes. However, he was fully aware from a course he had taken on assessment practices that for decades school systems had used standardized tests to unearth the same problem: Schools and school systems that did most poorly on such tests were identifiable by the social class and poverty of the students who attended them. There was no real mystery in this correlation. Poverty and low socio-economic status went hand in hand with low achievement on standardized tests and school people and policymakers had known of it for a very long time. Ratcheting up stakes using increased pressure from wider deployment of standardized testing practices, especially as he had witnessed it in the early twenty-first century, seemed to Becker to simply be more of the same. If significant resources (human and material capital) did not follow into the neediest schools and to the neediest students that the test results identified, little would change.

Some shifts in resources Becker had witnessed. However, what appeared to him to be the necessary reallocations were in very short supply. He often wondered if, in a zero-sum game, the vast increases in resources spent on standardized testing practices across the country had left school system accountants and state departments of education groping in the dark for the money to fund investments in those needy children and the teachers who taught them. After all, he reasoned, there's research out there that points out time and again that it is the quality of teachers that matters most in the education of such children.[4]

Becker also wondered a number of times about how schools and teachers were supposed to change the material conditions of those poor children's lives. Yes, they could dedicate themselves to engaging those students in powerful learning experiences against all odds, but if their daily charges went home each night to squalor, hunger, jobless parents, and life on the street, would that not deeply limit what teachers and schools could accomplish in their classroom spaces? How will increasing the stakes in standardized-testing practices in school systems—only one of the many institutional structures in society—help solve the poverty conditions produced by other institutions that function best when they stratify the humans they employ? Becker was convinced that the jury would long be out on standardized-testing regimes' impact on the equity/equality problem, for the solution remained only too distantly connected to the problem in his judgment, despite the best intentions of the proponents.

Another argument concerning the wisdom of pursuing vast accountability practices (through standardized tests) that Becker found suspicious turned on the theory that such efforts would significantly improve student achievement. In shorthand in the policy literature, this was the excellence argument. By employing high-stakes, demanding exams, policymakers could coerce teachers into providing improved and more powerful learning opportunities for students. The linchpin here involved (a) producing high-caliber academic standards that (b) teachers interpreted consistently and accurately as they were designed, and (c) to which standardized tests would be aligned. In theory, the idea, Becker thought, was quite brilliant. Stated as such, the theory went straight at the idea of aligning curricular goals and teaching practices to student learning outcomes as assessed on standardized exams. However, as Becker was to learn from the research literature in history and social studies education, there was no evidence to suggest such alignments had occurred or that, even if they had, the desired outcomes were being produced.[5] Because of his interest in such curriculum-teaching-learning-assessment alignments, Becker poured through this literature looking for ways to understand the nature of this problem. His queries pushed him to conjecture about several explanations.

One involved the issue of the psychology of mass testing and the process of operationalizing the practice *en masse* that underpinned testmakers' efforts to design standardized tests. Faced with the prospect of crafting assessments that would be taken by tens of thousands of students, testmakers were faced with several difficult realities. Scale figured in decisions to make tests inexpensive and easy to administer and score. The more complex items became (not unlike Becker's), the more difficult they were to administer and score, particularly the latter. Complex items would require complex scoring practices that would raise costs almost exponentially. Essay prompts, such as Becker's, if administered on a massive scale, required legions of scorers armed with complicated rubrics. Those scorers, in order to achieve some modicum of inter-rater reliability, would need to be carefully educated to learn how to consistently apply the scoring rubrics. Education of this sort would be expensive in ways that few school systems or state testing agencies were willing to pursue. Becker knew first hand about this sort of complexity and the cost in time consumed it took him to score the essays his students write. If standards were high enough, the curriculum (as in learning opportunities provided to students) would likely need to be reasonably complex and demanding, necessitating tests that were aligned well enough to measure that complexity. Assessment costs rise correlatively with increasing demands for excellence. Excellence then as achieved via large-scale testing, Becker conjectured, is not something educational policymakers and school officials currently appear willing to afford.

Related to abrogation on the educational excellence impulse were psychometric theories that testmakers relied upon when thinking about standardized testing practices. Becker also had looked into this concern by reading in the research literature.[6] He found that testmakers were particularly prone to worrying about test reliability. They developed elaborate schemes for producing tests that could generate consistent, reliable results, heavily relying on multiple-choice items with single (and with hope, unambiguous) correct answers. These efforts gave way to item-response theories in which, generally speaking, practices were designed to predict and test how any given item in a test would perform. Items that performed in ways outside the slope of the famous bell-curve distribution because they were too easy or too difficult would be dropped from a test. As a result, reliable tests tended to generate predictable bell-curve distributions repeatedly. If they did not, testmakers would begin examining items looking for the culprits. One effect of this process was for scores to converge to a mean at the center of the bell curve. If the curve was skewed substantially in one direction or the other from previous administrations, the test results were typically deemed unreliable. The question of whether there were genuine gains or drops in student performance would often pale in comparison to the question of reliability. Standardized tests under these assumptions and theories, Becker learned, were ill-equipped to fully gauge changes in achievement and therefore a location on a trajectory toward excellence.

The question of the validity of such tests was also of interest to Becker, and especially the idea of a standardized test's construct validity. What Becker was curious about was how well such assessments mapped onto the key ideas, or constructs, of a discipline or subject matter. To him, solid mapping represented potentially strong alignment between the rich ideas of the discipline/subject matter and what the tests actually assessed about what students knew and what they could do with what they knew. Here again, Becker found, the deep worry over a test's reliability tended to trump concerns over its treatment of construct validity.[7] The principal villain again was complexity. The more complex the discipline's pivotal ideas—and history was a prime exemplar because of its loosely defined structure, consequential ambiguity, and deep interpretive practices—the more difficult it became to sample those ideas through reliable multiple-choice items with single correct answers. Becker came to see these standardized tests and the decisions made about how they were constructed to be a very poor match for what he was attempting to accomplish and the discipline-centric investigative approach from which he operated. They trafficked in concerns of reliability at the expense of validity, eschewed complexity and especially ambiguity, sought testing on the cheap, worked from outdated behaviorist learning theories, and had done little to date to advance the causes of either educational equity or excellence.

Despite being rather jaded by studying the literature on standardized testing and accountability, he still firmly believed in the power of assessments. To him they were the central link between his curricular and pedagogical theories and structures, his day-to-day practices, and what his students learned and understood. Imprecise a business as it was, assessing that link was his only option. He had to repeatedly resolve to engage it the best way he could, pursue goal clarity, assess regularly, learn from what the assessment results taught him, and consistently modify his theories and practices while continually honing his capacities to generate more powerful and valid assessments. His target, therefore, was twofold: (a) consistently work to sharpen alignment between subject matter goals, teaching practices, and assessments, and (b) continually modify all three to better service alignment.

Assessment as Diagnosis

Such an approach required that Becker adopt a view of assessments as diagnostic tools rather than summative, standardized evaluations on which to base high-stakes consequences. The latter had very little value to Becker because, as he observed every year, high-stakes standardized exam data, for example, would return to schools and teachers long after it had much power to reshape the latters' practices. To hold diagnostic power, assessments needed to give nearly instantaneous feedback to both teachers and students. Becker's assessments, he believed, more adequately accomplished this goal. And he was getting better at it as his experience writing such assessments became more skilled.

Improving an assessment's diagnostic power—that is, its power to improve his practices in ways that increased his students' historical thinking and understanding capabilities—continually called his attention to being clear about his subject matter goals and the questions he was asking. This in turn required him to sharpen his theories about the relationship between historical thinking and historical understanding. What sorts of cognitive performances would students need to engage in that would enhance and deepen their understandings? This led him to systematically hone his theories about that relationship (e.g., Chapter 3, Figure 3.1). It also led him repeatedly back to the research literature on student learning in history (see

Chapter 4) and to teaching practices that literature described that connected the two with the greatest promise. As we have seen, Becker came to the conclusion that common practices (e.g., teaching American history as a story of nation building with a *fait accompli* narrative register) simply were not up to the task, thus his reconceptualized, investigative approach.

To generate diagnostic power for both himself and his students based on that approach, Becker needed to work diligently at the problem of alignment. He needed to use the research literature and previous experiences with assessment outcomes to focus his goals, tailor them in a sense developmentally, in order to build student thinking and understanding capacity sequentially.[8] He could not teach everything at once. Teaching students to read historically (a strategic capability) was often one of the most important initial efforts Becker undertook. Therefore, early in the year, his assessments pressed on this agenda as a reflection of his teaching strategies. But reading simply to read? Hardly. Embedded also in this effort was Becker's early attention to the concept of evidence and its relationship to making interpretive claims. Developing history-specific reading strategies was pressed into the service of using what that reading generated to construct evidence-based interpretations, forms of historical understanding that become public, either orally or in writing. Assessment items, therefore, had to combine both strategic reading capability and some display of understanding that resulted if Becker was to make sense of the relationship between the two and where his students were in that respect. His Indian Removal unit was a case in point, wherein his classroom practices, the architecture of the unit, and most if not all the assessment's items served that purpose.

However, without some type of organized feedback loop that included his students, part of the diagnostic power of his assessments would be lost. As a result, Becker made a practice of spending the class period following an assessment going over its details with students. He posted score breakdowns on all the items and attended similarly to the essay results. This put pressure on him from two angles. First, he needed to find an efficient method of scoring and then reporting out the assessment results soon after the assessment was taken, a process he continues to refine. And second, opening up the assessment to his students and making his scoring practices transparent (e.g., rationales for distracter weights) frequently invited criticism, complaints, and scoring counter arguments. Becker accepted the pressure because his experience taught him that it helped him clarify his goals (and how he communicated them especially), sharpen his practices, and hone his assessment-crafting capabilities (e.g., improve construct validity). Perhaps more importantly, the open-feedback process benefited students in ways that he had difficulty fully gauging. In short, students became astute at assessing their own assessment strategies, consistently improved almost to a student, and seemed to actually enjoy arguing with Becker about the assessment outcomes, which in turn appeared to enhance their interest levels. Becker found that their investment in and responsibility toward their own learning increased across the semester.

Part of this was linked to Becker's ability to demonstrate some flexibility in his assessment scoring process while connecting it to an understanding of the interpretive nature of the subject and its attendant ambiguity. Even the assessment process, then, possessed an educative function for his students, rather than merely some instrumental means to a course-grade end. However, Becker was quick to remind students that criteria for making historical claims existed (e.g., evidentiary basis) and that his American history classes were not places in which any story would do.[9] Assessment-results discussions provided yet another forum for Becker to offer up important ideas about what it means to understand the past, to construct histories, and to develop a sense of the guild-honed criteria for doing so. It also provided him additional opportunities to hear how his students were thinking about the history they were trying to learn as they verbalized their questions and challenges to his assessment items.

PERFECT ASSESSMENTS—AN UNATTAINABLE IDEAL?

Assessment conceived of in this way became integral to Becker's practice. Becker could not imagine what he would do without the diagnostic feedback it provided. It helped him become a better history teacher. It helped him understand his students, both collectively and individually. It assisted him in making sense of where his students were along a trajectory toward becoming more powerful thinkers, ones who understood history rather than simply memorized (or not) a panoply of details that they soon forgot. It also helped him attend to individual students who experienced particular cognitive impasses that limited their capacity to understand the past about which he wanted them to learn. Was approaching assessment in this vein a complex undertaking? Of course. However, it was well worth the energy he needed to invest in it because the consequential benefits far exceeded the costs. Was he the master assessment expert? No, but that was part of the charm. Becker welcomed the challenge of learning to become better at it, all while realizing that expert assessment practices characterized by perfect alignments and thus all-powerful diagnostic capabilities would likely forever be an unattainable ideal. But some assessments were clearly better than others. Becker was comfortable with those realizations.

CHAPTER 7

Theorizing Investigative History Teaching

During graduate school, Becker often heard his fellow classmates complain about how the teacher-education portion of the program seemed particularly long on theory and far too short on the practice-related strategies and tools they would need to navigate their classrooms. They wanted more saws, hammers, and nails for their pedagogical toolkits. They had a difficult time translating the theories of schooling and curriculum, teaching and learning into such toolkits for action. Sometimes Becker shared their frustrations.

However, the more he thought about it, he realized that having a bag full of tools with some knowledge about *how* to use them, while important, promised no understanding about *when* to use them, under *what* circumstances, and *why*. When do you use a hammer or nail gun as opposed to a screwdriver? Both fasten things together but have quite different properties. Well, he ruminated, it depends on whether you need to use a screw or a nail to fasten that something together. Which is best? Answering that question required a sense of what you were trying to accomplish, a theory about the relationship between the materials to be connected, and more theorizing about stress loads the materials would need to withstand within a particular application. Screws, for example, had better long-term adhesion properties and were stronger, but more time consuming and expensive to employ. Nails were cheaper and quicker to install, especially with a pneumatic nailer.

Applying this idea in a classroom was analogous. Knowing, for example, when to stop and ask particular questions of students or let them continue talking with each other required clarity about goals, which in turn was directly connected to a theorized relationship between goals, curricular materials, and pedagogical practices. All the tools in the world that a pedagogical toolkit could hold were virtually worthless without sound theories about how the use of those particular tools were related to how students learned, what materials best fostered that learning, and especially what targets teachers were setting for that learning from a sea of possibilities. In this chapter, I explore this set of relationships in an effort to theorize an investigative history pedagogy. I use what Becker knows and does—evidenced in the preceding chapters—as a backdrop against which to pursue this effort. My goal is to interconnect Becker's investigative goal framework (Chapter 2), subject matter knowledge (Chapter 3), research-based ideas about how students learn history (Chapter 4), and the practices he employed (Chapters 5 and 6) into a theoretical understanding that I am hoping can serve as a framework for assisting the learning process of history teachers who are predisposed to teach the way Becker does.

Accomplishing this task is a complex undertaking. The pieces fit together in distinctive ways. Pursuing a particular direction necessitates certain pedagogical choices and mitigates against others. Alignment is the watchword, as we saw for example, in the previous chapter. With most things, there are options, different pedagogically defensible choices a teacher could make. But the small-t theory I am endeavoring to sketch here constrains choices for the sake of that alignment. Is the theorizing I do here, using Becker as the foil, without flaw? No, however it does represent one take on what a close alignment exists between goals, materials, practice-related tools and strategies, and assessment decisions. The warrant for this particular theorizing involves a sense of the consequential validity Becker's investigative approach portends for student learning in the history domain as defined by a 30-year research literature. I argued that warrant in Chapter 2, but at the risk of belaboring the point, I will reference it again here.

A GOAL FRAMEWORK

Almost everything that Becker does with his students flows from his investigative goal framework. History teachers could certainly choose other types of goals for their students. Common practice, as we have seen, is deeply rooted in a different type of framework and therefore its goals serve different ends. The chief of these ends is to imbue students with the general contours of the nation-building, freedom-quest narrative. That narrative arc is designed to encourage identification with the nation state, its ideals, and its heroes and heroines. As we have seen, it traffics in commemoration rather than in investigation, and in the view of David Lowenthal, is heritage celebration rather than history. It is also marked by its *fait accompli* register, as though through relentless progress, the story is complete—ideals achieved with the nation state at its zenith. Although Becker wants his students to understand America's story (or stories perhaps more accurately), he does not consider the story to have ended or its various episodes to be fully understood. Too much remains yet to be investigated; too many perspectives exist to be explored anew. How does he know? He reckons that if the story was complete, most, if not all, Americanist historians would be looking for work. Therefore, he enjoins his charges in the search for new understandings of the American past.

The theory that underpins Becker's sense of the teaching–learning landscape in history education, as we saw in Chapter 3, looks something like this. If he wants his students to make sense of the American past, to understand its many compelling, but often conflicting story lines,[1] he begins by asking himself: Who currently best epitomizes depth of understanding of that past? The best answer he has come up with is that it's the historians who study it. He has looked around for other candidates, but always returns to the historians—the experts. Their understanding remains incomplete, which is precisely why they continue their pursuits. But despite their lack of a full and complete apperception, they remain the experts, those with the deepest understanding.

If the goal is to move students in that direction—that is, to cultivate and deepen their understandings—then it would make sense to ask, how do the experts come to their expertise? Becker reasons, based on his reading of the expertise research, that they dig about in the past, investigating its traces and residua in search of answers to the questions they pose, questions that remain to be addressed, questions that surface in response to previous experts' interpretations, ones that beg new questions and new explorations.[2] They follow a set of practices for doing so. Yes, they disagree with each other about how those practices are to be deployed. But generally speaking, there are particular guild-honored and sanctioned procedures that result in the production of understandings (histories by another name). Becker wants to teach his students about these practices on the trite aphorism, but one he thinks is very real nonetheless, that, if you give someone a fish, they can eat for a day; but if you teach them how to fish, they will never go hungry.[3] The challenge, of course, is "teaching them to fish." It requires the convergence of (a) subject matter knowledge, (b) a theory of how students best learn history, (c) powerful pedagogical principles and practices (aligned with a and b), and assessments that measure the results of that convergence while providing clear diagnostic feedback for improvement. Figure 7.1 attempts to depict a model of that convergence.

Several matters deserve closer attention regarding Figure 7.1. They turn on unpacking Becker's theorizing.

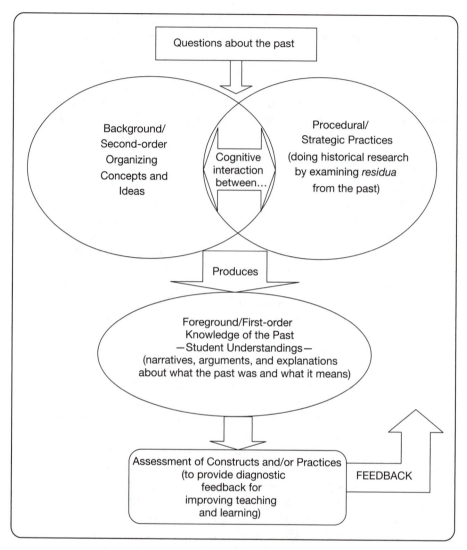

Figure 7.1 Becker's model of how understandings are produced and assessed

Sociocultural Context

The large rounded rectangle enveloping the three circles and the arrows connecting historical questions to cognitive interactions and how they produce histories (arguments, interpretations, explanations) represents the sociocultural context in which Becker's theorizations about how history education practices occur. Both Becker's and his students' positionalities are inextricably bound up in this process. Students engage and reason from a host of sociocultural, race–class–ethnicity-based positional anchors and assumptions. Becker operates from his. Both have positionalities deeply interpenetrated by life at home and by mass culture's historical messages and iconographies. All of it comes together on the stage of investigative action in the classroom. Historical investigators cannot completely get outside of or suspend these anchors and assumptions while thinking about the past. They depend on them in the first place to make sense of what they are doing. Trying to step outside of these positionalities would be like trying to walk away from your own two feet.

What Becker theorizes he can do is to place stress on the importance of contextualizing the past as his students study it, as we saw in his Indian-removal unit. This serves, he hopes, to draw contrasts and comparisons for his students between their contemporaneous positional moorings and those of whom they investigate. As a result, students become increasingly aware of themselves, their beliefs, convictions, and dispositions, while also reflecting on their origins. This is what Becker means by exploring America's past in search of not only America, but also self. One teaches the other. In short, all historical study operates from/within a sociocultural approach, whether school teachers, curriculum designers, test writers, or historian experts acknowledge it or not.

Three-Dimensional Subject Matter Knowledge

Subject matter knowledge has three dimensions. In Becker's mind, it simply is not solely about (1) first-order knowledge, that is, what happened in the past, when, involving whom, and creating what results. It involves knowing about these things, but as a consequence of knowing also about (2) the kinds of organizing ideas that can be used to order and construct that knowledge and (3) the practices and strategies for getting there. It is the thinking and reasoning characterized by (2) and (3) that get you to (1). Put a different way and as I have repeatedly noted, historical thinking/reasoning is the *sine qua non* of historical understanding. Becker finds that common school history privileges first-order knowledge to the exclusion of the other two types of subject knowledge. Consequently, students do not learn how to think historically and their understandings pale, as evidenced by repeated poor showings on those periodic National Assessment of Educational Progress exams, for example.

Becker has worked diligently to build a coherent theory for himself about how these three types of subject matter knowledge and their connecting operations fit together, and he continues to refine the ideas and relationships. He recognizes that historian experts sometimes focus their attention on what other historians have written about a particular period or historical movement. He knows that the accounts they study, although classified as *residua*, do not come from the original-source archive from which he drew many of the accounts he used in the Cherokee-removal unit. In that sense, they work from and on the historiographic landscape and, under those circumstances, build new histories from other experts' accounts.

Yet, even these historians make use of the same tools and practices as they move toward the same goal—producing interpretations, or reinterpretations, if you will—that he wishes to teach his students. It's only that the accounts they study are often not original sources. The difference for Becker and his students, as his theory goes, is that his students know very little about the historiography, say, of Indian removal. So he chooses to immerse his charges in exploring what he considers "first questions," those that begin with "what happened here," ones that necessitate investigations of original sources. Effectively, how knowledge is developed (i.e., subject matter understanding) entails the same investigative processes, cognitive interactions, and a three-dimensional structural relationship regardless of whether the focus is on what happened in America's past or what have other investigators say happened. Only the target accounts used to address the investigators' questions vary in importance and focus. Again, it is all accounts of one sort or another, all the way down.

THEORIZING LEARNING AND ITS RELATIONSHIP TO TEACHING AND SUBJECT MATTER

Becker considers his high school students as reasonably intelligent novices when it comes to studying and learning history. In his apprenticeship-model, novices are marked off from experts in terms of what they know and can do with what they know. As we saw, it is a difference of degree not kind. This is why he is interested in "first questions"—what happened here, why, how do we know? He is building up understandings from a relatively low plateau compared to the experts. He would like to see signs of expertise in the thinking and doing of his students. But he is not interested in creating experts—he simply prefers that his students become *competent* historical learners, ones who have mastered the basic structural components, understandings, processes, and criteria that frame the structure of the discipline. If they choose to become full-fledged experts, they can follow that path on through college to graduate school.

He often hears his colleagues complain that their students possess such little prior knowledge about the history they want them to know. This complaint puzzles him. It's as though they think that students should develop prior historical knowledge through some mysterious process of osmosis from passive exposure to historical studies in previous school courses, coming fully armed with reasonably deep understandings when they reach the high school classroom. As Becker thinks through this complaint, he imagines that his colleagues are working from an old idea that in order to think deeply about and analyze the past, something they claim they wish to see, students must possess what they call deep prior content knowledge.

From Becker's viewpoint, "deep content knowledge" arises from thinking and analyzing. That is, students develop knowledge and understandings by thinking and analyzing and investigating and studying rich historical questions. The former is not a prerequisite for the latter; it depends upon it. So, Becker thinks his colleagues have it backwards. Then he realizes that they may still be influenced by remnants of behaviorist learning theories that maintain that knowledge, in order to be grasped and understood, must be broken down and learned in discrete bits and built up slowly piece by little piece. Becker cannot see how such a learning theory works for those experts who epitomize the depth of historical understandings. Such experts know what they know because they have made a practice of investigating the past using intellectual tools such as analyzing, evaluating, and synthesizing elements of that past in order to construct their understandings. As we noted, Becker's learning theory is rooted in the idea that thinking is the *sine qua non* of understanding, or put another way, deep prior knowledge is a consequence of ongoing investigation.

In the history classroom, investigation can be made to follow a process that results in the sorts of deep knowledge possessed by the experts. It coheres closely in this sense then with Becker's three-dimensional subject matter structure and its interrelationships. Yes, students do bring prior knowledge of the past with them to Becker's classroom. The ideas students hold are often at odds with or naïve with respect to this structure and the understandings it is designed to produce. Novice students' everyday understandings of history are not unlike their naïve understandings of astrophysics, for example. For a long time, youngsters are convinced that the sun orbits the earth, and they glean what appears to them *prima facie* evidence by "watching" the sun "move across the sky." History is no different. Novices rightly assume that the past happened, that it occurred in a particular way. From that they also then assume that we should be able know that past in all its richness and complexity and scope. We should be able to chart the path of the past in all its minute detail. It can take considerable effort for them to learn that the past is only available to us in the present via accounts that were left behind, ones that testify to what occurred. Early on, they encounter and read omniscient-toned text-books and succumb to the referential illusions that textbooks traffic in so imperceptibly: The illusion that the past to which they refer "really happened" exactly as it's stated, that they mediate a putative reality unerringly.[4] In this sense, they hold naïve objectivist epistemologies about the relationship of the past to history, that one is merely a copy of the other. Mass culture's historical messages and icons repeatedly reinforce this idea.

Becker recognizes that these everyday ideas, while reasonable given their sources, create powerful cognitive impasses for his students. Students, for example, who are convinced that the past and the histories that purport to describe it are one and the same, become intellectually handcuffed as soon as they encounter conflicting versions of the past. These conflicting versions are also part of the novice's experiences with the past and history, both in and out of school. Many students try to quell the cognitive noise they create by ignoring them. Becker tries to take advantage of that cognitive noise by plunging his students into those conflicts, by pushing them to confront the impasses their epistemological ideas lock them into. He works hard to create a supportive classroom culture in which his charges can struggle with these cognitive impasses, seek out more effec-tive epistemological positions (see the criterialist stance described in Chapter 4) that allow them to grow their historical understandings, and encourage them to do the hard work it takes. Becker theorizes that without a structured, supportive classroom culture that both presses on the problem of cognitive impasses while providing a reasonably safe place to stumble, and the guidance and support to move forward, students will simply not be able to shed unproductive naïve ideas that powerfully constrain their historical understandings.

What is this "learning" support structure? How does Becker theorize it? His three-dimensional subject matter structure is the key. It provides the equipment and tools for (a) recognizing the impasses, (b) developing capabilities to move beyond them, and (c) creating new, more satisfying and intellectually powerful understandings, ones that are useful both in and out of school. In theorizing this way, Becker is reminded of historian James Kloppenberg's observation that:

> Beyond the noble dream of scientific objectivity and the
> nightmare of complete relativism lies the terrain of pragmatic
> truth, which provides us with hypotheses, provisional syntheses,
> imaginative but warranted interpretations, which then provide the
> basis for continuing inquiry and experimentation. Such historical

writing can provide knowledge that is useful even if it must be
tentative. [. . .] As [investigators], we cannot aspire to more than a
pragmatic hermeneutics that relies on methods of science and
the interpretation of meanings. But we should not aspire to less.[5]

Becker appreciates the way Kloppenberg's ideas point toward "the terrain
of pragmatic truth," the space where "hypotheses, provisional syntheses,"
and "imaginative but warranted interpretations" can be entertained. These
serve "continuing inquiry and experimentation" and lead to useful new
ideas, even if only tentative ones that must be revisited. It's the space of
a pragmatic hermeneutics, to mix two of Kloppenberg's terms together.
Becker attempts to create that space in his classroom everyday. To do so,
he must closely wed his three-dimensional structure of discipline to a
learning theory (his novice-to-competence-to-expertise apprenticeship
model), and thread it tightly to a pedagogical process that is consistent
with and reinforces both.

Recognizing impasses

By beginning with questions, Becker's approach continually opens room
for students to step into a place where they must confront everyday ideas
that block their progress in understanding the past, such as the assumption
that the past and the stories we tell about it are isomorphic. Questions
invite investigations that in turn search for answers. To serve that end,
accounts of and *residua* from the past become pivotal. Accounts rarely
tell the same story even about the same event. Even when "accounting
for" the same events or details, authors created these accounts for different
purposes and were influenced by their own historicized positionalities.
Their perspectives thus vary. Students are invited to make sense of this
variation as they search out answers to their questions. In doing so and in
order to succeed, they must give up the idea that the past and how we
choose to understand it must be the same, that we can choose to understand
it in different ways.

However, this invites the possibility of another impasse. Becker is
keenly aware of it. It's what Kloppenberg referred to as "the nightmare
of complete relativism" (identified as the naïve relativist position in Chapter
4). Such relativism serves as a handy epistemological tool for getting past
the naïve objectivist impasse. Students move to it easily. Becker hears them
say, "Oh, so the past can mean whatever we want it too. So we can tell
whatever story we want!" But that ends up being a dead end. Students
who move here in his class get cognitively handcuffed a second time
because it does not take them long to realize that they still need to sort

out which story they wish to believe (or tell) from a welter of possibilities. Here, they run headlong into the problem of having no criteria for arbitrating among stories, or telling one that is most defensible. With a little prodding from Becker, they come to the realization that such a relativist position is not particularly useful except perhaps in matters of taste. This opens the gate for Becker to introduce criteria for deciding. The idea of evidence plays a crucial role.

Judging evidentiary support and weighing whether it is enough or not to provide at least a tentative, defensible history is a complex process. Here Becker must be at his pedagogical finest. If students are to learn how to operate in the arena of producing Kloppenberg's pragmatic truth from a pragmatic hermeneutical process (provisional as such productions may be), they must be taught criteria for judging it. In history, the strongest evidentiary support creates the more powerful argument. But first getting to that strongest evidence is complicated by how investigators (a) conceptualize the historical significance of the problem, how variation from one investigator to another can enter into that process, (b) think about causation with respect to human agency and intention, (c) theorize about progress/decline and change/continuity, and (d) manage the problems of historical contextualization and imagination. These background, second-order ideas all must be taken into consideration if Becker is to move his students past their relativist leanings and onto a criterialist, pragmatic epistemological plane, one that enables them to break free from the impasses created by their other unproductive beliefs.

However, as complex as this may be, if Becker were to teach history from the common, *fait accompli* approach, this disciplinary structure–learning–teaching space would be walled off, inaccessible to students because that one final story was all they needed. The referential illusion, the past-as-history—no matter how erroneous a belief and impasse generating that would be—would retain its hold. Becker's theorizing cannot conscience that approach.

Developing New Cognitive Capabilities

Once students have begun to recognize and name the ideas they possess that contribute to their cognitive impasses, they can begin to move forward. Here is where they need sturdy tools in their cognitive tool belts and knowledge of how to use them, when, and why one tool as opposed to another. Here, the tools are of two closely related types: Second-order organizing ideas and strategic, thinking procedures. Becker must teach them both, together and separately as occasions warrant. Some he targets deliberately. Early in the school year, he focuses considerable attention on the types of strategic reading and thinking practices his PAIR^e guide entails. His assumption is that, if he begins with questions and foments investigations into the past, conflicting testimonies and varying perspectives will arise almost immediately as students begin pouring through accounts on the way to addressing the questions he poses for them. They need thinking tools to engage the process effectively. He has to quickly equip them in order to facilitate their handling of this problem space. The PAIR^e guide and the chart on the classroom wall are designed to stimulate this sort of learning. He realizes that his charges will take time to develop and automatize these types of thinking practices.

Because his novices are deeply prone to assessing accounts through the prism of their own presentist understandings, he also begins early on teaching them about the importance of historically contextualizing the judgments that they make. He also realizes that this practice requires time to develop, that it is rather unique for students to reason this way, and that it goes against the grain of how they typically reason. Becker must be persistent, holding his students consistently accountable to requirements to read, think, and judge from a contextualized, historicized understanding. He has to teach this idea explicitly. It is linked tightly to the idea of moral judgment in history, a difficult problem and an inescapable process simultaneously.[6]

At the same time, Becker is also paying close attention to ideas such as historical significance, progress/decline, change/continuity, causation, agency, and imagination. He knows, however, that he cannot teach all these ideas at once for fear of confusing them and overwhelming his students. As a result, he attempts to match the first-order understandings he is attempting to teach with a key second-order, organizing ideas that he reasons are necessary for students to make sense of those understandings. For example, in his consideration of Cherokee removal and dispossession, one key idea he is after is an understanding of the role of Manifest Destiny in this American storyline. To that end, he works on it by calling explicit attention to questions associated with its function as part of nineteenth-century change and continuity.

At the same time, but only more subtly and without direct explicit attention, he is treating questions of agency/intention and causation. Such other second-order ideas will resurface more explicitly in future units, where they are better matched and grow out of the first-order subject matter. He is building up capacity and offering new second-order tools slowly and deliberately, using the substance of first-order subject matter as a guide and rationale for choosing them in a succession. He hopes by the end of the semester to have treated them all (some more than once in a spiraling fashion) and, consequently, built a degree of competence among his students in working with them. Progress can be slow and not every student moves along at the same rate of building competence. Becker knows he must cycle through the ideas and concepts repeatedly, and provide additional assistance to the students who are slower to gain capacity with these tools.

Constructing New Understandings

Perhaps most importantly, Becker needs to provide students with clear criteria for what counts as defensible new understandings, or "new histories" as he prefers to call them. He draws again off his sense of disciplinary structure here. The idea of evidence is central. As with reading and reasoning tools in his PAIR^e guide, evidence becomes an early, pivotal, and explicit second-order concept that he teaches. He does so on the premise that, to combat the slippery slide into "the nightmare of complete relativism" among his students, he must offer an antidote. To cieterialize the concept of evidence, Becker teaches the notion of preponderance of evidence directly. He points out that historical understandings or arguments (or histories) rise or fall in believability based on how they account for available evidence. Arguments that can deal with both supporting and disconfirming evidence are stronger than ones that, for example, simply ignore the latter because it does not fit an argument's intended story arc.

This concept and applying it consistently is a tough lesson for students to learn. Becker must put stress on it regularly and be prepared to call students out if they fail to attend to its criterial burden. It is made even more difficult because, at least in his experience, Becker finds that his students think it quite natural that you would simply ignore "stuff" (as they call it) that does not readily fit the argument you wish to make. They claim to do it successfully all the time. Becker must more than occasionally demonstrate how much more powerful an argument becomes if it can consider disconfirming evidence openly and still make a case with other preponderant evidence for pressing claims. Of course, Becker is attempting to teach this concept as historically important, but also as part of a student toolkit for life in a complex, multi-valenced world. It takes him all semester. Even then some students have not reached competence working from it. He persists nonetheless because of its value.

Reasonably early on, Becker also begins stressing the criteria of being able to convincingly speak and write histories. This is about criteria for communicating new understandings and ideas, and communicating to broader audiences than just friends and acquaintances. This is why he invariably asks his students to write essays on his assessments and clusters students in groups in class, so that they can interact with each other around their burgeoning understandings. As the semester unfolds and he sees enough essay writing and sits in on enough group conversations, he begins to diagnose what students need as far as constructing better historical arguments go. About mid semester in earnest, he begins to focus more attention on it. He teaches the idea, especially in essay writing, about the importance of arguing clear claims, how to support them with preponderant evidence and also attend to disconfirming accounts, and about structuring the essays to make ideas convincing. He demonstrates (by displaying examples he has written) and models (using essays written by historians), often after returning essay questions on his assessments. In short, he is teaching students how to write historically. Footnoting is also part of this practice.

Overall, Becker is trying to press his students down the path toward a criteria-arbitrated, pragmatic, but provisional historical truth. He wants his charges to leave behind the unproductive, impasse-generating epistemological frames that block their efforts to think about and learn history. He wants his students to see that naïve objectivist and relativist stances (he doesn't use those terms in class), although "feeling natural," get in the way of their moving forward and becoming smarter history students. As we have seen in the foregoing, Becker draws from the well of ideas, practices, and the subject-matter nature of the discipline as tools to accomplish this goal. Without them, his theorizing about student learning would be incomplete and therefore hollow. They provide the substance that enables him to theorize in the first place.

THEORIZING ABOUT ASSESSMENT

It is difficult to overstate the importance of assessment to the elements of Becker's theory. It provides the feedback loop that tests the efficacy of both his practices and his conceptualization of the relationship between subject matter and learning (characterized by the arrow in the bottom right corner of Figure 7.1). If he aligns the elements properly, what students come to learn and understand about the subject vindicates his practices and the theorizing that sits behind them. If he fails a coherent alignment, the assessment data tells him where he must rethink and rework what he does and how he theorizes about it. It also instructs him on the individual needs of particular students. It is an ongoing process, one never quite mastered completely. Becker sees this as an open-ended and inviting challenge.

At the level of his assessment theorizing, Becker parts company somewhat with practices of the discipline and its guild-sanctioned practices and ideas. In the discipline of history, assessment occurs for the most part in the vetting of understandings and accounts that are produced in written form. Much of this happens in the largely invisible world of peer review, often in double-blinded fashion for respected historical journals. For books, there is also prepublication peer review. However, book reviews make up a very large proportion of space in peer-reviewed professional journals. Here, historians take each other on with regard to how well they hoe to the guild's criterialist practices in generating histories.

In the secondary classroom, Becker is far less concerned with his students being able to pass full muster on generating such professional histories. His goal is to teach students to gain in their capacities to think and reason historically on the grounds that this will make them better citizens in an information- and argument-dominated democracy, in which the flood of ideas and attempts at persuasion are omnipresent. In the historical, professional sense, Becker's students remain novices after all, albeit intelligent ones and growing more so, Becker hopes, as a result of his machinations and interventions. If, however, a handful of students become sophisticated, professional-like historical thinkers, all that much better. But this is not his principal aim. His assessments therefore are explicitly designed to (a) give him direct feedback on his theorizing and practices, and (b) engage his students in the act of becoming self-assessing learners who can regulate their own achievement gains, diagnose problems they encounter, and develop strategies for overcoming the limits those problems create.

How Becker structures his assessments is crucial to the kind of feedback he receives about how well his teaching efforts are succeeding. In talking to some of his colleagues, he has discovered that when they use more investigative teaching strategies (e.g., raising questions and asking students to dig around in the documentary evidence), they often make the mistake (in Becker's judgment) of failing to align their assessment strategies to those investigative orientations. They fall back on employing assessment items that require a display of correct answers.

Becker wonders to himself why these colleagues bother to open up the investigative space if they already know what the answers to the questions are that they are posing. It makes little sense to him. He figures that if you go so far as to ask the questions, and the evidence for address-ing them frequently remains ambiguous and complex, as Kloppenberg alludes, then your assessment practices must be designed to honor that ambiguity and complexity. Otherwise, Becker thinks, you send powerful mixed messages to your students, ones that fundamentally derail your investigative efforts. Students read the investigations as disingenuous, perhaps a trap to make their work in class more complicated then it needs to be. They resist and complain. This is why recognizing the importance of alignment as a matter of both message and actual practice orientation is so critical to making his investigative approach work. Lack of alignment muddies the feedback assessments provide on both counts, rendering them only marginally useful. Without adequate alignment, the assessment results become only marginally useful to students as well.

Becker also wonders what educative and diagnostic power his colleagues' more traditional assessments possess. Yes, students discover that they got some answers wrong and others right with respect to the pre-ordained story his colleagues insist they commit to memory. However, the intellectual landscape this creates is relatively limited. If the authority in the classroom messages that this particular storyline is the correct one, and the assessments point toward grasping and recalling the details contained in that story, then students either get it or do not. Case closed. There is limited room to question why that particular account should attain epistemological superiority, little space to consider the complexity and ambiguity of evidence, few opportunities to think more deeply, and little chance of wrestling with the very richness the study of the past creates. It turns out that it is all about constraints and boundaries when assessments are configured to match the recall of a given storyline and its details. To Becker, it feels more like indoctrination rather than education. And it runs deeply counter to the investigative approach he pursues.

Becker desires that his students become skilled self-assessors. He cannot see how to structure assessments differently than he does if he chases that goal. His assessments, he theorizes, open up broad intellectual space in order to allow his students to engage in critical examinations of their own historical thinking efforts and learning outcomes. In short, although he creates the assessments, how his students reason on them, and perhaps more importantly, reason *toward* and *after* them, shifts the responsibility for learning directly to their efforts. He becomes a choreographer, but his students come to realize that they are responsible for carrying out the dance. If they engage enough in the opportunities to self-assess their own performances, Becker's assessment approach gives them clear opportunities to adjust the dance (re-choreograph it, if you will) on the occasion that they can provide sound reasons for doing so. This is why he thinks it so important to stage the post-assessment discussion sessions he conducts. Effectively, during these sessions, he reveals how his assessments "work," how they are linked to his goals. Becker uses the process to model what is prized in his investigative approach and to reinforce messages he wishes to send to students about how important it is for them to shoulder the self-assessment responsibility.

Even in his arguably short career, Becker has gathered powerful evidence for the efficacy of his approach, of the growing level of responsibility his students assume over their own learning process once he opens the assessment terrain and invites students onto it as co-participants. Early on, Becker struggled with getting his students to trust his approach. Because students had been fooled in other courses by more exploratory, investigative teaching practices that were then misaligned to the mark-the-correct-answer assessments students eventually saw, they thought what he was doing was a trick. Consistent messages and repeated invitations to post-assessment discussions combined with modeling practices and follow through on changing assessment results when students argued strong positions would eventually impress even the biggest doubters. Occasionally, Becker would misfire and his students would catch him in an inconsistency or a weaker argument. This would only reinforce the strength of the feedback loop his assessment theory entailed. He also interpreted such moves as evidence of his students becoming the self-assessors he prized most especially.

★　★　★　★　★

In summary, Becker's theorizing draws together several sub-theories, if I can speak of that way. He theorizes a tripartite structure for the discipline/subject matter of history that is rooted fundamentally in his idea that historians epitomize depth of knowledge in that arena, that what they *do* to attain their historical understandings can serve as a model for student learning, if the goal is to build at least a degree of academic competence in the subject matter. Becker also theorizes that such competence also serves significant broader, sociocultural, and out-of-school learning goals, the ones I have noted.[7]

Becker weds his tripartite subject matter structure to a theory of learning that is roughly developmental (or progressional, as British researchers might term it) in that he assumes students construct knowledge gradually at different rates. In wedding the two, he postulates that students are capable of learning to think and understand historically, not unlike that of the experts, if they are consistently invited to participate in an apprenticeship process that is designed to monitor and adjust for different rates of cognitive growth. He sees himself as a choreographer of this process. But the net responsibility for gaining competence has to be on students; in the end they must become responsible for their own historical learning. Becker's responsibility is to provide ceaseless counsel and support, while gently encouraging growth as he firmly presses them to assume responsibility for their own learning. Yet, as more-knowledgeable other, he always remains close at hand.

To facilitate these interrelationships, Becker uses an assessment system that provides feedback on the process to both him and his students. It is an open practice that invites student participation in its results. Having a system that offers feedback to *both* is critical to his students' success in becoming competent historical thinkers and understanders as well as to his success at becoming a better practitioner. The assessment approach and the theories that guide it are deeply contingent on the idea of consistent alignment. That alignment must run from his goals through the tripartite subject matter structure to his learning theories and the pedagogical practices and moves that support it. Inconsistent connections among these elements defeat his purposes and derail his students. Becker's entire theoretical structure is therefore in a constant state of more or less significant revision as diagnostic feedback pours in. He would have it no other way.

It is not difficult to appreciate the complexity of these structural and practice-based theorizations. Learning to maintain consistent linkages and send commensurate messages between and among its constituent elements is complex enough. Accomplishing all this in the context of diverse classrooms with the thorny, dilemma-laden circumstances they generate only adds to the knowledge burden teachers such as Becker must shoulder. But as we have seen, shoulder them Becker does. Where are history teachers who may wish to emulate someone like Thomas Becker supposed to learn to teach as he does? I posed this question early on. Given the importance of education and an educated citizenry for a text- and information-dominated twenty-first century world, it is a profoundly important question. But it is an equally complex and challenging one. Now that I have used Becker as an exemplar to illustrate the approach and its constituent parts I have had in mind, I take up an effort to address this question in the next and final chapter.

CHAPTER 8

How Are History Teachers to Learn to Teach Using an Investigative Approach?

It is no secret that teaching the way Becker does is a complex undertaking. Learning to teach that way hinges on contributions from a number of facets of a loosely coupled system of education in the United States.[1] That the system is indeed loosely coupled increases the complexity and broadens and deepens the challenges involved. In part, the demise of the Amherst Project in the 1970s, in which similar efforts to reform history teaching were taken on, could perhaps be traced to this loose coupling. Although the educational system and the preparation of teachers for it have become more centralized and tightly linked since the 1970s, policy control over it remains rather diffuse. Despite efforts by states to wrest control away from local education agencies and centralize, say, curricular requirements, and the federal government's attempts to tell states what to do, much of the daily decision making and policy applications still occur at local school and school-district levels.

During the 1990s, standards reform led policy analysts to conceptualize arguments that called for what they termed systemic reform. As standards were developed, the bar for what students were to learn in public schools across the country ostensibly rose. Some maintained that the bar rose considerably. By extension, if students were to achieve higher standards of learning, teachers would need to be equipped with more knowledge in order to facilitate their growth. As a general consequence, systemic reformers and policy analysts conceptualized the problem of educational reform as fundamentally one of teacher knowledge. That is, in order to grow student knowledge and affect changes in achievement toward increased learning of more demanding curricular standards, teachers needed to possess more of that knowledge themselves. Deeper knowledge of subject matter and reconceptualized teaching practices were two key domains that captured the attention of the systemic reformers. Their argument was that all elements of the educational system would need to produce coherent efforts to address the teacher knowledge problem if standards-based change was to occur. A key assumption—supported, however, by decades of research—turned on the idea that what mattered most for student knowledge growth and increased achievement was the teacher, what that teacher knew about the subjects h/she taught and how s/he theorized his/her practice vis-à-vis the new standards. The system would need to *systemically* grow those teachers' knowledge.[2]

My efforts in this chapter to address the question I pose in its title operates from roughly the same line of reasoning pursued by systemic reformers. For history teachers to teach as Becker does—a deeply compelling yet demanding type of practice that possesses significant promise for enhancing students' historical understandings—I am arguing that reformers and policymakers would benefit by conceptualizing the change curve as primarily a knowledge problem. This sharpens my title's question: Under what circumstances and in what range of contexts are history teachers to have opportunities to grow their knowledge in ways that enable them to teach as Becker does? Taking the systemic reform tact, I argue in what follows that a number of facets of the educational system, elements that all currently contribute to what history teachers know and can do in classrooms with what they know, are implicated in addressing the knowledge problem. From a long list, I consider the following five elements that I believe can contribute most directly to addressing the challenge: State departments of education, the federal government, school districts and local schools, historians, and schools of education and specifically their teacher preparation programs.

As I think is clear by now, the pivotal assumption that drives the reform ideas I consider here is the claim that decades of research evidence indicate that what we currently are about in history classrooms is largely broken and needs an infusion of new ideas, new knowledge, and a different approach. Doing more of the same only more fervently, as some reform strategies would suggest, will not produce the results that we appear to want for our twenty-first century students, those digital natives who have more perplexing ideas, assertions, information, and enticements at their immediate disposal than many thought possible just 25 short years ago.

As I note this, I am keenly mindful of the fact that stakeholders do not all agree on the direction history education should move in this twenty-first century. The loose coupling of the educational system that decentralizes control over policy exacerbates the problem of developing coherent educational policies and thus can ameliorate an embrace of what I am arguing for here. Nonetheless, I make a plea for taking the ideas offered here seriously, on the principal grounds that a sizable corpus of empirical research points quite clearly to the need to reformulate how we teach history if we truly care about growing the historical understandings of our students. And that research steers us in quite particular directions, as I have labored to show. Becker's efforts epitomize that direction. What he knows, what he can do with it to the benefit of his students, and the contexts in which he learned it form the basis of the observations and recommendations that follow.

THE SOURCE? TEACHER PREPARATION PROGRAMS

It has been fashionable to criticize teacher education programs for their propensity to prepare under-qualified and under-prepared teachers, in history and in many other teaching fields. United States Secretaries of Education have been known to travel about the country proclaiming the shortcomings of such programs as though they were the only preparatory organizational structure responsible for what teachers know and how they teach in classrooms. It turns out that teacher preparation programs are merely one facet of a much more complex process of building a teaching force. And it also turns out that they may be regarded as one of the weaker influences, not for lack of ability or for taking their missions cavalierly, but for the markedly limited role they play in the overall education of teachers. Some simple arithmetic makes this point clear.

If we assume that prospective teachers learn much about what it means to teach from years of watching it done in pre-K-16 classrooms in which they were a captive audience—what sociologist Daniel Lortie once called the apprenticeship of observation—then learning to teach school begins very early.[3] Following this line of reasoning, a child begins school at age four, shall we say for the sake of argument, and observes what it means to teach through a schooling career that ends with a bachelor's degree at age 22 from an accredited college or university. A quick calculation shows that this translates into 18 years of a systematic apprentice of observation. If teaching practices in American history courses, for example, are as relatively uniform (the sage on the stage regaling charges with a story of national development presented as *fait accompli*, shorn of the questions and investigations that produced the story in the first place) as the decades of research demonstrate, then by the time prospective history teachers enter a formal teacher preparation program in the junior year of the collegiate career, the evidence suggests that they already think they know how to teach history. They simply mimic and/or channel their predecessors. And as we have seen, channeling predecessors' common practices results in highly questionable learning outcomes. Or put another way, students of these channelers learn little if any history, but rather appear to come away from the experience with a gilded, simple, commemorative story that is long on selective, celebratory amnesia and preciously short on historical detail, nuance and depth of understanding.[4]

Most traditional bachelor-level, college teacher preparation programs, particularly those that prepare secondary history teachers, despite claims to the contrary, have very little time to offer an antidote to the deeply reinforced ideas about teaching history prospective teachers possess as they enter such programs. At best, graduates spend on average about a year and a half within the confines of the actual teacher preparation program, about half of which is consumed by internships (part and full time) in local school systems, internships mandated by licensure standards controlled and set by state departments of education, *not* by teacher education programs. Here, the teacher candidates are back in the very classrooms of those history teachers who can again reinforce and perpetuate the wisdom of common practices, the ones already deeply familiar to the prospective history teachers. Such sets of structures and organizational efforts provide powerful cloning mechanisms, the will of teacher preparation programs to draw on research to reform teaching practice and thus deepen student learning and understanding notwithstanding.

A simple arithmetic time-ratio calculation makes the point clear. The denominator: Give or take 18 years of teacher preparation via repeated apprenticeships of observation. The numerator: Approximately two semesters or one year of coursework (calculating generously by estimating time spent in school-based internships conservatively) in a formalized teacher preparation program designed to grow history teachers' knowledge and assist them in rethinking common practices. The fraction: 1/18. Expressed as percentages, a prospective history teacher spends about 95 percent of the time learning to teach history via the apprenticeship of observation and a mere 5 percent of the time in a teacher education program that might offer opportunities to rethink the nature and limitations of that apprenticeship. It is not difficult to see why formal teacher preparation programs have such a circumscribed influence. Given the time-ratio discrepancies and the consequential attenuated impact a preparation program can have on prospective teachers, it seems odd for policymakers to criticize them. It's a bit like blaming the minnows for the inability of much larger fish to live in a polluted river.

Alternative teacher preparation programs face the same daunting challenges because the time-ratio relationship also fails to favor them. The problem, as I have alluded is systemic; you cannot produce different results without in some measure affecting all the parts of the system that contribute to those results. In a loosely-coupled system, with a number of agencies and interests vying for power and competing for control over the education, the teacher preparation "problem," and the roles schools of education play in it (or alternative programs for that matter), is only one factor among a complex set of influences. However, this does not mean that teacher preparation programs have no role, or even decisively limited ones. As educational agencies, they arguably remain at the forefront of efforts to grow teachers' knowledge.[5] The question is why, if we assume that they are indeed growing their prospective teachers' knowledge and helping them become more skilled and powerful educators (and on this point, I will for the moment give them the benefit of the doubt), this knowledge does not transfer to the classrooms these new teachers inherit?

POLICY SUPPORT INFLUENCES

The Role of State Departments of Education (SDEs)

State departments of education play pivotal roles in what history teaching looks like in classrooms. They set limits, ranges, and types of certification, thereby controlling almost all aspects of teacher licensure, targets to which teacher education programs must comply if their graduates are to become practitioners. They develop subject matter standards and identify learning benchmarks that local schools systems are increasingly required to meet. To drive standards and learning outcomes, they test the states' children *en masse* and administer high-stakes sanctions tied to the test results. Not every state tests in, say, American history, but a number do. What those tests measure to one degree or another drives instruction. Perhaps no other institution/structure within the overall system of education has as much overall control over and responsibility for what is supposed to happen in classrooms as SDEs, and the individuals who work for them in shaping policy. The different types of control and responsibility SDEs exercise all contribute collectively and independently to classroom practice.

Teacher Licensure. Effectively, SDEs set the bar for the type of knowledge prospective history teachers must possess in order to be licensed to teach history. They can do this in a number of ways. They can demand minimum numbers of course credits in particular college history courses that then count as a proxy for subject knowledge competence. This can be the case in discipline-based courses such as history, but also with regard to professional education courses. In the past, SDEs have left it to college-level programs, for example, to identify and build courses that would generally meet licensure demands. More recently, SDEs have begun specifying certain types of course or internship requirements that must be met, without necessarily specifying exactly what the content of these courses or internships must be. In order to qualify as a teacher preparation program that prepares state certifiable teachers, programs must be vetted by a third-party accreditation agency (e.g., National Council for Accreditation of Teacher Education) that operates from some sort of teacher standards identified by accepted teacher organizations (e.g., National Council for the Social Studies, National Council of Teachers of Mathematics).

To augment this course credit-count approach, SDEs also have been known to assess prospective teacher knowledge competence via standardized tests (e.g., PRAXIS). Again, the results of the tests serve as a proxy for knowledge competence. Pass the test(s), satisfy specific credit counts, and complete an accredited program (or its equivalent in alternative pathways) and apply for licensure. Much of this licensure process is technical in orientation with bars set by credit counting, college GPA assessments, test score results, and the like. Actual in-class performance-success measures remain a rather weak component of SDEs licensure provisions.[6]

However, in each of these technical cases, if the bar is set low, becoming a licensed history teacher, for example, is not a particularly challenging matter. There are understandable reasons why SDEs would desire to keep the bar relatively low. A pressing problem a number of states face involves satisfying the need to provide licensed teachers for every public school classroom. Fluctuations in student populations in school systems can create significant staffing problems. High turnover and attrition rates among teachers can exacerbate it. Maintaining a steady supply of licensed teachers becomes an increasingly important SDE goal. If SDEs set the licensure bar (and, arguably, by extension the knowledge bar) too high, a teacher-shortage problem can ensue, opening public school systems and SDEs to charges that they fail to adequately produce enough qualified, licensed teachers to satisfy the mandate to properly educate public school children.

A second factor also militates against high licensure bars. It helps school systems meet needs for teachers if SDEs keep specific subject matter licensure endorsements sufficiently broad. As a result, if you can categorize a new secondary history teacher's teaching endorsement as "Social Studies" (as opposed to say "American History"), a school principal can assign this new teacher to teach any course under its umbrella (world and/or American history, psychology, sociology, economics, government, geography) regardless of how much, or more likely, how little knowledge or background the new history teacher has in any one of these subjects. To illustrate, think of our new history teacher as having majored in American history, but taken only one or two college-level courses in psychology, not an unusual arrangement in a broad social studies license and given the finite credits a bachelor's degree requires. Under the broad-category endorsement provision, a principal, should she need to meet enrollment demands, could assign our new teacher to teach two World History courses and three Psychology courses without having to defend against the claim that this new teacher was under prepared for the assignment. After all, our new teacher is "licensed" to teach social studies broadly defined. There are a variety of such means that SDEs rely on to keep the knowledge bars related to licensure relatively low.

In elementary teacher licensure, where the press is to produce subject matter generalists, the entry-level knowledge bar in many states is even lower. Even though at fifth grade in most parts of the United States, teachers are required to teach a type of year-long, survey American history course to their students, these teachers have on average little more than one collegiate American history course as part of their knowledge repertoire.[7] And that course often was a 100-level survey lecture course taught by a talking head in the pit of a 200-person lecture hall.

Without systemic changes in how these types of low knowledge-bar standards are set and controlled by SDEs, it seems highly unlikely that teacher preparation programs will by themselves be able to produce the next generation of Thomas Beckers. Lessons with opportunity-costs teach us that teacher education programs that demand more of their graduates (as in greater and more sophisticated types of knowledge that take *longer* to teach and grow) than SDEs require for licensure will see steadily declining enrollments as potential candidates opt to attend institutions that demand and, therefore, cost less. It's hard to argue with that economic logic.

Subject Matter Standards and Learning Benchmarks. The same set of policy rules described in the foregoing analysis applies here. As with licensure, there are a number of factors that conspire to keep the standards and learning benchmarks reasonably low. Two deserve attention here: the actual nature of history curriculum standards and the testing practices that ostensibly measure students' capacity to learn them.

Despite the standards movement of the 1990s, many states' history standards continue to provide a recipe for reinforcing what research has come to understand as common practice, with all its limitations intact. As Becker's case makes clear, teaching historical thinking that deepens understanding (a goal most everyone seems to endorse) requires time and concerted effort coupled with an investigative, question-rooted orientation. As an approach, it is complex and requires considerable teacher knowledge, but, as we have seen, pays powerful dividends for the effort. State history standards that champion and sanction an approach structured around and operating from a *fait accompli* idea, say, in American history is deeply familiar, relatively simplistic, and therefore appears easy to measure. Because of its familiarity alone, the approach and its carrying ideas are quickly codifiable into formal state standards. It's as though, during the standards movement, SDEs in many states said, "Good. We got it right; standards and curricular work done. Check it off the reform list."

And the low bar remains, in part from the inability to imagine a viable alternative and/or to summon the moral and political will to pursue one. Few incentives exist at present to revisit that terrain other than intractably low student test scores (consistently predicted by the history education research), making them appear to be the most pressing problem to tackle rather than assuming that the problem might be located in the opportunities students have to learn, or SDE curriculum standards by any other name.

The public nature of current test scores that ostensibly reveal how much children know relative to curricular standards presents real, visible problems for SDEs. The public has been trained to think that test scores serve as a valid proxy of their children's knowledge growth and retention and have responded by becoming critical of school systems and by extension SDEs when results appear to flag. Hypothetically, if test scores among a majority of school districts in a given state fail to meet targeted benchmarks associated with public state curriculum standards, an SDE can anticipate a barrage of criticism for not doing enough to promote the educational welfare of the state's children. One strategy for dealing with this problem is to keep standards and benchmarks manageable, predictably familiar, and easy to assess. This can quickly translate into a low curricular bar, as I just noted with respect to history standards in many states. Another strategy is to adjust what some call cut scores (usually downward if test results are poor), the magical number below which students are considered failing.[8]

A good illustration of how the second strategy works can be found in Virginia, in the case of its history Standards of Learning (SOLs). Media outlets and independent, self-proclaimed standards evaluators have frequently given Virginia's SDE high marks for its history SOLs.[9] However, the state's students consistently scored poorly on the tests that measured those SOLs. In fact for a number of years, of the dozen or so subjects the Virginia SDE tested, students performed the poorest on the history exam, until, that is, the SDE adjusted the cut score downward to almost instantly improve the results.[10] Adjusting the cut scores downward effectively reduces knowledge demand and thus lowers the bar. But it may have the perceived salutary effect of making the SDE (and its state's school systems) appear as if it is doing a better job of discharging its responsibility—of course, as long as the public does not scrutinize the process too closely.

Testing. A third strategy for dealing with the problem of embarrassingly high failure rates involves the testing process itself. Because the actual, active testing process tends to be shrouded in mystery—a function of trying to protect test-item identity and prevent gaming the tests—SDEs can adjust the mix of items using item-response analyses to lower the bar and reduce the difficulty of the test. It is difficult to know how often the SDEs' psychometricians engage in this strategy because of all the secrecies that surround testing practices. However, in the quest to protect reputation and ward off criticism, it is reasonable to assume that SDEs rely on this strategy with some frequency. The wisdom of the strategy hinges on allowing SDEs to maintain the appearance of demanding publicly accessible curriculum standards and learning benchmarks while simultaneously sampling only a fraction of them (the easier ones to assess using current inexpensive technologies[11]) through high-stakes testing practices that are largely shrouded from public view and therefore accountability. The irony here should not go unnoticed. A lowering of the educational bar is not an intended consequence, but an outcome related to palpable fear of public criticism in a high-stakes, accountability-driven policy context. History teachers, for example, and the teacher education programs that prepare them have virtually no control over this process. This is strictly the domain of SDEs, who in the aughts came under federal oversight via the stringent accountability provisions contained in the "No Child Left Behind" law.

As long as the knowledge bar remains relatively low for students in history classes, the knowledge bar for their teachers can also remain relatively low. Unless state curriculum standards and learning benchmarks become more demanding and testing practices are much more closely aligned to them (which would raise unwanted costs), there is little pressure on SDEs to substantially or substantively raise licensure standards, beyond the occasional adjustments in technical requirements, such as the demand for secondary teachers to have majored in a discipline so as to achieve the current federal law's technical demand for "high quality" instructors. However, as Becker's case demonstrates, holding a bachelor's degree in American history may be necessary, but it is hardly sufficient. The knowledge he holds and uses to theorize his practice and deepen his students' historical thinking and understanding goes far beyond what a collegiate major in American history, for example, provides, at least as we currently know it. In order to promote the preparation of more teachers like Becker, SDEs would need to fundamentally alter their licensure provisions, moving beyond tinkering with technical requirements and working closely with teacher preparation organizations to reshape knowledge demands.

Perhaps no other single link in the loosely-coupled educational chain is poised currently to affect as much widespread change in history education as SDEs. Unfortunately, in the present high-stakes accountability climate, state policymakers tend to allow political and economic circumstances to trump educational decision making, circumstances that conspire to keep the bars low for both teachers and students. Part of my aim here is to demonstrate that, if growing and deepening student thinking capacity and historical understanding—as Thomas Becker does—is indeed a worthwhile goal, then more of same will not do. SDEs need to be on the forefront of policymaking change that helps to bring that goal to fruition.

Should SDEs choose to exercise some of their influence to improve history teaching and learning, it would require the following types of changes:

- Those who work in SDEs could pay much closer attention to the research in history education, to glean what it teaches us about how to *align* revised curricular standards with learning theory/research and assessment practices.
- They could help history teachers by reducing the breath of their history standards and curricular sweep, refocusing that curriculum sequence on powerful questions (the sort that Becker relies on), and promoting an approach that is investigative. Encourage the teaching of history, as opposed to nation-state commemoration or selective and collective memorializations through revised standards and learning benchmarks.[12]
- They could assist history teachers by finding ways to use revised standards and curricula to grow their knowledge, providing them with aligned assessment aids, fully funding exemplary subject-specific professional development opportunities, and developing a rich panoply of classroom resources (e.g., documents, readers, teaching and assessment guides) aligned to a state's revamped curricular approach.
- And, as I noted, they could work with teacher preparation programs, accreditation agencies, and local school systems to rethink and redevelop history teacher education efforts that help grow and deepen teacher knowledge (of the sort described in the research literature), while simultaneously raising licensure bars that stretch beyond simple, technical guidelines.

Unfortunately, without incentives to reconceptualize low bars, and standards, curricula, and assessment orientations that retain a tight hold on common, age-old approaches, little will change with respect to student achievement. A century of test results have made this abundantly clear as I have often noted. In many ways, serious change initiated by SDEs remains the *sine qua non* of reform in history education, at least along the lines I have been arguing for here.

Perhaps in the end, flatlined student achievement and renewed questions about low-standards bars in history education, despite accountability regimes ostensibly designed to eradicate both, will be the impetus for new directions. We can only hope. In the meanwhile teacher preparation programs will be held hostage to current SDE licensure requirements and low-bar standards and accountability provisions that conspire to lock them in place. The role of federal policymaking more recently has been to force the educational reform hand of SDEs. But has it been a constructive force?

The Role of the Federal Government

As Americans celebrated the century mark, states had barely finished their 1990s curriculum standards and learning benchmarks work when they were confronted by the long reach of federal government's educational policymaking hand. With the passage of law, dubbed "No Child Left Behind," states were required to hold school systems and teachers accountable to those standards and benchmarks through a barrage of testing efforts across a range of grade levels and subjects. States who refused to comply would be denied access to millions of dollars in federal Title funds they had grown to depend upon. Testing approaches had to pass federal approval to keep Title funds flowing. Sanctions would visit schools and school systems whose children did not meet the bars set by the states. The law contained provisions to financially support schools and school systems that were classified as failing or in need of improvement. However, in actual practice, little of that money actually followed. So much money was spent on the massive testing and accountability effort, that few additional resources remained for schools, or more importantly for teachers, who, it appeared initially, needed to increase their knowledge in order to teach to the tests more effectively.

No mention of history-achievement accountability was made in the law. However, almost half the states pressed testing/accountability provisions in history and social studies anyway.[13] Since much of what passes for social studies in the nation's schools is history, and U.S. history in particular, it become a tested subject in many states (especially large ones such as California, Texas, and New York) alongside reading, mathematics, and science. In those states, failure to meet cut scores in history did not jeopardize the flow of Title funds into a state and/or school system, but states attached other sanctions instead, such as the denial of high school diplomas for failing students.

Almost a decade after its inception, we can say that the federal law's impact has been powerful, but not necessarily in the way it was intended.

It was designed primarily to (a) leverage higher achievement among students across the country and, ostensibly, (b) close the achievement gap separating European and Asian ethnics from their ethnic African-American and Latino/a counterparts. As we have seen, it did not take states long to figure out how to satisfy the law's demands while continuing to retain relatively low curricular standards and learning benchmarks and/or toying with testing effects to give the appearance that standards and learning targets were being met. To date, there has been evidence of a very gradual closing of achievement gaps, but analysts maintain that this trend began before the passage of the law and progress since has not shown any substantial acceleration in that closing. Neither of these outcomes should come as any surprise. Research consistently points out that there simply is no strong relationship between heavy stresses on high-stakes testing and accountability and increases in student achievement or achievement gap closures.[14] This is no less the case with regard to history achievement.[15]

From a systemic-reform angle, one of the principal ironies in federal policymaking and its consequences is that it applies a technical solution—high-stakes testing—to a knowledge problem—among teachers and through standards setting. Testing alone will not increase teacher's knowledge nor necessarily raise the standards and learning bars. In fact, if anything the high-stakes, negative-sanctions nature of the technical solution increases the likelihood that both the teacher knowledge and standards bars will be kept low rather than raised, particularly in the absence of resources necessary to enhance knowledge or standards.

In the case of history education and as Becker's case makes clear, to teach as he does—in ways that foster student historical thinking in order to deepen historical understanding—depends to a significant degree on the knowledge (of subject, learners, teaching and assessing strategy) he deploys in his practice. As policy analyst and systemic reform advocate David K. Cohen once ruefully noted, "systemic reform envisions profound changes in teacher professionalism, including steep elevation of professional knowledge and skill, extraordinary complication in teachers' roles, and radically new and demanding conceptions of professional conduct." He then adds, "The chief agencies of such change could only be revolutions in teachers' knowledge and professional values, and it seems unlikely that such changes could be 'driven' by nonprofessional systems of external rewards and punishments, administered by agencies of the state."[16]

If we conceptualize improvement in education, of history education in particular, as a systemic reform problem, the recent efforts by federal interventions in schooling via high-stakes testing and accountability mandates wildly miss the mark. Although perhaps an understandable political impulse, a high-stakes testing/accountability solution appears considerably premature. If states had resisted the temptation to keep the standards, benchmarks, and licensure bars low and actually responded to the standards reform period of the 1990s by significantly raising the knowledge bar, it would still take a decade or better of investments in growing teacher knowledge to realize the types of deeper understandings and revolutionized practice Cohen envisions. Again, for political rather than educational reasons, federal policymakers jumped the gun with their accountability reform. They chose to invest in tests rather than teachers. And it appears that almost a decade in, we have gained little from those vast expenditures.

To facilitate the type of knowledge-growth reform I have been describing, the federal role in policymaking would need to shift. Fundamentally, it would need to amount to a legislated resources-reallocation process, away from high stakes accountability provisions and toward investments in teachers—history teachers among them. The federal government could reauthorize the law in ways that relaxed the testing requirements and instead asked states to shift resources to agendas that followed the integrated lines I described in the preceding section (pay attention to the research, significantly raise licensure standards while working with teacher preparation programs to grow more deeply knowledgeable teachers, revisit and seriously rethink standards and learning benchmarks, allocate for subject-specific forms of professional development, grow teachers' knowledge about how to use assessments to facilitate improvements *in their own practices*); map a long-term process for reinstituting high-stakes testing, but only after states were first able to spend the time, energy, and resources to cultivate their own teachers' knowledge; and make history education an integral part of the teacher reinvestment process. In short, use the policymaking power of the federal government to incentivize states and local school systems toward genuine increases in standards, benchmarks, and teacher knowledge bars.[17] Learn from the limits encountered, say, by the Amherst Project, and keep messages and resources focused on encouraging growth in the quality and knowledge of teachers such as Thomas Becker.

POLICY SUPPORT AND KNOWLEDGE DEVELOPMENT INFLUENCES

The Role of Local School Districts

Because they are on the front lines of providing prospective history teachers with internship/apprenticeship experiences, school districts and the schools that constitute them play an important role in cultivating new teachers' knowledge. However, the nature of that role is mitigated by a number of other factors that deal with the wider policy context in which they are situated.

Like teacher preparation programs, school districts are often pawns in the current process of reform by accountability. SDEs control the high-stakes testing regime they put in place as the federal government keeps a watchful, sanction-ready eye on the proceedings. Public, state floggings of schools and school systems sell newspapers and play along the headlines of Internet news outlets and the blogosphere. School systems recoil then entrench themselves in a battle to reach test-dependent "annual yearly progress" (AYP) statistics in a frenzied race to fend off public criticism. Teachers are ordered to teach to the test, more so in schools that have difficulty meeting AYP targets. If the bar is low because the standards and/or the benchmarks are weak, and we know they tend to be in history education, there is little a school or school district can do about it.[18]

However, school districts can expend more classroom time on high-stakes test preparation. Where the standards-testing bar is low, then the test results tell schools, school systems, and teachers little more than where pockets of poverty are and which schools serve those students. In these cases, the few additional resources left over after all those test-preparation packages and tests are bought and administered can go into helping teachers do better at teaching their students to the test. School systems are beholden to the state as the state is beholden to the federal law. Like SDEs, school systems, especially poorer ones, have few incentives within the current policy matrix to pursue raising the standards-testing bar and few residual resources for investing in their teachers' knowledge growth, even if that is what they truly wished to do.[19]

Wealthy school systems may have other options. Because their students typically fare well on high-stakes tests, there is little pressure to expend scarce resources on additional test preparation. Teachers are freed to do other things and school systems are able to experiment with raising their own internal teaching and learning standards because they have the resources to do so. They can also offer higher teacher salaries and provide better working conditions. Deeply knowledgeable teachers are easier to hire given those incentives. Wealthy school systems then can make a habit of raiding other, less fortunate school systems and recruiting off the better, more knowledgeable teachers. Such teachers' classrooms can make for rich learning apprenticeships for prospective history teachers.

Unfortunately, not all prospective teachers can apprentice in wealthy school systems, nor would we want them to. It is possible to make a compelling case that children of disadvantage deserve the very best teachers and therefore teacher preparation programs ought to be preparing teachers to teach in them by apprenticing them in just those classrooms. However, at present, it is in those classrooms that history teacher apprentices are most likely to find the most traditional, least compelling practices and often lower levels of knowledge among possible mentors.[20] Teacher preparation programs encounter these sorts of realities every day as they attempt to provide their graduates with the best apprenticeships they can find, while also committing themselves to helping to prepare teachers for the needs of challenged schools.

Yet, school systems can engage in a variety of efforts to grow their history teachers' knowledge. This in turn could result in producing teachers among them who would teach as Becker does and therefore could serve as mentors for young teacher apprentices. The following are some specific ideas school systems could pursue. I offer them with the understanding that they are likely to be undertaken at the expense of school systems already at the limits of their budgets. And they have few means to raise additional revenues to support such efforts. Here again, how states and the federal government make choices about what to invest in (e.g., teachers over tests, or vice versa) has deep implications for what role school systems can play in developing a new generation of history teachers:

- Encourage teachers to read the research literature in history education and find opportunities to build learning communities among history teachers in which they can discuss this literature.
- Summon the political will to push back against SDEs concerning weak licensure standards for history teachers and poorly conceived history standards and learning benchmarks. Use the results of the research literature to demonstrate weaknesses (e.g., too much breadth, not enough depth; too many superficial ideas, too focused on nationalistic collective memorializations rather than historical thinking and understanding) and suggest alternatives (e.g., pursuing historical questions that spark investigations rather than insisting on the repetition of someone else's preconceived, memory-infused storyline).
- In states that have no high-stakes history tests, school systems might encourage history/social studies coordinators to in turn encourage their history teachers to experiment with research-based teaching approaches. To support those experiments, coordinators could make efforts to adapt local history curricula in ways that foster research-based practices (e.g., reformulating the history curriculum to reflect reduced breath and greater depth, focusing on rich historical questions, encouraging practices that teach historical thinking as students are invited to wrestle with addressing those questions).

- Identify history teachers who are prone to teach like Becker and encourage and support them to become mentors of new history teachers in concert with local teacher education programs. Also encourage these Becker-like teacher mentors to be as transparent as possible about what they know that enables them to teach as they do.
- Invest in and use subject-specific professional development experiences to encourage risk taking in classroom history teaching and assessment practices. Draw from the research to defend and support such practices. Pursue Teaching American History grant professional-development partnerships with museums, historians, and teacher education programs that share the mission of a re-conceptualized, re-imagined form of school history education.
- Work closely with local universities and colleges and their history education faculty to select mentors and devise apprenticeships that are likely to enhance new teachers' knowledge, rather than dropping apprentices into a class simply because a teacher said he would take one. The latter only ensures the conservatism of traditional practices and their learning-limiting outcomes. It is difficult to underestimate this part of the role school systems can play in breaking the cycle of reproducing practices that research indicates will do almost nothing to improve student thinking capacity nor historical understanding.

Local school systems can play vital roles in dealing with the knowledge problem of history teachers. However, they need support and incentives. That support could best come from enlightened state and federal policies that take the knowledge problem seriously and look beyond technical accountability solutions that do not possess, by themselves, the capacity to address it.

KNOWLEDGE DEVELOPMENT INFLUENCES

The Role of Historians

Historians, whether they like it and recognize it or not, stand on the very front lines of educating future history teachers. They are inextricably bound up in the knowledge development of those teachers, if only because future teachers learn from historians through observational apprenticeships what history is and therefore how it can be taught as such.[21] But herein lies a frequent disconnection.

A good share of the rewards historians accumulate within their profession relate to the scholarship they produce, meaning the books, papers, essays, book reviews, and conference proceedings they generate. Although many colleges and universities champion the high quality teaching that goes on within its classrooms and attempt to demonstrate how much they value it, close analyses reveal that, at least within the more general culture of the history guild, you become known nationally and internationally by virtue of your published scholarship and only at best locally by your teaching. Of course, there are variations on this rule, but those variations only serve to exemplify the rule.

Given the focus on published or authored scholarship, and the fact that historians spend much of their professional lives engaging in and with it (much to their delight), they are understandably predisposed to think about their teaching roles as largely pivoting on the task of conveying/sharing/transmitting (pick your metaphor) that scholarship to those uninformed, undergraduate prospective history teachers sitting in the lecture halls and seminars. Frequently this is a unidirectional process: historians talk, students listen and take notes on the usually accurate assumption that they will soon be tested on their capacity to make sense of and recall the scholarship (historical texts broadly defined) to which they were exposed. As observational apprentices in the classes of expert historians, they learn quickly (and they are already predisposed to such ideas through 12 years of pre-collegiate experience) that what it means to teach history involves conveying/sharing/transmitting scholarship to uninformed students' minds. Such experiences simply reinforce what prospective history teachers thought they already knew about what history teaching requires.

Because of their sturdy preoccupation with the results of historical thinking and investigative practice, historians seldom reveal to their students in any specific way what goes on behind the scholarship curtain, that research and inquiry-driven machinery that produces those results in the first place. Typically, history majors—among them certainly not too few prospective school history teachers—must wait to encounter their first opportunity to apprentice in the practices that produce scholarship until their senior year, when they are asked to produce a seminar paper or thesis on a particular topic.[22] History majors I have talked to, many of whom have held school-teaching aspirations and do not intend to go on to do graduate work in the discipline, remark that such courses were difficult, tedious, and seemed more like drudgery than anything else. They seldom mention that they learned much from their research efforts, and are more likely to say that they simply did not understand why they had to learn to "do history" if their aspirations were only to teach it. In this sense, they are remarkable only for the ways in which their ideas about what history is depart from how Becker thinks about them. The research seminar was like the addition of a sour ice cream on a piece of pie they had already found sufficiently palatable. The pie was their observational apprenticeship.[23]

The addition was unwelcome and alien because few had bothered to explain how important the research-intensive, investigative process was to the way historical scholarship is produced. In these prospective history teachers' cases, seldom was it explained that interested explorers can come to very deep understandings of the past—as epitomized by historians themselves—by a carefully tuned, criteria-laden, archive-focused investigative process that renders that past more comprehensible than only reading or hearing about others' synthetic accounts makes possible. Canadian historian Chad Gaffield put it aptly:

> In the history courses I took in school . . . we read about history, talked about history and wrote history; we never actually did history. If I had learned basketball this way, I would have spent years reading the interpretations and viewpoints of great players, watching them play games, and analysing the results of various techniques . . . [but I would not have learned to play the game]. In my history courses . . . the focus was on learning the various viewpoints of historians rather than directly coming to grips with the past. In basketball terms, I began to play the sport only at the doctoral thesis level.[24]

However, this horizon has begun to change during the last decade or so, as historians have re-entered the conversations on teaching history and the preparation of teachers.[25] Three promising developments suggest the direction I envision historians taking in the mission to re-imagine history education.

With support from the Carnegie Center for the Advancement of Teaching, some historians have begun to explore their teaching practices as a form of scholarship in itself. In doing so, they have begun to rethink the guild's transmission-style signature pedagogy. Rather than focus students energies solely on Gaffield's "interpretations and viewpoints of the great players," they have reformulated their roles in the direction of calling their students' attention to how the history game gets played. Drawing from cognitive research on what it means to learn history, these historians have begun working with their students from variations on a tripartite disciplinary knowledge structure I outlined in Chapter 3. This means that prospective history teachers sitting in such classes begin to have their apprentices of observation remade. They learn more about the investigative machinery that produces history. In short, they have an opportunity to emerge from such experiences with different ideas about what history is, how textual productions based in questions and investigations can come to be called histories, and why. This work forms a seedbed for knowledge development that cultivates teachers such as Thomas Becker. It, therefore, becomes crucial to growing teachers like him. It also lays groundwork for teacher preparation programs that seek to build upon it.

As I noted in Chapter 1, in this new century historians have taken it upon themselves to call greater attention to the roles they play as teacher educators. For example, I refer again to the conference at the University of Virginia in 2006, from which a white paper emerged, titled "The Next Generation of History Teachers: A Challenge to Departments of History in American Colleges and Universities." As I obsverved, it produced key recommendations centered on the roles historians could play in growing the knowledge of history teachers.[26] One recommendation in particular called for the historians and history departments to create new opportunities for history majors to begin thinking like history teachers as well as history students. Another suggested the importance of history departments collaborating more closely with teacher preparation programs at their institutions in order to help cultivate the knowledge and understandings of history teachers. Such efforts, if taken seriously, point toward bringing historians and their work into closer alignment with the types of knowledge-growth reforms I have been describing. What would make such work doubly important would be the linking of scholarship of teaching history with these efforts by history departments to (re-)embrace their teacher–educator roles.

It is also a welcome development that professional organizations such as The American Historical Association and the Organization of American Historians have invested considerable energies in their teaching divisions. They publish teaching articles routinely in their professional journals, newsletters, and on their websites. These moves have the capacity to bring the scholarship of teaching into sharper focus for historian readers. These organizations provide numerous sessions at annual conferences devoted to teaching and offer history teachers resources through their websites and teacher-organization affiliates. The Teaching American History program also has put increasing numbers of historians directly in contact with practicing teachers, where presumably the combination of the scholarship of practice and historical knowledge has another opportunity to intersect with the knowledge needs of practicing teachers.

Growing the knowledge capacity of history teachers who aspire to teach like Becker will continue to depend on historians. They are principally positioned in this effort. But historians will need to recognize that future Beckers must come to understand the structure of the discipline, as Jerome Bruner might say. Historians then will need to be as transparent as possible about that structure, showing off its procedural-knowledge elements as well as its substantive-knowledge results and giving prospective history teachers plenty of chances to conduct authentic historical research. Historians likely will also need to work in the epistemic space characterized by the challenging impasse-generating ideas incoming history teachers possess. This will necessitate the tough act of trying to move these teachers toward the type of pragmatic criterialist epistemologies they will need to traverse the path toward teaching as Becker does. Here, working with colleagues across the quad in history teacher education programs could pay some real dividends.

In these respects, historians are part of a systemic solution to the problems that plague history education. If historians seek nothing more than smarter students who sit in those freshmen lecture halls, and more knowledgeable history majors who exit their programs, helping to raise up a generation of Thomas Beckers from among them can go a considerable distance in helping historians realize that desire.

The Role of Teacher Education Programs—Revisited

Despite the limited time teacher preparation programs have to do the complex work of educating future history teachers like Thomas Becker, they can still play a significant role. Yet, their challenges will remain daunting. They need help from historians because, as we have seen, they too work in the difficult space of reshaping the impasse-generating epistemic stances that the years-long observational apprenticeships of current prospective history teachers have reinforced. What makes this work even trickier is that, given current licensure policies, secondary teacher preparation programs (TPPs), for example, must prepare future history and government and economics and geography teachers. If to cultivate teachers like Becker requires helping them understand the structures of the discipline they are to teach, TPPs will have a number of different structures to tackle. Although the disciplines I have listed have overlapping structural features, they are unique enough nonetheless that each deserves its own attention.

Take the differences between history and disciplines such as political science (on which government teaching depends) and geography. The former shares much more in common structurally and in practice with the humanities, while the latter disciplines relate more to structures and practices found in the social sciences, who in turn draw many of their cues from the natural sciences. Epistemically speaking, they share different types of intellectual space and thereby necessitate different practices. As a result, TPPs that take those distinctions seriously need their own curricular structures in place to do justice to those differences. That takes time, a precious resource of which TPPs have relatively little. Therefore, as near as I can tell given their pressing time constraints, TPPs must make hard choices when it comes to how many disciplinary structures they can teach. As my arguments imply, I think one of those structures must be history, particularly since it is one of the most commonly required subjects in the K-12 school curriculum.

Perhaps most importantly, should TPPs assume this disciplinary-structure approach, a principal role they would need to perform involves the alignment challenge that I described in Chapter 7. That is, TPPs in history education would need to organize their curricular landscape in ways that provide alignments between (a) disciplinary structure (generally as I have described it in Chapter 3), (b) learning theory that takes advantage of the research on what it means to learn history (outlined in Chapter 4), (c) correlative teaching practices (illustrated in Chapter 5), and (d) assessment efforts (identified in Chapter 6). Attention also would need to be directed to (e) the sociocultural backgrounds of students on which learning history in school classrooms would play out. Of course, this is no small task. However, it is worth noting because it typically departs from standard social studies TPPs that attempt to treat all of the subject matters contained under the umbrella called social studies.[27] It turns out that, if it is teachers like Becker that TPPs are after, the typical all-subjects-considered approach ends up producing less understanding of any one of those subjects and the crucial disciplinary referents from which they are drawn. Under current arrangements, there is no time to provide justice to each, largely because the epistemic entanglements that can ensue in each subject, by themselves, can take considerable efforts and time to treat successfully.[28]

The wisdom of the disciplinary-structures approach has its roots in the capacity to draw especially on research related to learning. How students learn a particular subject is deeply important to thinking about how to teach it, arrange curricular opportunities that maximize learning, and assessing that learning in ways that strengthen teaching practices. In many respects, the learning research is pivotal. Without it, it is difficult to build up and align teaching, curriculum, and assessment efforts. Although there is learning research in subjects and disciplines other than history, most of the progress has been made in that field most recently. Therefore, it makes additional sense for TPPs to build first from and around the learning research in history as they prepare teachers to teach that subject. A coherent, deeply aligned TPP in history education is possible, and it could be of considerable help in growing a new generation of history teachers. After all, my characterization of Thomas Becker's knowledge is deeply rooted in the research on learning history. In that sense here, I am trying to illustrate one specific role TPPs can play in growing that knowledge.

Should those programs be housed in an undergraduate delivery structure, one that prepares certified history teachers who are also, say, history majors in the traditional four years? Or should these be graduate, masters-type programs of the sort Becker went through? And what about alternative programmatic and/or Internet-based models? By my lights, the most important consideration here is time. As I have labored to show, cultivating the type of knowledge and theorizing Becker possesses is not something that can happen quickly. The single more pressing impediment is the epistemic roadblocks that novice history teachers often possess (e.g., thinking that history and the past are one and the same, holding to an impoverished sense of what constitutes a historical account). It takes time and concerted effort to assist history teachers in overcoming these road-blocks. Then there is the business of alignment: thinking about teaching practices and curricular approaches in concert with learning research and theory and assessment design. This is complex space requiring even more time to cultivate adequately. And then there is the need for opportunities to intern in contexts that support practice in learning to teach this way.

I am tipping my hand. Graduate type programs (e.g., five-year, six-year, seven-year models) can operate on extended time frames because their prospective teachers have already completed their undergraduate disciplinary majors. Unlike four-year, bachelor-degree trajectories, TPPs are not attempting to sandwich their learning opportunities around under-graduate schedule openings. However, my preference is less about model (traditional, alternative, Internet based) and more about the opportunities provided to deal with the complex learning demands necessitated by learning to teach in ways that enhance the historical understandings of those students whom prospective teachers will one day teach. If it takes two years or more in combination with classroom internships to accomplish this feat, then so be it. This is the sort of investment in teachers (rather than, say, tests) that I have been advocating. Yes, this is more expensive. But then as they say, if you think education is expensive to a society, try the alternatives (e.g., illiteracy, prisons, unemployment).

In summary, I am advocating that TPPs pay close attention to what I have been suggesting as five preparation pillars:

(a) structures of the discipline, history in this case;[29]
(b) learning theory and research that is subject specific, again history here;

(c) curricular shape and practice configurations (as in opportunities to learn);

(d) assessment design linked to diagnostic feedback for teachers and students; and

(e) the sociocultural landscape on which diverse learners are situated.

Deep knowledge of each and of their interrelationships is crucial to preparing history teachers who can teach as Thomas Becker does. TPPs cannot, however, accomplish this effort alone. As I have noted, they will need coherent policy support assistance from school systems, state departments of education, and the federal government. They will also need knowledge-development support from historians and history-teacher mentors in schools in which prospective teachers do their internships. This is the meaning of systemic history education reform.

GOING FORWARD?

We keep saying that we want smarter kids who are more adept at navigating the complex, globalized world of the new century. But smarter kids will require much smarter teachers. As I have said repeatedly, it is fundamentally a knowledge problem that must be addressed, not a technical one. All the high-stakes testing and accountability systems in the world will not make for more knowledgeable students, if their teachers do not first possess the knowledge required to teach them well. Growing teachers' knowledge will take time, effort, resources, and concerted, coherent efforts on the part of all those organizations and institutions that play roles in the process. In the end, cultivating smarter teachers will require smarter policies.

With respect to history education, we can look in the rearview mirror to find antecedents. I am arguing that one might be the Amherst Project. As I conceive it, it represents a symbolic marker of an unfinished effort that is worth revisiting. In the foregoing, I have attempted to describe a way forward from that largely abandoned—as opposed to unsuccessful—effort. What buoys my advocacy is the burgeoning history-education research on student learning that suggests how important the investigative approaches of teachers such as Thomas Becker (and Nancy Todd) are in leveraging the growth of the smarter students we say we want. Perhaps all that remains is our capacity to summon the collective will necessary to move (again?) in that direction.

Appendix

REFERENCES FOR ACCOUNTS, IMAGES, AND MAPS USED IN TEACHING THE INDIAN REMOVAL UNIT

Images

"Original Extent of Cherokee Lands" (map) http://cherokeehistory.com/
original.gif

"Cherokee Lands, 1791" (map) http://cherokeehistory.com/cne1791.gif

"Cherokee Nation, 1838" (map) http://cherokeehistory.com/cne1838.gif

"Treaty of New Ochota" (image) www.footnote.com/page/83001570_
the_cherokee_trail_of_tears/

"Andrew Jackson Portrait" http://usinfo.org/enus/government/overview/
pres23.html

"Painting of John Ridge" http://mesda.org/onlineExhibits_sprite/Georgia/
mesda_major-ridge-and-john-ridge.html

"*Cherokee Phoenix*, front page" www.pbs.org/kcet/andrewjackson/edu/
cherokeephoenix.pdf

"Two Artistic Renderings of Indians on the Trail of Tears" www.
legendsofamerica.com/NA-TrailTears.html and http://community-
2.webtv.net/Skyes_Blues/ASLONGASWATERSFLOW/page2.
html

Documents

"Andrew Jackson, excerpts from a speech to his troops, 1814." In Ronald
Takaki, *A Different Mirror: A History of Multicultural America* (Boston:
Little, Brown & Co., 1993), pp. 85–86.

"Andrew Jackson, letter to General Coffee, 1832." In Ronald Takaki, *A Different Mirror: A History of Multicultural America* (Boston: Little, Brown & Co., 1993), p. 91.

"Chronology of Cherokee Removal" http://ngeorgia.com/history/cherokeetimeline.html

"Treaty of New Ochota, 1835" http://ourgeorgiahistory.com/documents/treaty_of_new_echota.html

"John Ridge Letter to Albert Gallatin, 1826" www.stolaf.edu/people/fitz/COURSES/Cherokee.htm

"Excerpts from Cherokee Constitution, 1827" www.cherokee.org/Docs/TribalGovernment/Executive/CCC/2003_CN_CONSTITUTION.pdf

"*Worcester v. Georgia*, 1832" (excerpts) www.civics-online.org/library/formatted/texts/ worcester.html

"U.S. Senate and House of Representatives: 'Speeches on Indian Removal,' 1830" (excerpts). In *The North American Review, 31* (69) (October 1830), pp. 396–442.

"Andrew Jackson, 'Seventh Annual Message to Congress,' 1835" (excerpts on removal) www.presidency.ucsb.edu/ws/index.php?pid=29477

"Indian Removal Act, 1830" (excerpts) www.uintahbasintah.org/papers/removalact.pdf

"Lewis Cass, on Indian removal, 1830" (excerpts) http://national humanitiescenter.org/pds/triumphnationalism/expansion/text4/cassre moval.pdf

"Elias Boudinot, 'Editorial in the Cherokee Phoenix,' 1829" (excerpts) www.cerritos.edu/soliver/Student%20Activites/Trail%20of%20Tears/web/boudinot.htm

The following are from Theda Perdue and Michael D. Green, *The Cherokee Removal: A Brief History with Documents* (Boston: Bedford/St. Martin's, 2005)

"Young Wolf, 'Last Will and Testament, 1814'" (excerpts, pp. 29–30).

"Georgia State Assembly, 'Laws Extending Jurisdiction Over the Cherokees,' 1829, 1832" (excerpts, pp. 76–79).

"Survey of John Ross's Plantation, 1832" (image, p. 85).

"Memorial of Protest of the Cherokee Nation, 1836" (excerpts, pp. 87–92).

"Zillah Haynie Brandon, 'Memoir,' 1830–1838" (excerpts, pp. 95–100).

"William Penn [Jeremiah Evarts] Essays, 1829" (excerpts, pp. 105–110).

"Cherokee Women, 'Petitions,' 1817, 1818, 1831" (excerpts, pp. 131–134).

"Elias Boudinot, 'Letters and Other Papers Relating to Cherokee Affairs,' 1837" (excerpts, pp. 161–166).

"John Ross, 'Letter in Answer to Inquiries from a Friend,' 1836" (excerpts, pp. 154–159).

"Evan Jones, 'Letters,' 1838" (excerpts, pp. 171–176).

"George Hicks, 'Letters From the Trail of Tears,' 1839" (excerpts, pp. 176–177).

"Rebecca Neugin, 'Recollections on Removal,' 1932" (p. 179).

Note: Becker also consulted (but opted not to use) several excellent sources from the National Park Service's "Teaching with Historic Places" website.

Notes

1 Seeking a More Potent Approach to Teaching History

1 John Bodnar, *Remaking America: Public Memory, Commemoration, and Patriotism in the Twentieth Century* (Princeton, NJ: Princeton University Press, 1992). See especially Chapter 1, pp. 14–18.

2 See, for example, Larry Cuban "History of Teaching Social Studies." In James Shaver (Ed.), *Handbook of Research on Social Studies Teaching and Learning* (New York: Macmillan, 1991), pp. 197–208; Edwin Fenton (Ed.), *Teaching the New Social Studies: An Inductive Approach* (New York: Holt, Rhinehart, Winston, 1966) pp. 443–451. James Shaver, O.L. Davis, J., and Mary Helburn, "The Status of Social Studies Education: Impressions From Three NSF Studies," *Social Education, 43* (February, 1979), pp. 150–153.

3 In part, she learned to think about teaching history this way in a history education seminar during her M.Ed. program. The course was co-taught by a historian and a teacher educator who had done research in history classrooms. There, she was introduced to a scholarship of history teaching penned by the likes of David Pace and Lendol Carter. See David Pace, "The Amateur in the Operating Room: History and the Scholarship of Teaching and Learning," *American Historical Review, 109* (October, 2004), pp. 1171–1192. Lendol Carter, "Uncoverage: Toward a Signature Pedagogy for the History Survey," *Journal of American History, 92* (March, 2006), pp. 1358–1370.

4 She was influenced here by reading Suzanne Donovan and John Bransford (Eds.), *How Students Learn: History in the Classroom* (Washington, DC: National Research Council, 2005), particularly Chapters 2, 3, and 4.

5 Her caveats and skepticism about standard history textbooks had blossomed after she read a research review by Richard Paxton on how such books disappear their authors, and a book chapter by Stuart Foster on how immigrant contributions are treated in those books. See Richard J. Paxton, "A Deafening Silence: History Textbooks and the Students Who Read Them," *Review of Educational Research, 69* (Autumn 1999), pp. 315–339; Stuart Foster, "Whose History? Portrayal of Immigrant Groups in U.S. History Textbooks—1800–Present." In Stuart Foster and Keith A. Crawford (Eds.), *What Shall We Tell the Children? International*

Perspectives on School History Textbooks (Greenwich, CT: Information Age, 2006), pp. 155–178.

6   See especially Larry Cuban, "History of Teaching Social Studies." For other examples, see the case of George Blair in S.G. Grant, *History Lessons: Teaching, Learning, and Testing in U.S. High School History Classrooms* (Mahweh, NJ: Lawrence Erlbaum Assocites, 2003); David's case in Cynthia Hartzler-Miller, "Making Sense of 'Best Practice' in Teaching History," *Theory and Research in Social Education, 29* (Fall, 2001), pp. 672–695; the case of new teacher, Angela, in Stephanie van Hover and Elizabeth Yeager, "Making Students Better People? A Case Study of a Beginning History Teacher," *International Social Studies Forum, 3* (2003), pp. 219–232; and the case of Ed Barnes in Suzanne Wilson and Sam Wineburg, "Wrinkles in Time and Place: Using Performance Assessments to Understand the Knowledge of History Teachers," *American Educational Research Journal, 30* (Winter, 1993), pp. 729–769.

7   See Maurice Halbwachs, *On Collective Memory* (trans. by Lewis A. Coser) (Chicago: University of Chicago Press, 1992).

8   In 1992, Brinton was deeply affected by reading the late Arthur Schlesinger, Jr.'s book, *The Disuniting of America*, after which he redoubled his efforts to teach his students about the importance of strong national leaders who unified the country. See Arthur Schlesinger, Jr., *The Disuniting of America: Reflections on a Multicultural Society* (New York: Norton, 1991).

9   See, for example, Schlesinger, *Disuniting*.

10 Although exceptions are rare, several cogent examples can be found in Donovan and Bransford (see note 4); Bob Bain, "Into the Breach: Using Research and Theory to Shape History Instruction." In Peter Stearns, Peter Seixas, and Sam Wineburg (Eds.), *Knowing, Teaching, and Learning History: National and International Perspectives* (New York: New York University Press, 2000) pp. 331–352; Bruce VanSledright, *In Search of America's Past: Learning to Read History in Elementary School* (New York: Teachers College Press, 2002).

11 The print version of this address appears as, Richard Brown (1966), "History as Discovery: An Interim Report on The Amherst Project." In Edwin Fenton (Ed.), *Teaching the New Social Studies: An Inductive Approach* (New York: Holt, Rhinehart, Winston, 1966), pp. 443–451.

12 See Jerome Bruner, *The Process of Education* (Cambridge: Harvard University Press, 1960).

13 See Chapter 5 especially in David Jenness' book, *Making Sense of Social Studies* (New York: Macmillan, 1990).

14 Richard Brown, "Learning How to Learn: The Amherst Project and History Education in the Schools," *The Social Studies, 87* (1996), pp. 267–273. (Online: http://weblinks2.epnet.com.proxy.umresearchport.umd.edu). Page numbering in the digitized version is 1–7. The quotations cited here are from pages 1 and 2.

15 Brown, p. 3.

16 Ibid.

17 Ibid. pp. 4–5.

18 See Carter, "Uncoverage" and Pace, "The Amateur."

19 American Historical Association, "The Next Generation of History Teachers: A Challenge to Departments of History at American Colleges and Universities." (Washington, DC: Author, 2007), p. 2. (Online: www.historians.org/pubs/Free/ historyteaching/pdfs/HistoryTeaching.pdf).

20   See David Hicks, Peter Doolittle, and John Lee, "Social Studies Teachers' Use of Classroom-based and Web-based Historical Primary Sources." *Theory and Research in Social Education, 32* (Summer, 2004), pp. 213–247.

21   See Michael Lapp, Wendy Griggs, and Brenda Tay-Lim, *The Nation's Report Card: U.S. History 2001.* (Washington, DC: National Center for Education Statistics, 2002).

22   Donovan and Bransford, *How Students Learn.*

23   Larry Cuban, *How Teachers Taught: Constancy and Change in American Classrooms* (New York; Teachers College Press, 1993) and Cuban, "History of Teaching in Social Studies."

24   For examples, see Bruce VanSledright and Margarita Limon, "Learning and Teaching Social Studies: A Review of Cognitive Research in History and Geography." In Patricia Alexander and Phillip Winne (Eds.), *The Handbook of Educational Psychology, 2nd Edition.* (Mahweh, NJ: Lawrence Erlbaum Associates, 2006), pp. 545–570.

2   On the Limits of Collective Memorialization and Persistent Instruction

1   Arthur Schlesinger, Jr., *The Disuniting of America: Reflections on a Multicultural Society* (New York: Norton, 1991).

2   By their chronological structure, periodization schemes, and emphasis placed on soup-to-nuts topical coverage, curriculum policies in most states and school districts sanction the repeated telling of the narrative of nation building and the identity-formation program that underlies the process. History teachers are generally powerless in reshaping these curricular policies because, in a time-honored tradition, those policies are typically crafted by district administrators and state departments of education.

3   Florida House of Representatives, H.B. 7087 (Tallahassee, FL: Author, 2006).

4   For more on this, see Gary Nash, Charlotte Crabtree, and Ross Dunn, *History on Trial: Culture Wars and the Teaching of the Past* (New York: Vintage, 1997).

5   Bruce VanSledright, "Narratives of Nation State, Historical Knowledge, and School History Education." *Review of Research in Education, 32* (2008), pp. 109–146.

6   Kevin O'Connor, "Narrative Form and Historical Representation: A Study of American College Students' Historical Narratives," paper presented at the Conference for Pedagogic Text Analysis and Content Analysis, Harnosand, Sweden (1991). Anecdotally, I conducted a general approximation of O'Connor's study, using the same prompt with a group of 27 undergraduate prospective elementary teachers in 2002. Twenty-four of the 27 wrote responses that virtually mirrored those written by students in the earlier study.

7   James V. Wertsch, *Mind as Action* (New York: Oxford University Press, 1998); James V. Wertsch, "Specific Narratives and Schematic Narrative Templates." In Peter Seixas (Ed.), *Theorizing Historical Consciousness* (Toronto: University of Toronto Press, 2005), pp. 49–62; and James V. Wertsch and Kevin O'Connor, "Multi-voicedness in Historical Representation: American College Students' Accounts of the Origins of the U.S.," *Journal of Narrative and Life History, 4* (1994), pp. 295–310.

8   Keith Barton, "Narrative Simplifications in Elementary Students' Historical Thinking." In Jere Brophy (Ed.), *Advances in Research on Teaching, Volume 6* (Greenwich, CT: Elsevier, 1996) pp. 51–84. Jere Brophy and Bruce VanSledright, *Teaching and Learning History in Elementary Schools* (New York; Teachers College

Press, 1997) also found a number of the features of the narrative present in the thinking about U.S. history of the 9- through 11-year-olds they studied in Michigan.

9   Michael Frisch, "American History and the Structures of Collective Memory: A Modest Exercise in Empirical Iconography," *Journal of American History, 75* (March, 1989), pp. 1130–1155. Frisch does not provide readers with a breakdown of the ethnoracial composition of the students from whom he collected data. Presumably, they were predominantly white and of European lineage.

10   John Bodnar, *Remaking America: Public Memory, Commemoration, and Patriotism in the Twentieth Century* (Princeton, NJ: Princeton University Press, 1992).

11   Frisch, p. 1150.

12   Ibid. p. 1154.

13   Brinton is acutely aware of his students' difficulty in this regard and expends considerable effort in making sure few conflicts get in the way of forward progress in narrating the American story. This is principally why he avoids using multiple accounts and relies exclusively on the textbook. For more on students' challenges in dealing with conflicting historical accounts and the helplessness that results if they are not taught strategies and criteria for adjudicating among them, see, for example, Peter Lee, "Putting Principles into Action: Understanding History" in M. Suzanne Donovan and John Bransford (Eds.), *How Students Learn: History in the Classroom* (Washington, DC: National Research Council, 2005), pp. 31–78, and Bruce VanSledright, *In Search of America's Past: Learning to Read History in Elementary School.* (New York: Teachers College Press, 2002).

14   See Terrie Epstein, *Interpreting National History: Race, Identity, and Pedagogy in Classrooms and Communities* (New York: Routledge, 2009).

15   VanSledright, "Narratives of Nation."

16   David Lowenthal, *The Heritage Crusade and the Spoils of History* (Cambridge, UK: Cambridge University Press, 1998).

17   See, for example, Michael Lapp, Wendy Grigg, and Brenda Tay-Lim, *The Nation's Report Card: U.S. History 2001* (Washington, DC: National Center for Education Statistics, 2002).

18   This pattern of less than salutary results on such tests of historical memory is not only a recent phenomenon. Poor scores have been turning up since at least the early 1900s. For a discussion of the politics of testing in history and the limits of current history assessments, see Richard Rothstein, "We Are Not Ready to Assess History Performance," *Journal of American History, 90* (March, 2004), pp. 1381–1391. For a review of earlier testing practices in history, how such tests work, and with what results, see Sam Wineburg, "Crazy for History," *Journal of American History, 90* (March, 2004), pp. 1401–1414. For more on how students have difficulty remembering what some of them perceive to be a steady stream of historical tidbits organized around a general narrative, see Bruce VanSledright, "I Just Don't Remember—the Ideas Are All Jumbled in My Head," *Journal of Curriculum and Supervision, 10* (Summer, 1995), pp. 317–345.

19   Larry Cuban, "History of Teaching in Social Studies." In James Shaver (Ed.), *Handbook of Research on Social Studies Teaching and Learning* (New York; Macmillan, 1991), pp. 197–208; James Shaver, O.L. Davis, Jr., and S.W. Helburn, *An Interpretive Report on the Status of Pre-College Social Studies Education Based on Three NSF-Funded Studies* (Washington, DC: National Science Foundation, 1978); John Goodlad, *A Place Called School* (New York: McGraw Hill, 1984).

20   See Thomas Haladyna, J. Shaughnessy, and A. Redsun, "Correlates of attitudes toward social studies," *Theory and Research in Social Education 10* (Winter, 1982), pp. 1–26; Mark Schug, R. J. Todd, and Richard Beery, "Why Kids Don't Like Social Studies," *Social Education 48* (September, 1984), pp. 382–387; and Bruce VanSledright, "And Santayana Lives On: Student's Views on the Purposes for Studying History," *Journal of Curriculum Studies, 29* (Fall, 1997), pp. 529–557.

21   For an example, see Linda Levstik, "Articulating the Silences: Teachers' and Adolescents' Conceptions of Historical Significance." In Peter Stearns, Peter Seixas, and Sam Wineburg (Eds.), *Knowing, Teaching, and Learning History: National and International Perspectives* (New York: New York University Press, 2000), pp. 284–305.

22   For a discussion about how students come to understand themselves as good students in typical schooling contexts, see Robert Sternberg, "What is an Expert Student." *Educational Researcher, 32* (September, 2003), pp. 5–9.

23   VanSledright, *In Search of America's Past.*

24   Lowenthal, *The Heritage Crusade.*

25   Frisch, "American History and the Structures of Collective Memory," p. 1154.

26   Ibid.

27   I take up the shortcomings of such assumptions in Chapter 7.

28   For some examples, see a review of history education research by Bruce VanSledright and Margarita Limon, "Learning and Teaching Social Studies: A Review of Cognitive Research in History and Geography." In Patricia Alexander and Phillip Winne (Eds.), *The Handbook of Educational Psychology, 2nd Edition* (Mahweh, NJ: Lawrence Erlbaum Associates, 2006), pp. 545–570.

29   See David Pace, "The Amateur in the Operation Room: History and the Scholarship of Teaching and Learning," *American Historical Review, 109* (October, 2004), pp. 1171–1192; Lendol Carter, "Uncoverage: Toward a Signature Pedagogy for the History Survey," *Journal of American History, 92* (March, 2006), pp. 1358–1370; and Bruce VanSledright, "Why Should Historians Care About History Teaching?" *Perspectives: Newsletter of the American Historical Association, 45* (February, 2007). (Online: www.historians.org/perspectives/issues/2007/0702/ 0702tea2.cfm). I revisit this issue in the final chapter.

30   See Jerome Bruner, *The Process of Education* (Cambridge: Harvard University Press, 1960).

31   VanSledright, *In Search of,* especially Chapter 7.

32   There have been some exceptions to this general rule. For example, the Amherst History Project of the 1960s and 1970s provided some initial forays onto this landscape. See again Chapter 1 in which I describe in more detail those efforts.

33   Illustrations I borrow from, for example, would include the cases in the Donovan and Bransford (2005) volume, *How Students Learn: History in the Classroom,* Chapters 3 and 4, my own work teaching students as represented in *In Search of America's Past,* and Bob Bain's (2000) illustration of his own teaching efforts as found in his chapter "Into the Breach: Using Research and Theory to Shape History Instruction," in Stearns, *et al., Knowing, Teaching, and Learning History.*

3   The Case of Thomas Becker: Using Knowledge of History as a Domain to Structure Pedagogical Choices

1   Becker derived this thesis from reading Robert V. Remini's, *Andrew Jackson and His Indian Wars* (New York: Viking, 2001).

2   Remini, *Andrew Jackson*; Ronald Takaki, *A Different Mirror: A History of Multicultural America* (New York: Little Brown, 1993); and Anthony F.C. Wallace, *The Long Bitter Trail: Andrew Jackson and the Indians* (New York: Hill and Wang, 1993).

3   Gloria L. Jahoda, *The Trail of Tears* (New York: Wings, 1993).

4   The contradiction that most intrigued Becker involved the professed ideals of democracy residing up against the practice of rather severely limiting the franchise, a key piece of his master's thesis work.

5   Becker would have preferred that his students had more ready access to the Internet in the classroom in order to facilitate explorations of documents and historical residue online via digitized archives. However, at Sentinel High School, classrooms came equipped with only two Internet-linked computers and no smart boards or related digital technology.

6   On this problem endemic to studying the past, see Joan Wallach Scott, "After History," paper presented at History and the Limits of Interpretation: A Symposium, Rice University (February, 1996). (Online: www.ruf.rice.edu/~culture/papers/ Scott.html).

7   Robert Sternberg, "Who Is an Expert Student," *Educational Researcher, 32* (September, 2003), pp. 5–9.

8   I revisit Becker's planning process in Chapter 5.

9   Lee Shulman observes that, "hypothesis-guided inquiry is only strainful in task environments where the inquirer has no organized bodies of knowledge on which to draw. In the far more typical case, when the inquirer has a good deal of prior relevant knowledge, organized sets of intellectual skills, and experience using the knowledge and skills jointly in problem solving, the finding is reversed, and it is hypothesis-guided inquiry which brings about the least cognitive strain." From "The Psychology of School Subjects." In Suzanne Wilson (Ed.), *The Wisdom of Practice: Essays on Teaching, Learning, and Learning to Teach* (San Francisco: Jossey-Bass, 2004), p. 112.

10   Bruner, *The Process of Education* (Cambridge: Harvard University Press, 1960). See also Joseph J. Schwab, "Education and the Structure of the Disciplines." In Ian Westbury and Neil Wilkop (Eds.), *Science, Curriculum, and Liberal Education* (Chicago: University of Chicago Press, 1978), pp. 229–273; and Joseph J. Schwab, "The Structure of the Disciplines: Meanings and Significances." In G.W. Ford and Lawrence Pugno (Eds.), *The Structure of Knowledge and the Curriculum* (Chicago: University of Chicago Press, 1964), pp. 22–37.

11   See, for example, different treatments by Frank Ankersmit and Hans Kellner (Eds.), *A New Philosophy of History* (Chicago: University of Chicago Press, 1995); David Carr, *Time, Narrative and History* (Bloomington, IN: University of Indiana Press, 1986); R.G. Collingwood, *The Idea of History* (Oxford: Oxford University Press, 1946/1993); Louis Mink, "Philosophical Analysis and Historical Understanding," in Brian Fay, Eugene Golob, and Richard Vann (Eds.), *Historical Understanding* (Ithaca, NY: Cornell University Press, 1987) pp. 130–149; Pierre Nora, *Realms of Memory: The Construction of the French Past.* (New York: Columbia University Press, 1996); Jorn Rusen, *Studies in Metahistory* (Pretoria, 1993); and Hayden White, *Tropics of Discourse: Essays in Cultural Criticism* (Baltimore: Johns Hopkins University Press, 1978).

12   Lee Shulman has noted that in the studies of expert history teachers he and his students conducted at Stanford in the 1980s, the differences observed among them

and their approaches to teaching practice were determined most by the differences in their understandings and epistemologies of historical knowledge. See Shulman, "Aristotle Had It Right: On Knowledge and Pedagogy," in *The Wisdom of Practice*, pp. 400–415. For an example of such differences found in these studies, see Suzanne Wilson and Sam Wineburg, "Wrinkles in Time and Place: Using Performance Assessments to Understand the Knowledge of History Teachers," *American Educational Research Journal, 50* (Winter, 1993), pp. 729–769. Other researchers have observed similar patterns. See, for example, the two teachers profiled by S.G. Grant in *History Lessons: Teaching, Learning, and Testing in U.S. High School Classrooms* (Mahweh, NJ: Lawrence Erlbaum Associates, 2003) and the three teachers in Jere Brophy and Bruce VanSledright, *Teaching and Learning History in Elementary Schools* (New York: Teachers College Press, 1997).

13   Peter Novick, *That Noble Dream: The "Objectivity Question" and The American Historical Profession* (Cambridge: Cambridge University Press, 1988).

14   R.G. Collingwood defined historical practice as the effort to understand how the minds of the past thought. See his *The Idea of History*. On how the ways in which telling the unmediated truth about the past is denied, see, for example, Scott, "After History."

15   For more on these issues of knowledge in history, their epistemological considerations, and their relationships to teaching the subject, see Collingwood, *The Idea of History*; Peter Lee and Rosalyn Ashby, "Empathy, Perspective Taking, and Rational Understanding," in O.L. Davis, Jr., Elizabeth Yeager, and Stuart Foster (Eds.) *Historical Empathy and Perspective Taking in the Social Studies* (Lanham, MD: Rowman & Littlefield, 2001), pp. 21–50; Denis Shemilt, "Beauty and the Philosopher: Empathy in History and Classroom," in Alaric Dickinson, Peter Lee, and Peter Rogers (Eds.), *Learning History* (London: Wobern 1984), pp. 39–84; Bruce VanSledright, "On the Importance of Historical Positionality to Thinking About and Teaching History," *International Journal of Social Education , 12* (Winter, 1998), pp. 1–18; and Bruce VanSledright, "From Empathic Regard to Self-Understanding: Im/positionality, Empathy, and Historical Contextualization," in O.L. Davis, Jr., Elizabeth Yeager, and Stuart Foster, *Historical Empathy and Perspective Taking in Social Studies*, pp. 51–68.

16   David Lowenthal, *The Past is a Foreign Country* (Cambridge: Cambridge University Press, 1985).

17   In graduate school, Becker read Richard J. Paxton's "A Deafening Silence: History Textbooks and the Students Who Read Them," *Review of Educational Research, 69* (Autumn, 1999), pp. 315–339.

18   See John Bodnar, *Remaking America: Public Memory, Commemoration, and Patriotism in the Twentieth Century* (Princeton: Princeton University Press, 1992).

19   Ibid. Bodnar might refer to these as vernacular histories.

20   Becker's structural ideas bear some resemblance to those of the British educational philosopher and curriculum theorist, Paul H. Hirst. See, for example, Paul H. Hirst, *Knowledge and Curriculum: A Collection of Philosophical Papers* (London: Routledge, 1975).

21   For examples of how historians' conceptual frameworks shape their accounts, see especially James W. Davidson and Mark H. Lytle, *After the Fact: The Art of Historical Detection* (New York: McGraw Hill, 1992).

22   There are, of course exceptions to this general rule, as Becker would no doubt point out. One good example is Laura Thatcher Ulrich's, *A Midwife's Tale: The Life of Martha Ballard* (New York: Knopf, 1990); and the essays that populate Davidson and Lytle's, *After the Fact*. What makes these to works relatively unique is that their authors slide their organizing background ideas, concepts, and presumptions rather seamlessly into the foregrounded narrative space of the stories they tell, and/or demonstrate how background organizing concepts and theories help structure narrative arcs.

23   Again, for a variety of explicit examples of this process, see Davidson and Lytle's *After the Fact*.

24   On this point see, for example, Hayden White, *Tropics of Discourse*.

25   Geoffrey Parrington attempted to outline a cluster of criteria for measuring historical significance. His list included relevance, durability, quantity, profundity, and importance. Geoffrey Parrington, *The Idea of Historical Education* (Windsor, UK; NFER Publishing, 1980). For a detailed unpacking of these five criteria, see Stephane Levesque, *Thinking Historically: Education Students for the Twenty-First Century* (Toronto: University of Toronto Press, 2008), especially Chapter 3. See also Robert Phillips, Historical "Significance—The Forgotten 'Key Concept'?" *Teaching History 106* (2002), pp. 14-19; and Peter Seixas," Conceptualizing the Growth of Historical Understanding." In David Olsen and Nancy Torrance (Eds.), *The Handbook of Education and Human Development* (Oxford: Oxford University Press, 1996), pp. 765–783.

26   See, for example, Shemilt, "Beauty and the Philosopher" and VanSledright, "From Empathic Regard."

27   For example, see Peter Lee and Rosalyn Ashby, "Progression in Historical Understanding among Students Ages 7–14." In Peter Stearns, Peter Seixas, and Sam Wineburg (Eds.), *Knowing, Teaching, and Learning History* (New York: New York University Press, 2000), pp. 199–222.

28   Here Becker adapted the three source-work reading strategies from Bruce VanSledright and Peter Afflerbach, "Assessing the Status of Historical Sources: An Exploratory Study of Eight Elementary Students Reading Documents," in Peter Lee (Ed.), *Children and Teachers' Ideas About History, International Research in History Education, Volume 4* (London: RoutledgeFalmer, 2005), pp. 1–20.

29   On the issue of developmental trajectory, see Patricia Alexander, "Toward a Model of Academic Development: Schooling and the Acquisition of Knowledge," *Educational Researcher, 29* (2000), pp. 28–33, 44. For more on progression, see Peter Lee and Denis Shemilt, "A Scaffold Not a Cage: Progression and Progression Models in History," *Teaching History, 113* (2003), pp. 13–24.

4   Learning History: What Do Students Know and What Can They Do with that Knowledge?

1   See Terrie Epstein, *Interpreting National History: Race, Identity, and Pedagogy in Classrooms and Communities*. (New York: Routledge, 2009); Peter Seixas, "Historical Understanding Among Adolescents in a Multicultural Setting," *Curriculum Inquiry, 23* (Autumn, 1993), pp. 301–327; Sam Wineburg, Susan Mosberg, Daniel Porat, and Ariel Duncan, "Common Belief and the Cultural Curriculum: An Intergenerational Study of Historical Consciousness," *American Educational Research Journal, 44* (January, 2007), pp. 40–76.

2   See, for example, Angela Valenzuela, *Subtractive Schooling: U.S.-Mexican Youth and the Politics of Caring* (New York: SUNY Press, 1999).

3   See Epstein, *Interpreting.*

4   See James V. Wertsch, *Mind as Action* (New York: Oxford University Press, 1998).

5   Eric Foner, *Who Owns History?* (New York: Hill and Wang, 2002). Both quotes are from p. xv.

6   John Bodnar, *Remaking America: Public Memory, Commemoration, and Patriotism in the Twentieth Century* (Princeton, NJ: Princeton University Press, 1992).

7   Becker's ideas here were shaped by his reading of Michael Kammen's, *Mystic Chords of Memory: The Transformation of Tradition in American Culture* (New York: Knopf, 1991); and his "History is Our Heritage: The Past in Contemporary American Culture," In Paul Gagnon (Ed.), *Historical Literacy: The Case for History in American Education* (Boston: Houghton Mifflin, 1989), pp. 138–156; as well as by David Lowenthal's, *The Heritage Crusade and the Spoils of History* (Cambridge, UK: Cambridge University Press, 1998); and Peter Lee's, "Putting Principles Into Practice: Understanding History," In Susan Donovan and John Bransford (Eds.), *How Students Learn: History in the Classroom* (Washington, DC: National Research Council), pp. 31-–78.

8   See Bruce VanSledright and Margarita Limon, "Learning and Teaching Social Studies: A Review of Cognitive Research in History and Geography." In Patricia Alexander and Phillip Winne (Eds.), *The Handbook of Educational Psychology, 2nd Edition.* (Mahweh, NJ: Lawrence Erlbaum Associates, 2006), pp. 545–570; and Samuel Wineburg, "The Psychology of Teaching and Learning History," In Robert Calfree and David Berliner (Eds.), *Handbook of Educational Psychology* (New York: Macmillan Reference, 1996), pp. 423–427.

9   Denis Shemilt, *History 13-16 Evaluation Study* (Edinburgh: Holmes McDougal, 1980); Peter Lee and Rosalyn Ashby, "Progression in Historical Understanding among Students Ages 7–14." In Peter Stearns, Peter Seixas, and Sam Wineburg (Eds.), *Knowing, Teaching, and Learning History* (New York: New York University Press, 2000), pp. 199–222; Peter Lee and Denis Shemilt, "A Scaffold Not a Cage: Progression and Progression Models in History," *Teaching History, 113* (2003), pp. 13–24.

10 Patricia Alexander, "Toward a Model of Academic Development: Schooling and the Acquisition of Knowledge." *Educational Researcher, 29* (2000), pp. 28–33, 44; John Seely Brown and Paul Duguid "Organizational Learning and Communities-of-Practice: Toward a Unified View of Working, Learning, and Innovation," *Organization Science, 2* (March, 1991), pp. 40–57; Jean Lave and Etienne Wegner, *Situated Learning: Legitimate Peripheral Participation* (Cambridge: Cambridge University Press, 1991); Samuel S. Wineburg, "Historical Problem Solving: A Study of the Cognitive Processes Used in the Evaluation of Documentary and Pictorial Evidence," *Journal of Educational Psychology, 83* (1991), pp. 73–87.

11 Becker's categorizations derived from his reading of Lee and Ashby, "Progression in Historical Understanding"; Peter Lee, "Putting Principles into Action: Understanding History" in M. Suzanne Donovan and John Bransford (Eds.), *How Students Learn: History in the Classroom* (Washington, DC: National Research Council, 2005), pp. 31–78; Lee and Shemilt, "A Scaffold Not a Cage," Peter Seixas, "Conceptualizing the Growth of Historical Understanding." In David Olsen and Nancy Torrance (Eds.), *The Handbook of Education and Human Development* (Oxford: Oxford University Press, 1996), pp. 765–783; Bruce VanSledright and Margarita Limon,

"Learning and Teaching"; and more recently, Stephane Levesque, *Thinking Historically: Education Students for the Twenty-First Century* (Toronto: University of Toronto Press, 2008).

12   This idea is so central to Becker's understanding and approach that, as a pivotal theme, it therefore appears here, in the preceding chapter, and it reappears in later chapters all at the risk of belaboring the point.

13   Bruce VanSledright and Peter Afflerbach, "Assessing the Status of Historical Sources: An Exploratory Study of Eight Elementary Students Reading Documents," In Peter Lee (Ed.), *Children and Teachers' Ideas about History, International Research in History Education, Volume 4* (London: Wobern, 2005) pp. 1–20. Maggioni and colleagues refer to such naïve realists as "copiers," because they tend to see historical accounts, particularly officialized textbook versions, as direct, unmediated copies of that past. See Liliana Maggioni, Bruce VanSledright, and Patricia Alexander, "Walking on the Borders: A Measure of Epistemic Cognition in History," *Journal of Experimental Education,* 77 (2009), pp. 187–213.

14   As Becker learned from talking to other teachers in his school district, the "Americanization" process starts in elementary school and continues on into middle school (with a U.S. history course in eighth grade). In the elementary grades, youngsters get a steady dose of the freedom-quest collective memory built around the celebratory "holidays curriculum" (Columbus Day, President's Day, Martin Luther King Day, Thanksgiving, and African-American and Women's history months). That curriculum is reinforced—to the extent U.S. history is taught as a course at all—in fifth grade with a chronological treatment from "Native Americans in North America" through "Colonization and the Founding of the United States" and on to "Westward Expansion" of the early nineteenth century. In eighth grade, the 10-pound U.S. history textbook with its authoritative, national-development narrative arc makes its arrival, and more often than not, as we have seen, is followed chapter by chapter for the duration of the year. Students learn that to be good at U.S. history means being able to recall correctly as many details as one can about the nation-building story and the role patriots and pioneers played in its development.

15   VanSledright and Afflerbach, "Assessing the Status." Maggioni and colleagues refer to the naïve relativist as a "borrower," because the naïve relativist tends to think that histories come from borrowing and pasting pieces of multiple accounts into some sort of coherent storyline. When asked to generate histories themselves, these "borrowers" deploy that cutting and pasting strategy, while realizing that almost anyone who is able to read can likely do so as well. Therefore, history becomes more someone's opinion than an established set of understandings tested and underpinned by evidence corroboration procedures. See Liliana Maggioni, Bruce VanSledright, and Patricia Alexander, "Walking on the Borders."

16   R.G. Collingwood (1994). *The Idea of History* (Oxford, UK: Oxford University Press; original work published in 1946).

17   See again VanSledright and Afflerbach, "Assessing" and Liliana Maggioni, Bruce VanSledright, and Patricia Alexander, "Walking."

18   Those decisions and how they play out for Becker are the subject of the next chapter.

19   As noted, there are clearly exceptions to this general rule, Laurel Thatcher Ulrich's, *A Midwife's Tale: The Life of Martha Ballard Based on Her Diary, 1785–1812* (New York: Knopf, 1990) being among the more powerful ones. However, as Becker well knew, such histories seldom graced the desks of pre-collegiate readers. See

also James West Davidson and Mark Hamilton Lytle, *After the Fact: The Art of Historical Dectection, 5th Edition* (New York: McGraw Hill, 2004).

20 See Robert Philips, "Historical Significance—The Forgotten 'Key Concept.'" *Teaching History* 106 (2002) pp. 14–19. See also the treatment of this second-order idea in Levesque, *Thinking Historically*, Chapter 3. Becker would later abondon this intention in the interest of time.

21 For more on the strategic reading capabilities of accomplished readers, see, for example, Michael Pressley and Peter Afflerbach, *Verbal Protocols of Reading: The Nature of Constructively Responsive Reading* (Mahweh, NJ: Lawrence Erlbaum Associates, 1995).

22 During his searches, he stumbled on a small book he became particularly fond of, written by Cleo Cherryholmes, entitled *Reading Pragmatism* (New York: Teachers College Press, 1999). The ideas in this book were more helpful to Becker in building his approach to reading in history than all the content-area reading texts he consulted throughout his state-required content-area reading course during his master's program.

23 He first encountered these four in a short article by Bruce VanSledright, "What Does it Mean to Think Historically . . . and *How Do You Teach It?*" *Social Education, 68* (2004), pp. 230–233.

24 Becker used a streamlined version of this chart in class with his students. He had modified it several times since he began using the initial iteration of it in his first year of teaching.

25 Bruce VanSledright, "From Empathic Regard to Self-Understanding: Im/positionality, Empathy, and Historical Contextualization," in *Development of Historical Empathy: Perspective Taking in Social Studies*, O.L. Davis, Jr., Elizabeth Yeager, and Stuart Foster (Eds.) (Lanham, MD: Rowman Littlefield, 2001), pp. 51–68.

26 Samuel S. Wineburg, *Historical Thinking and Other Unnatural Acts* (Philadelphia: Temple University Press, 2001), pp. 63–88.

27 Rosalyn Ashby and Peter Lee, "Information, Opinion, and Beyond," paper presented at the American Education Research Association annual meeting (San Diego, CA, April, 1998).

28 Margaret MacMillan, *Dangerous Games: The Uses and Abuses of History* (New York: Modern Library, 2009), p. 165.

29 Becker was influenced here by the work of Peter Lee and Denis Shemilt, "Progression in Understanding about Historical Accounts," *Teaching History, 117* (2004), pp. 25–31, the figure on page 27 especially.

30 Collingwood, *The Idea*.

31 Becker's teaching experience has taught him that, for his students, "seeing is often believing." Therefore, he uses contemporary visual historical accounts in DVD-style formats rather sparingly because his students tend to reify what they see. Becker has needed to repeatedly stress that such accounts are human creations, prone to all the issues that affect, for example, written sources. Use of PAIR[e] strategies are equally necessary in considering them. In effect, such visual accounting is no more or less reliable than others. One must judge their reliability in the same way any other type of account must be. He hears himself say frequently in class, "It's all one historical account or another, all the way down," as if he's channeling Jacques Derrida's famous dictum that there is no outside text. See *Of Grammatology* (Baltimore: Johns Hopkins Press, 1976).

5   Teaching about Indian Removal: Describing and Unpacking the Investigative Approach

1   As he heard himself asking these questions, he again remembered what historian Robert Rosenstone once said (paraphrasing him in his head), "History is not a collection of details. It's an *argument* about what those details mean!" He had seen the sentences quoted without citation in Katherine Masur, "Edmund Morris's *Dutch*: Reconstructing Reagan or Deconstructing History?" *Perspectives: American Historical Association Newsletter*, 37 (December, 1998), pp. 3–5.

2   Perdue and Green, *Cherokee Removal, 2nd Edition* (Boston: Bedford/St. Martin, 2005).

3   Becker was reminded of historian Thomas Holt's interesting reflections on his own efforts to teach history, titled *Historical Thinking: Narrative, Imagination, and Understanding* (New York: College Board, 1990), from which he recalled the phrase "other people's facts."

4   Perdue and Green's treatment of Cherokee removal is seen among experts on removal as careful, detailed scholarship, built up from systematic analyses of archival material, and reasonably balanced. For these reasons, many generally respect its narrative arc and use of evidence, even if not all scholars of the period agree with every narrative turn the authors take.

5   Assessment practices are the subject of the next chapter.

6   This book's structure had the side, but equally important benefit of providing readers with a prima facie example of how historians build up arguments about what the past means by drawing off from available evidence, and when that evidence is thin, hedging and cautioning and suggesting alternative ways of thinking about the past that the available evidence does not explain. A high school history textbook, Becker knew, should be so fortunate.

7   Becker wrote into his plan Groups D, E, and F, anticipating that, if he left it at only three sets of questions and thus only three groups, the groups possibly might be too large and unwieldy to allow students to work together effectively. He reserved the option to have two groups simultaneously exploring each of the three question clusters. He would eventually decide to exercise this idea when he began photocopying materials.

8   See again Chapter 3, Figure 3.1 and p. 50, 'A characterization of history domain knowledge'.

9   At the beginning of the school year, when he first introduced a streamlined version of the template—the one he placed on the classroom wall (see Chapter 3)—Becker took great pains to go over it in detail, offering definitions of terms, addressing questions students had, and reassuring them that it would take time and effort to come to some mastery of the practices it entailed. He told them that he would keep this in mind in his assessment and grading approach.

10 Students in Becker's fourth-period class were Abby (White female), Amanda (African-American female), Angie (White female), Britney (African-American female), Carlita (Latina), Cynthia (Latina), James (White male), Javon (African-American male), Jorge (Latino), Jonathan (White male), Juan (Latino), Max (White male), Melissa (White female), Michael (African-American male), Paul (White male), Reggie (African-American male), Regina (Latina), Salvator (Latino), Serena

(African-American female), Sonia (Latina), Thomas (White male), and Zenith (African-American female).

11   According to the reading test scores, petite bespectacled Serena was reading well above grade level, beyond everyone else in class. She was also the most studious student and typically the most articulate despite being occasionally reticent to put her ideas out there in public view.

12   Overnight, Becker would study Group D's notes and return them to the group the following day.

13   Becker's check of the Guides the night before revealed that students generally had scribbled in quick responses to the four sourcing practices. Most of the R^e (Reliability/Evidence) sections were left blank, largely because, he hunched, students waited to respond until after they had held a group discussion, and then failed to complete the process as they became engrossed in conversation and debate. Such debates about account reliability could be common. The practice, as Becker knew, was difficult and often only partial, and therefore only partially successful. Nonetheless, he knew by looking over the Guides that he would need to press on his students about being more fastidious and conscientious with all four types of history-specific reading practices in future units if they were to make such a cognitive practice habitual and automatized. The Guides were effectively a record of their efforts. Perhaps, he thought, he would announce in the next unit that he would be collecting and grading them.

14   The actual substance of the test is described and discussed in the next chapter.

6   Assessing Student Learning

1   Item numbers correspond to initial items generated, not final assessment item numbers.

2   He had been reminded recently of the importance of teaching such capacity to write historically by reading Chauncey Monte-Sano, "Qualities of Historical Writing Instruction: A Comparative Case Study of Two Teachers' Practices," *American Educational Research Journal, 45* (December, 2008), pp. 1045–1079.

3   Becker's hunching and theorizing here was linked to his reading of Terrie Epstein, *Interpreting National History: Race, Identity, and Pedagogy in Classrooms and Communities* (New York: Routledge, 2009), and Peter Seixas, "Historical Understand Among Adolescents in a Multicultural Setting," *Curriculum Inquiry, 23* (Fall, 1993), pp. 301–327.

4   See, for example, Linda Darling Hammond and C.D. Prince (Eds.), *Strengthening Teacher Quality in High Need Schools—Policy and Practice* (Washington, DC: The Council of Chief State School Officers, 2007).

5   Becker had been impressed by the cogent analysis of S.G. Grant and Cinthia Salinas, "Assessment and Accountability in Social Studies," In Linda S. Levstik and Cynthia A. Tyson (Eds.), *Handbook of Research in Social Studies Education* (New York: Routledge, 2008), pp. 219–236, especially pp. 227–232.

6   See, for example, two articles by Lorrie Shepard, "The Role of Assessment in a Learning Culture," *Educational Researcher, 29* (October, 2000), pp. 4–14; and "Psychometricians' Beliefs About Learning," *Educational Researcher, 20* (October, 1991), pp. 2–16. Becker also read Sam Wineburg, "Crazy for History," *Journal of American History, 90* (March, 2004), pp. 1401–1414.

7   Becker found an interesting story about this consequence and its influence on history teachers in Virginia. See Stephanie D. van Hover and Walter F. Heinecke, "The Impact of Accountability Reform on the 'Wise Practice' of Secondary History Teachers: The Virginia Experience." In Elizabeth Yeager and O.L. Davis, Jr. (Eds.), *Wise Social Studies Teaching in an Age of High Stakes Testing: Essays on Classroom Practices and Possibilities* (Greenwich, CT: Information Age, 2005), pp. 89–116.

8   Becker found the work of the CHATA Project in England to be especially helpful in thinking about what Project researchers called progression in students' historical ideas. See the chapters by CHATA researchers in M. Suzanne Donovan and John Bransford (Eds.), *How Students Learn: History in the Classroom* (Washington DC National Research Council, 2005).

9   As we saw in Chapter 4, such ideas are often found among novices who, upon confronting ambiguity, gaps in the record, and/or conflicting perspectives in historical accounts, decide that it's the opinion one holds about the matter at hand (usually unsupported by evidence) that is most important. Part of the challenge for Becker and all history teachers who teach history through investigative approaches is to help students learn to work from the types of criteria for making and supporting claims employed within the historical community of practices. Such criteria bestow on students considerable power both in making sense of the past and in persuading others of the sense they make. Becker's essay questions, for example, are structured with this idea at the forefront. For an interesting set of recent essays on what these criteria look like, see Allan Megill, *Historical Knowledge, Historical Error* (Chicago: University of Chicago Press, 2007), Chapters 5, 6, and 7 in particular.

7   Theorizing Investigative History Teaching

1   Behind this more general goal of deepening understanding of the American past, is Becker's profound conviction that such understanding ultimately leads to a more intense understanding of self. In this sense, he sees his investigative approach as identity enhancing but in a very different way than the more indoctrinating approach traditional school history pursues by pushing its foreclosed narrative arc.

2   See, for example, Sam Wineburg, "Reading Abraham Lincoln: An Expert/Expert Study in Historical Cognition," *Cognitive Science, 22* (1998), pp. 319–346.

3   This same principle undergirded the Amherst Project. See Chapter 1.

4   See Roland Barthes, "The Reality Effect." In Theodore Todorov (Ed.), *French Literary Theory Today: A Reader* (Cambridge: Cambridge University Press, 1968, Translated by R. Carter), pp. 11–17; and Roland Barthes, "The Discourse of History." In *The Rustle of Language* (New York: Hill and Wang, 1986, Translated by R. Howard), pp. 128–139.

5   James T. Kloppenberg, "Objectivity and Historicism: A Century of Historical Writing," *American Historical Review, 94* (October, 1989), pp. 1011–1030. The quote can be found on page 1030.

6   See for example, Peter Seixas, "Conceptualizing the Development of Historical Understanding." In David Olsen and Nancy Torrance (Eds.), *The Handbook of Education and Human Development* (Oxford: Oxford University Press, 1996) pp. 765–783.

7   For a pointed description of these, see note 29 in Chapter 8.

8   How Are History Teachers to Learn to Teach Using an Investigative Approach?

1 The term loosely coupled comes from the cogent analyses of two sociologists of education, John Meyer and Brian Rowan. See their "Institutionalized Organizations: Formalized Structures as Myth and Ceremony." *American Journal of Sociology, 83* (1977), pp. 340–363. On p. 343, for example, they note of large loosely-coupled organizations such as those found in education that "structural elements are only loosely linked to each other and activities, rules are often violated, decisions are often unimplemented, or if implemented have uncertain consequences, technologies are of uncertain efficiencies, and evaluation and inspection systems are subverted or rendered so vague as to provide little coordination."

2 See, for example, Julia Koppich, Daniel C. Humphrey, and Heather Hough, "Making Use of What Teachers Know and Can Do: Policy, Practice, and National Board Certification," *Education Policy Analysis Archives, 17* (April, 2006), pp. 1–28; and Linda Darling Hammond and C.D. Prince (Eds.), *Strengthening Teacher Quality in High Need Schools—Policy and Practice* (Washington, DC: The Council of Chief State School Officers, 2007).

3 Daniel C. Lortie, *Schoolteacher: A Sociological Study* (Chicago: University of Chicago Press, 1975).

4 On this point, see especially Michael Kammen, *Mystic Chords of Memory: The Transformation of Tradition in American Culture* (New York: Knopf, 1991).

5 Momentarily, I will revisit this issue of the role teacher preparation programs can play in growing history teachers' knowledge along the lines evidenced by Thomas Becker.

6 An exception to this general rule would be teachers applying for National Board for Professional Teaching Standards accreditation, a proxy of knowledge and performance success only available to already licensed teachers.

7 This claim is based on an extrapolation I am making from what happens in my own state of Maryland. I justify the claim on the grounds that extrapolation is warranted in that Maryland has licensure reciprocity with 42 other states.

8 For more detail on how SDEs tinker with cut scores and disconnect standards from what's tested, see the essays in S.G. Grant, *Measuring History [Achievement]: Cases of State-Level Testing Across the United States* (Greenwich, CT: Information Age, 2006). For an especially instructive testing case in state of New York and the less than salutary results it produces, see Grant's chapter, "Research on History Tests," pp. 29–52.

9 As an example, see the Fordham Foundation's efforts to rate and rank state history standards. See www.edexcellence.net/. A closer examination of the Foundation's standards evaluation work suggests that it lacks the full expertise to assess history standards adequately. Standards, for example, are not assessed against any criteria that could be adduced from the history education research of the last three decades, making ratings and rankings at least partially suspect.

10 For a more detailed account of this matter, see Stephanie D. van Hover and Walter F. Heinecke, "The Impact of Accountability Reform on the 'Wise Practice' of Secondary History Teachers: The Virginia Experience," In Elizabeth Yeager and O.L. Davis, Jr. (Eds.), *Wise Social Studies Teaching in an Age of High Stakes Testing: Essays on Classroom Practices and Possibilities* (Greenwich, CT: Information Age, 2005), pp. 89–116.

11   See again my discussion of this issue in Chapter 6. For more detail on how this
     works in history-achievement testing, see for example Catherine Horn, "The
     Technical Realities of Measuring History [Achievement]," in S.G. Grant (Ed.),
     Measuring History [Achievement]: Cases of State-Level Testing Across the United States
     (Greenwich, CT: Information Age, 2006), pp. 57–74.

12   For more on the distinction between what it means to teach history as opposed to
     nationalistic commemoration/collective memorialization, see David Lowenthal, *The
     Heritage Crusade and the Spoils of History* (Cambridge: Cambridge University Press,
     1998); and Alan Megill, *Historical Knowledge and Historical Error* (Chicago: University
     of Chicago Press, 2007), especially Chapters 1 and 2. On the negative consequences
     of a nationalistic collective-memorialization school curriculum and standards, see
     Bruce VanSledright, "Narratives of Nation State, Historical Knowledge, and School
     History Education," *Review of Research in Education, 32* (2008), pp. 109–146. All
     three authors recognize that history and memory are deeply interconnected, that
     it is fundamentally impossible to talk about one without the other. However, the
     authors come to the conclusion that it is the excessive exuberance emitted by those
     who press collective memory's celebratory, commemorative register that push it to
     distort understandings of the past (e.g., in school history) that history labors hard
     to avoid.

13   As of 2004, 23 states had history tests built into their accountability regimes. See
     Grant, *Measuring History*.

14   See especially Linda Darling-Hammond and Beverly Falk, "Using Standards and
     Assessments to Support Student Learning." *Phi Delta Kappan, 79* (1997), pp.
     190–199. See also William Firestone and David Mayrowetz, "Rethinking 'High
     Stakes': Lessons From the United States and England and Wales," *Teachers College
     Record, 102* (2000), pp. 724–749; Gary Orfield and Mindy Kornhaber (Eds.), *Raising
     Standards or Raising Barriers? Inequality and High-Stakes Testing in Public Education*
     (New York: Century Foundation Press, 2001); and Daniel Koretz, *Measuring Up:
     What Educational Testing Really Tells Us* (Cambridge: Harvard University Press, 2009).
     For a collection of reports on the unintended consequences of the law, many of
     which contain empirical evidence, see the Social and Institutional Policy *Special
     Issue on No Child Left Behind, American Educational Research Journal, 44* (2007), pp.
     456–629. Of the five articles offered in the special issue, all demonstrate serious
     unintended, negative consequences on student learning and teaching practices
     related to the implementation of the federal law.

15   See again Grant, *Measuring History*.

16   Cohen, "What's the System in Systemic Reform?" *Educational Researcher, 24*
     (December, 1995), pp. 11–17, 31.

17   The current "Race to the Top" venture pressed by the U.S. Department of
     Education may suggest some promise in this regard, particularly with respect to its
     provisions to incentivize SDEs to rethink and raise their curriculum standards and
     learning benchmarks.

18   Grant, *Measuring*.

19   For over two years in the middle aughts, I served on a task force charged by the
     state superintendent of education in Maryland to wrestle with the problem of the
     diminishing role social studies and history education played in the state's school
     systems under the heavy pressure of federal accountability guidelines. The task force
     found prima facie evidence that, because those subjects were not covered by the

federal law's accountability umbrella, their role in the curriculum of the state's children was diminishing. The most egregious examples were found in school systems that had difficulty meeting AYP in reading and mathematics. As some might have predicted, the task force recommended banded, high-stakes testing in history in particular on the idea that, if it does not get tested, it won't get taught. Superintendents of school systems in the state, once they got word of the task force testing recommendations, campaigned vehemently *against* such a new testing mandate largely on the grounds that their school systems simply could not afford to fund any more testing. Part of the subtext was the abiding fear that more high-stakes tests would only increase the chance that they could be visited by additional negative sanctions. As a consequence, nothing changed and history remains an untested subject and a low-visibility part of the curriculum in Maryland. My point is to illustrate how local school systems respond to the threat of negative sanctions by pursuing efforts to limit rather than expand the source of those potential threats, even to the extent that, in this case, they effectively imbalance the learning opportunities they provide their students.

20 Of course, there are certainly exceptions to this rule. However, given the low bars most state standards and/or testing systems maintain in history education, the pressure to meet AYP targets (assuming the schools are in states that test in history/social studies) in schools serving socio-economically disadvantaged students virtually guarantees history education practices will look very little like what Becker does.

21 For more on this, see Bruce VanSledright (2007, February). "Why should historians care about history teaching?" *Perspectives: Newsletter of the American Historical Association, 45* (February, 2007), pp. 23–25. (Online: www.historians.org/Perspectives/issues/2007/0702/0702tea2.cfm).

22 Even here, many history majors focus their inquiries and analyses on histories produced by historians rather than dig into archival, original source material in search of producing their own histories. They often need to wait until graduate school in order to undertake the latter. See note 24.

23 Historians reading this might complain that my portrait here is an unfair caricature. I have two responses to that criticism. First, I have literally spoken to thousands of practicing and prospective history teachers about their collegiate history coursetaking experiences over 20 years. Over the past eight years, I have also sat in innumerable sessions, watching historians teach history teachers under the auspices of Teaching American History grant programs. Everything I have repeatedly heard about and personally observed bears ample anecdotal evidence to support my characterization. There have been few, but precious few, exceptions. See again Note 24.

24 See Gaffield, "Towards a Coach in the History Classroom," *Canadian Issues* (October, 2001), pp. 12–14.

25 As the Amherst Project attests, historians were once deeply involved in thinking about teaching, their own and that of history teachers in the nation's schools. From the early 1900s to about 1940, they were also quite active in conversations involving K-12 school curricula and the role American history in particular should play in it. On this latter point, see, for example, David Jenness, *Making Sense of Social Studies* (New York: Macmillan, 1990), Chapter 4.

26 See the American Historical Association, "The Next Generation of History Teachers: A Challenge to Departments of History in American Colleges and

Universities." (Online: www.historians.org/pubs/free/historyteaching/recommendations. htm).

27   For a sense of how social studies TPPs tackle this all-subjects problem, look at popular social studies teaching-methods textbooks. Many of them devote chapter-length treatments to each of a rather dizzying array of social studies subjects taught in secondary schools on the presumption often that roughly a chapter a week would be devoted to each. This approach implicates a mile-wide, inch-deep set of curricular opportunities for prospective social studies teachers. It does have the implicit attractiveness, however, of mapping onto common, broad-brush teacher-licensure policies in many states, and consequently many of the bestselling textbooks attempt to so align.

28   It is for this latter reason especially that I look with some skepticism on typical, subject-integrated social studies TPPs. From a teaching perspective, subject-integrated programs (often advocated, for example, by organizations such as the National Council for the Social Studies) place complex epistemic demands on prospective teachers because they appear to require that such teachers possess rich understandings of the differing epistemological and knowledge-production frameworks of each disciplinary referent from which school social studies subjects are drawn. As we have seen, understanding the epistemological terrain in history alone is complex enough. The additional demand for epistemic understandings of knowledge frameworks in economics, sociology, psychology, and geography as an underpinning for teaching integrated social studies, *all within the short preparation time spans available to TPPs*, is most likely a recipe for the development of superficial knowledge that would have limited pedagogical transferability to and for the investigative approaches I am advocating. Becker, for example, is able to plan, teach, and foster learning as he does, precisely because he has a reasonably deep understanding of history and its epistemic structure. It takes time and focused effort to grow those types of understandings even within one subject matter, let alone multiple ones—more time and effort than most current TPPs have at their disposal. For an example of the challenges involved in preparing history-focused teachers, in which such deep knowledge demands were taken seriously, see Daisy Martin and Chauncey Monte-Sano, "Inquiry, Controversy, and Ambiguous Texts: Learning to Teach for Historical Thinking." In Wilson Warren and D. Antonio Cantu (Eds.), *History Education 101: The Past, Present, and Future of Teacher Preparation* (Charlotte, NC: IAP, 2008), pp. 167–186.

29   This disciplinary-structures pillar stands on the idea that historical understanding among learners is the primary goal we seek and that the route to deep understanding is epitomized by the practices defined by that set of structures. Yet, on my view and as I have noted, it is the correlative benefits that arise for students who possess such deep understandings that ultimately provide the most powerful rationale for this pillar's anchoring: Deepening self understanding; broadening sense of self in the world so as to constrain ethnocentrism, parochialism, unwarranted partisanship, and grow tolerance and respect for diversity; cultivating capacity to read carefully in order to detect spin, hyperbole, crisis mongering, and propaganda; and the promotion of engaged, participating civic selves who look to their futures in hope rather than in fear.

Index

Abby (student) 96, 108, 123, 209n10
accountability 181, 182, 183–184, 185, 194, 213n13
African-American students 5, 25–27, 61, 77, 183; in Becker's fourth-period class 60, 61, 68, 95, 209n10; *see also* students of color
agency/intention 164, 165
alienated students 31
alignments 3, 87, 156; assessments and 150, 152, 153, 168–169, 171; state policy and 181; teacher preparation programs and 192, 193
Amanda (student) 100, 102, 109, 111, 209n10
American Civil War 5–8, 9, 10, 11, 12
American Historical Association 190
Americanization: of the Cherokee 103, 126, 129, 139; history education's role in 21–22, 34, 64, 207n14
American Memory website 18, 43
Amherst Project 14–17, 172, 194, 202n32, 214n25; legacy of 18–19
Angie (student) 97, 209n10
annual yearly progress (AYP) 185, 214n19, 214n20
apprenticeships: model of learning 63, 79, 160, 170; of observation 174, 175, 187, 188, 189; teaching internships 175, 176–177, 185–186, 187, 194
Asian-American students 5, 62, 77, 95, 183; *see also* students of color

assessments 6–7, 10, *158*, 194; Becker's belief in power of 152; in Becker's class 117–119, 125–127, 139–143, 145–148; deciding on essay questions 137–138; deciding on multiple choice items 128–137; as diagnosis 137, 152–154; NAEP 27–28, 159; politics of 201n18; scoring 10–11, 143–145, 153–154; self-assessment 168, 169–170; theorizing about 167–170, 171; *see also* high-stakes testing; standardized testing
attribution 75, 76, 98

background (second-order) knowledge 49–50, *52*, 68–71, 72, 78, *158*
Becker, Thomas (invented, history-teacher protagonist) 3; analyzing pedagogy of 101, 107, 110, 116–117, 124–125; education 40; epistemological underpinnings 46–48; knowledge of assessment 148–154; knowledge of his students 60–62; knowledge of history 44–46
Becker's fourth-period U.S. history class 94–127, 209n10; Class 1 95–102; Class 2 102–108; Class 3 108–111; Class 4 111–115; Class 5 117–125; Class 6 125–127; results of assessment of 145–148
Becker's Investigations Template 91–93, 96–97, 99, 209n9

eBooks – at www.eBookstore.tandf.co.uk

A library at your fingertips!

eBooks are electronic versions of printed books. You can store them on your PC/laptop or browse them online.

They have advantages for anyone needing rapid access to a wide variety of published, copyright information.

eBooks can help your research by enabling you to bookmark chapters, annotate text and use instant searches to find specific words or phrases. Several eBook files would fit on even a small laptop or PDA.

NEW: Save money by eSubscribing: cheap, online access to any eBook for as long as you need it.

Annual subscription packages

We now offer special low-cost bulk subscriptions to packages of eBooks in certain subject areas. These are available to libraries or to individuals.

For more information please contact webmaster.ebooks@tandf.co.uk

We're continually developing the eBook concept, so keep up to date by visiting the website.

www.eBookstore.tandf.co.uk